Democracy across Borders

He assumes
deliberation in
not pub spheres
just movers!! *

(p 61)

Then transnat
communicate
must link

dispersed   o inchoate
         publics

⊕ Internet must become
      a public

      public.
      it must be
      shape ie effective
     - requires an
       institutions
       context

* o ltar
it is
unified

The EU (is) almost there:
Democratic deficit is
not an
deliberative
deficit

Studies in Contemporary German Social Thought (partial listing)
Thomas McCarthy, general editor

Democracy across Borders

From *Dêmos* to *Dêmoi*

James Bohman

The MIT Press
Cambridge, Massachusetts
London, England

MIT Press books may be purchased at special quantity discounts for business or sales promotional use. For information, please email special_sales@mitpress.mit.edu or write to Special Sales Department, The MIT Press, 55 Hayward Street, Cambridge, MA 02142.

This book was set in New Baskerville by SPi, and was printed and bound in the United States of America.

Library of Congress Cataloging-in-Publication Data

Bohman, James.
Democracy across borders : from Dêmos to Dêmoi / James Bohman.
    p.   cm.—(Studies in contemporary German social thought)
Includes bibliographical references and index.
ISBN-13: 978-0-262-02612-3 (hc : alk. paper)
1. Democracy. 2. Regionalism (International organization). 3. World citizenship. I. Title.

JC423.B623   2007
321.8—dc22

                                                                    2006046909

10 9 8 7 6 5 4 3 2 1

Contents

Preface and Acknowledgments

The Greeks invented the word *democracy*, if not democracy itself, but it is we who must now use the word for our time. Democracy quite literally means popular government, rule by the *dêmos*, the people. Democracy came to mean rule by a people, or *dêmos*, rather than by peoples, or *dêmoi*. In the singular, *dêmos* originally signified a specific territorial space and meant "district, country, or land," and thus by extension its inhabitants or peoples. Along with its varied institutional forms, the concept of democracy has had a long history, often discussed in terms of the differences between its ancient and its modern form. Yet throughout it has retained its singular noun and its territorial connotation. The main concern of this book is to rethink the deep assumptions this conceptual archeology covers. In the age of globalization and significant authority delegated beyond the nation state, I contend that democracy needs to be rethought in the plural, as the rule of *dêmoi*. This small change of one letter has enormous normative, political, and institutional significance and permits us to better understand how it is that citizenship and membership need to be transformed. Much as a cubist painting alters the given world of objects through the use of multiple perspectives, transnational democracy challenges single perspective politics and fixed jurisdictions.

The transformation of democracy in the current era is a topic of much debate in social science, economics, international law, and political theory. I will refer to this literature, as well as to current discussions of the impact of globalization. However, my main purpose here is philosophical. I want to show that many of the basic categories of democracy need to be rethought, including the very basic conceptions of the people, the public, citizenship, human rights, and federalism. Given my emphasis on the potential for a transnational polity, many of the examples in this book are taken from the European Union—even if it now falls short of a deliberative democracy across borders.

This book incorporates, in a greatly revised form, material from previously published articles and chapters, and I gratefully acknowledge the work of the editors of those journals and anthologies. Parts of chapter 1 were first published in *Ratio Juris*, *Ethics and International Affairs*, and *Journal of Political Philosophy*. Some parts of chapter 2 were first developed in *After Habermas: Perspectives on the Public Sphere*. Material from chapter 3 appeared in the *Canadian Journal of Philosophy*, and some sections of chapter 4 in the *European Journal of Political Theory*. Parts of the conclusion were published in the *Journal of Social Philosophy*. I also want to thank Larry May, Matthias Lutz-Bachmann, Jürgen Habermas, Andreas Niederberger, Simone Chambers, Archon Fung, Samantha Besson, Charles Sabel, Philip Pettit, David Held, and Thomas McCarthy for helpful feedback and comments, as well as the anonymous reviewers for this Press. I give my special thanks to Michael Allen and Mark Piper, who were excellent critics as well as research assistants. Many audiences have shaped my thinking, including those at the American Philosophical Association, the American Political Science Association, the International Studies Association, the Critical Theory Roundtable, the Philosophy of Social Science Roundtable, ARENA, Yale University, the University of Frankfurt, Roskilde University, University of Aix-Marseille, University of Maryland, University of British Columbia, and Carnegie Mellon University, among others. A grant from Saint Louis University helped me complete the manuscript.

Above all, I want to thank Gretchen, Lena, and Clara for their love and support. I dedicate this book to Lena and Clara, through whose eyes I see the future.

Introduction

According to the current wisdom, we live in the golden age of democracy. In the absence of any viable alternative, liberal democracy is taken to be the only feasible form of democracy and goes unchallenged. Democracy is now recognized in international documents as "the best means to realize human rights," so that some now argue that international law, formerly unconcerned with internal affairs of states, establishes a "democratic entitlement."[1] At the same time, it is often claimed that democracy has never been weaker. It is increasingly unable to solve collective problems or gain legitimacy, thus leading to economic crisis, the declining legitimacy of states in ever more numerous demands for succession, and greater internal conflicts, even civil wars. As a result, some electoral and representative democracies cede many areas of social life to delegated and increasingly nondemocratic forms of authority. Possible responses to these facts lie between two extremes of a continuum. On the one hand, communitarians call for the renewal of social consensus through a democratic ethos, and some participatory democrats demand decentralization into smaller units. On the other hand, cosmopolitans argue that only supranational levels of governance can solve the many collective action and coordination problems, ranging from global warming to sustainable growth to grave human rights abuses and genocide.

Both of these responses are correct in certain respects and indeed are hardly as mutually exclusive as their proponents believe. In this book I argue that all democracies at some point face a period of renewal and transformation. Indeed, many democracies are currently struggling to discover better ways to organize jurisdictions, units, and levels in order to govern well. Contrary to both cosmopolitan and communitarian proposals, good democratic governance needs both bigger *and* smaller units. However, most important in this regard is not size, but the ways in which polities and their subunits are organized and interrelated. The proper solution to the problems of democracy is not to find some optimal size or ideal democratic procedure, but rather to establish a more complex democratic ideal. I call this ideal "transnational democracy."

Since the task of this book is to redefine democracy so as to make it appropriate for transnational settings, it would be premature and misleading to offer a definition of democracy in advance. Defining democracy is made even more difficult by the fact that it should take different forms in different institutions. But as a working definition I offer the following: Democracy is that set of institutions by which individuals are empowered as free and equal citizens to form and change the terms of their common life together, including democracy itself. In this sense, democracy is reflexive and consists of procedures by which its rules and practices are made subject to the deliberation of citizens themselves. Democracy is thus an ideal of self-determination, in that the terms and boundaries of democracy are made by citizens themselves and not others. It does not, however, require the more specific conception of self-determination that has guided much of democratic theory since the eighteenth century—self-legislation in a bounded political community—that is thoroughly imbricated with democracy's current difficulties. If it is self-rule, it is the rule of the many and not of the few.

The modern nation-state has historically been the most successful institutional location for realizing democracy. As opposed to ancient city-states, it has over time achieved universal political rights for all adult citizens regardless of race, class, or gender. More than that, these struggles have expanded the scope of rights to include not just negative rights and immunities, but also various social rights to benefits and services. In light of these achievements, most critics of current democracy still assume the state is the proper institutional location for further democratization. In the wake of globalization, this assumption no longer goes unchallenged. Indeed, states now seem both too big and too small: too big to generate the loyalty and legitimacy needed for a demanding democratic ideal, and too small to solve a myriad of social problems. Powerful multinational corporations evade state power even as international financial institutions dictate the terms of cooperation to weak states. In the interest of promoting free markets and trade, states now voluntarily delegate their powers to international bodies and private authorities. Antiglobalization protesters challenge such policies in the name of local control and democracy. What unites these diverse phenomena is a shift to forms of political authority that are no longer accountable to a measure of popular influence and control—one of the necessary, though not sufficient, conditions for any form of democracy.

Whatever the shortcomings of states, it is no longer clear how they will be able to extend and revise democratic practices under their current circumstances. Deeper than their political and institutional geography, these shortcomings have more to do with the ways in which past practices inform our thinking about democracy at the most basic conceptual level. If the world in which these concepts have developed is undergoing a basic transformation, current democratic theory may no longer provide the proper framework in which to propose solutions. This failure extends to the vocabulary in which demands for democratic justice are made, even when these demands are supposed to be against globalization.

This predicament leaves the democratic theorist with two main methodological choices: either to continue to use these concepts as methodological fictions out of the conviction that they are inseparable from the norms of democracy, or to revise the inherited concepts and norms most people associate with democracy itself. In his *Law of Peoples,* John Rawls chooses the first alternative, at the risk of not taking notice of the post-Westphalian world around him. In contrast, John Dewey in "The Public and Its Problems" takes the second route in responding to new problems of scale and complexity, rejecting the fiction of the public as the people assembled in a single forum. While not directly Deweyan in orientation, my framework here is pragmatic to the extent that it sees new social facts as demanding a new normative and conceptual understanding of democracy and its political geography. Furthermore, my approach is both constructive and reconstructive. On one hand, I will try to determine the fundamental principles from which to argue for this alternative transnational conception. On the other hand, such principles cannot be developed without first examining and reconstructing the democratic potential of recent innovative democratic practices already crossing the borders of nation states as well as of new polities such as the European Union. Finally, my approach is progressive in that these arguments are based on Jane Addams's well-known adage— perhaps the statement of the democratic faith most common to the Progressive Era—that "the cure for the ills of democracy is more democracy." While the transnational circumstances are relatively new, the need for democratic renewal is not.

When Dewey takes up Addams's common faith, he immediately introduces several qualifications that are particularly important in thinking about the possible emergence of new transnational forms of democracy. Democratic institutions cannot produce more democracy by "introducing more machinery of the same kind as that which already exists." Just recognizing the necessity of new frameworks and machinery highlights the need for philosophical work to free democratic theory from the conceptual straightjacket of its historical exemplars. The goal, as Dewey puts it, is "to criticize and remake its political manifestations."[2] These new conditions and their publics, Dewey reminds us, "bring about their own forms"[3] and their own novel practices, which far outstrip the current philosophical discussion of democracy and cosmopolitanism.

In this pragmatic spirit, my task here is twofold. First, I describe the new circumstances of politics so as to show why more of the same democracy is not the solution. By "the same democracy," I mean liberal democracy that remains tied to specific institutional innovations of the early modern past. Liberal democracy's many enduring solutions to modern social problems include the transformation of practices of self-government into practices of representation and the adaptation of democracy to the already existing and historically contingent state form, whose structure of sovereign power and commitment to exclusive political identity is at odds with the universal principles of democracy. Globalization fundamentally challenges these institutions and their assumptions of congruence between decision-takers and decision-makers, or the ruled and the rulers, in a territorially bounded political community. However, nothing should be immediately inferred about democracy from the mere fact that globalization has changed the scale of significant social relationships, unless this change can be shown to affect the feasibility of core democratic values and principles. My first task is to rethink these values and principles under the changed circumstances of politics and the distribution of political authority.

My second task is to take up Dewey's intellectual problem and criticize and remake the idea of democracy. For this purpose, I justify my account of transnational democracy based on republican rather than liberal premises. Republican premises, I argue, supply the necessary orientation to the *terra nova* that democracy becomes when it occurs outside the familiar container of the state. As I noted in the preface, I mark this new conceptual terrain by using the plural form of the Greek term *dêmos, dêmoi*. Such a conception goes beyond the eighteenth-century model of a self-legislating *dêmos* that is at once the author and the subject of the laws guiding most of philosophical thinking about democracy. Instead this conception of democracy goes beyond the nation-state and takes as its political subject *dêmoi* within a larger political community of humanity. The central feature of this democracy as I understand it is that it is a reflexive order, an order in which people deliberate together concerning both their common life and the normative and institutional framework of democracy itself. Democracy in this view is popular control over decision making in a specific sense: it is the interaction between communicative freedom as it is manifested in the public sphere and the normative powers by which people create and control their rights, obligations, and deontic statuses. Fundamental human rights are then precisely such normative powers, the most basic of which is the right to initiate deliberation. This freedom is the basis of what I call "the democratic minimum." Such an account of democracy is certainly broad enough to encompass states and their political communities. It is, however, not necessary that such normative powers be exercised only in such contexts. Indeed, human rights and nondomination are better realized in a variety of institutions and overlapping political communities. In this sense, transnational democracy—democracy as realized in a variety of institutions and communities—is not only more democratic, but is the only feasible way (for the medium term at least) in which to realize the democratic minimum and the rights of members of the human political community. Transnational democracy is first and foremost a response to the increasing potential for political domination that cannot be addressed by traditional interpretations of the democratic ideal.

Nondomination and the Ends of Transnational Democracy

Sociological skeptics of democracy have frequently appealed to long-term social trends to justify their criticisms. For example, Weber argued that democracy was one of many victims of a self-undermining modern rationalism and its "iron law of oligarchy," according to which large organizations tend toward hierarchical and centralized structures of authority.[4] Similarly, Schumpeter argued that the increasing division of epistemic labor from the political role of expertise would lead to a strong distinction between the ruler and the ruled. Democracy would then devolve into the act of voting to choose the elite who would be the guardians of the people. These arguments share a common emphasis on changes in the structure of political authority that undermine the conditions needed for democracy as rule by the people. Some critics use facts about globalization to make the case for this sociological skepticism, arguing that the state is no longer able to fulfill even these minimal democratic conditions. Because it lacks the proper congruence between the rulers and the ruled, the state no longer has the legitimacy it once did; in failing to possess or exercise exclusive authority over its own territory, it also fails to protect its citizens from subjection and domination. Moreover, many no longer support the idea that there are special characteristics of social interaction that limit "especially intense interdependence and mutual subordination" to one's compatriots, or to those in close proximity.[5] The very policies implemented to deal with these new exigencies (such as the active denationalization of new international legal regimes) also widen the gap between the effective exercise of citizens' important normative powers and the authoritative demands of powerful institutional actors. My argument does not

depend on strong versions of the claim that various social and economic interactions have reached "unprecedented levels," but only that
such interactions are sufficient to impede the ability of sovereign states
to secure nondomination.[6] Conversely, a positive impact of globalization on democracy is the emergence of sufficient cross-border communication to form transnational public spheres.

What is unique to this debate about globalization and democracy
is not just that it calls into question the state's authority by challenging the idea that democracy currently resides in a viable unit. It also
implicitly challenges the model of self-legislation that is the basis of
democracy in the constitutional state: namely, that the people who
are subject to the laws are also their authors. Given such challenges,
globalization seems then to be a social fact that potentially affects
how we think of democracy in much the same way that Rawls thinks
pluralism "profoundly affects the requirements of a workable conception of justice."[7] Social complexity and interdependence affect
not only justice, but also the capacity of the *dêmos* to exercise control
over social processes. Two consequences follow: first, the task is not
to determine some special institutional design of an ideal cosmopolitan democracy in which a global *dêmos* could be formed. Second, the
main task of transnational theories of democracy is rather to analyze
the basic conditions of global democratization, the aim of which is
the emergence of a democracy of *dêmoi*.

Historically, democracies have responded to extensive interdependence in a variety of ways. They may attempt to exert control,
limiting the complexity and extent of global social, political, and
economic interactions by strengthening their boundaries, thus
increasing centralized authority. This response is no longer effective, as shown by the denationalization of central state powers in a
variety of regimes and institutions. It is also more likely than not
that such an attempt would lessen rather than increase democracy
within states. Another possible response is the division of labor
and political delegation of authority that produces a proliferation
of principal/agent relationships in which agents govern citizen-
principals in many areas of life. Certainly, large areas of economic
life, from the Federal Reserve to the International Monetary Fund,
show this reversal of agency where the terms of the relationship are

dictated by the agent rather than by the principal. A more effective response to increased interdependence has been federalism, with the recognition that the large and populous democratic polity must be divided into numerous units to be well governed. Many federalists who argued for such arrangements were republicans who saw federalism as a means of overcoming the potential for domination seen in colonialism and classical tyranny; they also saw that republican principles and arrangements could be applied across borders. In this book, I offer a contemporary account of such a republican federalism, the normative core of which is freedom as nondomination, interpreted in such a way as to apply to emerging forms of global political authority.

As opposed to the liberal ideal of noninterference, the republican emphasis on nondomination develops the concept of freedom depending on the social and political statuses of its bearers. The traditional republican contrast is between slave and citizen, where the former is subject to the arbitrary will of a master. The status of citizen brings with it the robust capacity to command the nondomination of others. Those who lack this status are not slaves, but rather rightless persons who lack even the right to have rights. Besides producing rising numbers of stateless persons, the current distribution of global political authority produces situations in which many people lack the very minimum of normative powers and control over their own rights and duties: they lack the capacity to make claims of justice and to initiate deliberation, and in lacking this power are subject to normatively arbitrary political authority. Members of democratic communities can, however, recognize others as participants in various publics. In so doing they can initiate a fundamental condition for democratization: communicative freedom—that is, the freedom to address others and be addressed as members of publics.

In order to account for such powers and freedoms in their transnational context, a republican cosmopolitanism must introduce a richer conception of nondomination and of the political order that realizes it. Rather than develop Philip Pettit's conception of government as a nonarbitrary interferer, the notion of domination needs to be reexamined within the transnational context. In particular, I argue that Pettit's nonnormative definition of domination as arbitrary interference concedes too much to the idea of negative liberty it is meant to replace.[8] It also confuses the ancient problem of tyranny with the problem of modern domination that is accentuated under conditions of complexity, pluralism, and interdependence. Modern democracies may successfully undermine tyranny, but they still have their own potential to produce specific legal and political forms of domination.

Under these modern democratic political circumstances, domination is neither simple tyranny nor the ability to interfere arbitrarily. It is rather tied to another republican meaning of domination: rule by another, one who is able to prescribe the terms of cooperation. Thus political domination is the arbitrary use of normative powers to impose duties and obligations, and it can operate even against the democratic background of normative expectations. This means that domination is the result of the use of distinctly normative powers. However, to have robust nondomination is to have a particular kind of normative status, a status allowing one to create and regulate obligations with others. This is the status of being a citizen. It is a status for nondomination rather than self-legislation; it is to be not ruled by others. The two conceptions of freedom coincide in that citizens can only overcome domination if they have the capacity to deliberate on and change the terms of democratic cooperation, and thus have normative power over the distribution of normative powers, including our status as members of humanity.

If persons have such a status in virtue of being bearers of human rights, including political rights, such rights entail a commitment to the proper organization and constitution of the human political community. I argue that this commitment demands that rights be realized in a variety of overlapping institutions. Constitutionalism in the European Union (whether successful in its current attempt to expand its scope or not) provides the best example of this sort of a reflexive, democratic, and transnational order. In order to be successful it must move beyond the current juridical conception of rights toward a political conception that sees them as rights of membership in the human political community. It must also become more fully democratic, to the extent that it includes the capacity to reform itself democratically, a capacity it currently lacks sufficient legitimacy to execute.

Throughout this book, I use the European Union (EU) as a model of some of the main features appropriate for successful political integration at the transnational level. Even in its nascent form, such a model makes it possible to show two things. First, it is clear that some of the conditions necessary for transforming and extending democracy across borders already hold, and that the EU's institutions have at least begun to develop "the means by which a scattered, mobile and manifold public will recognize itself and define its interests."[9] These publics institute the conditions for communicative freedom. Second, we can begin to ask different questions about the democratization of a polity. The main issue is not the real or supposed democratic deficit, but the democratic criterion itself; the question is not what it would be for a transnational polity to be fully democratic, but to determine how a transnational polity might be adequately democratic "given the kind of entity we take it to be."[10]

Many nation-states are now internally pluralistic, with differentiated citizenship, institutional complexity, and many different levels of organization that repeat the same powers and competences. The difference between the nation-state and the European Union is a difference in *kind*, not one of size or scale (the problems that representative institutions putatively mean to solve). Rather, it is a difference between a democracy that organizes a *dêmos* and one that organizes *dêmoi*. Democracy of the first kind is insufficient to realize nondomination democratically in a polity of *dêmoi*. The conceptual foundations of democracy are in each case quite different, even if we hold some of the norms and principles constant across both. On the republican account I am defending, democratic institutions aim to secure the conditions for nondomination. The facts of authority and interdependence suggest that national democracy and political membership no longer secure these goods, if they ever did. The institutional conditions that enable citizens to be free from domination are realized in unitary states as shown by the republican impulse toward federalism with a variety of variously sized units. The form of republicanism I defend here has its roots not in the English Commonwealthman traditions, but in the republican anticolonialism and anti-imperialism of Diderot, Kant, and others. Their fundamental insight is that domination abroad undermines democracy and nondomination within the republic, and thus that secure nondomination is based on the common liberty of all rather than the escalation of executive and military power.

An Argument for Transnational Democracy

In the last section I described the tasks of a theory of democracy during times of transformation. This theory is broadly cosmopolitan, in both a moral and political sense, in that it demands a significant reorganization of current political institutions into highly differentiated structures containing multiple units and levels and many different *dêmoi*. As a way of framing the overall argument, I begin by mapping the cosmopolitan terrain in order to show the distinctiveness of my position vis-à-vis the main alternatives. Along with the reconstructive method I employ for a theory of democracy in times of transition, my positive argument must demonstrate three main things: first, that transnational democracy is a feasible extension of emerging preconditions, practices, and institutional orders; second, that it is possible to fulfill the democratic minimum in democracies of *dêmoi*; and, lastly, having fulfilled this minimum, that transnational democracy is a robust way of realizing human rights and establishing popular control over some of the normative powers exercised by political authority without appealing to a singular *dêmos* or unified will of the people. Whereas the idea of a singular *dêmos* has been tied to a fundamentally juridical model of self-legislation, the idea of nondomination decenters this conception and requires that citizenship powers be exercised in a variety of overlapping *dêmoi*.

This leads to the first question regarding the feasibility of a democracy of *dêmoi*: what sort of cosmopolitanism is required for democracy under the current circumstances of politics? Transnational democracy is certainly a form of political cosmopolitanism, to the extent that it sees new political institutions as fundamental in addressing concerns for global justice. While entirely consistent with cosmopolitan moral concerns, transnational democracy is neither directly a form of moral cosmopolitanism, nor are its institutions justified by an appeal to broad moral principles such as equal concern and respect for fundamental human dignity. Its political character can be determined from its emphasis on humanity—not merely as a moral property of individuals, but also as a political community in which the right to have rights is recognized.

Compared to some forms of political cosmopolitanism, transnational democracy emphasizes the plurality of institutions and communities necessary for the flourishing of humanity. In common with liberal nationalism, transnational democracy is opposed to the idea that the *dêmoi* ought to be subsumed into a cosmopolitan hierarchy with a single *dêmos* at its apex. As the term transnational suggests, states continue to have a role in the political life of the transnational polity, although not as the democratically favored form of organization; they are but one of the *dêmoi* and one of the polities organized within the human political community. At the same time, distinct peoples or sovereign states are not the fundamental units of transnational federalism. It is not democracy *beyond* borders but *across* borders; democracy across borders means that borders do not mark the difference between the democratic inside and the nondemocratic outside of the polity, between those who have the normative power and communicative freedom to make claims to justice and those who do not. It is not a democracy of a single community, but one of many different communities.

The overall argument here aims to provide just such a normative theory of transnational democracy, a theory that is much less dependent on inherited juridical conceptions than are theories of cosmopolitan democracy. The first two steps of the argument develop the theory of the democratic transformation from *dêmos* to *dêmoi*. This argument begins with certain social facts: first of all, with those conditions that constitute the social field of constraints and opportunities in which democracy can be realized, including macrosociological facts concerning globalization outside the state and increasing pluralism within it. The second set of conditions is related to the nature of the public sphere, the existence of which is a basic presupposition for interaction in a democratic form of political life. The main issue regarding this set of conditions is this: if talk of a global public sphere in the singular is a nonstarter, what is the relevant alternative? The third step in the argument follows as a consequence of these conditions and is distinctly normative and republican in character. Rather than the threat of global institutions with regulatory capacities, an increased potential for domination at the transnational level is one consequence of uneven interdependence. Thus, a transnational democracy must no longer reconstruct rights as the claims of a juridical subject to immunities from interference, but rather as normative statuses and powers in the political domain sufficient to promote nondomination. This reconstruction of political rights as rights against domination also suggests the fourth and final step in the argument: the development of a distinctive form of transnational constitutionalism that is the basis of any democratic reflexive political order. When human political rights are multiply realized in a such a reflexive constitutional order, they provide the minimum sufficient conditions to establish the reasonable hope that such a democratic order could be a means of attaining global justice.

The first chapter begins both of the main reconstructive tasks, one negative and the other positive. The negative task is to reject the usual argument for cosmopolitan democracy. In David Held's well-known definition, globalization is a complex and multidimensional process that primarily denotes "the expanding scale, growing magnitude, speeding up and deepening impact of transcontinental flows and patterns of interaction."[11] From this account of globalization, many infer that the problem of democracy is one of scale, and thus contend that democracy can once again be effective so long as it develops on the same scale as the social processes it interacts with and often tries to regulate. But however the process of democratization is connected to this abstract description of globalization, these arguments do not take seriously enough the political circumstances of current asymmetrical globalization, circumstances which demand the deeper conceptual transformation of democracy beyond simply rejecting the assumptions of state sovereignty. Democracy must now not only change its institutional form, but also its political subject.

The reconstructive task of this chapter begins with the development of an exhaustive typology of current theories of democracy beyond the nation-state. There are four main axes that provide the basis for such an exhaustive classification of positions on this issue:

social or political, institutional or noninstitutional, democratic or nondemocratic, and transnational or cosmopolitan. In considering the major theories of Rawls, Habermas, Held, and Dryzek, I will show that only my position is political, institutional, democratic, and transnational, while Held's cosmopolitan democracy and Dryzek's transnational democracy cover only three such aspects each, to the detriment of their theories. While Held's conception of cosmopolitanism is multileveled in its institutional form, at the apex of its framework is a *dêmos* organized by standard parliamentary institutions. Dryzek, on the other hand, emphasizes civil society as the appropriate agent of transformation, and this emphasis tends to conceptualize democracy entirely in terms of contestation rather than deliberation. Both ignore the most fundamental necessary condition for democratization: the power to initiate effective public deliberation. For the purpose of accounting for this distinctive democratic power, I develop a conception of the democratic minimum: the minimum necessary conditions for democracy to be sufficiently self-transformative so as also to be a means of achieving global justice.

The second chapter shifts from theoretical concerns to the main practical precondition for the exercise of rights against domination: a vibrant public sphere in which people regard themselves as members possessing communicative freedom. The increasing level of cross-border communication is now a recognized social fact, leading many to assert the emergence of a new global public. Just as in the national case, it would be easy to overestimate the significance of global civil society for democracy. The emergent public sphere more clearly opens up spaces for deliberation across borders than does global civil society alone. Publics can begin to take on "some measure of political organization," as Dewey noted, when they establish a dynamic between the communicative freedom of publics and the normative powers of citizens as embodied in particular institutional processes.[12]

Here, too, we should not underestimate the differences between national and transnational publics and the conceptual task of developing an alternative, decentered conception of democracy. Rather than merely a location for associations and contestation, the transnational public sphere is also the potential source of communicative freedom and novelty when it begins to interact with and shape institutions. Historically, public spheres emerge and develop in inter-action with political authority, particularly when that authority tries to shape and restrict the public sphere itself—as was the case, for example, with early modern attempts at state censorship, which helped give participants a greater sense of identity as members of a public. Given the role of initiation and claim making that I empha-size in the first chapter, such public spheres establish crucial delib-erative conditions for the democratic minimum. The sorts of public best able to challenge and contest the new dispersed forms of dele-gated authority on the principal/agent model are what I call "dis-tributed publics," which have already emerged in network forms of communication such as the Internet. In the case of transnational democracy, the creative and generative side of communication is needed to establish new institutional frameworks. Those who create the new public spheres will act as new transnational intermediaries, replacing older democratic intermediaries whose agency opened up and maintained the spaces needed for the exercise of communica-tive power.

The third chapter turns to the normative basis of transnational democracy in the common currency of international politics, human rights. This chapter develops the conception of political rights as crucial normative powers to resist domination. Here international human rights law provides conceptual clues regarding the develop-ment of this normative conception in crimes against humanity and in the right to nationality owed to refugees and stateless persons. While many have thought of such a cosmopolitan requirement as instantiated politically in the constitutional state at a higher scale, this understanding of humanity is most fully realized in a multilevel, differentiated polity with multiperspectival forms of deliberation. Here humanity is not only the addressee of the claims of rightless persons, but it is also the proper perspective of the generalized other that is constitutive of humanity as a political subject across *dêmoi*. That the concept of humanity must play various roles in a democracy that realizes universal human rights also suggests that a differenti-ated institutional structure that translates human rights into norma-tive powers distributed throughout that structure is the best way to realize human rights, particularly human political rights. To the extent that human rights denote statuses, these statuses require a particular political community—the republic of humanity—and thus at least some global institutions to secure common liberty and nondomination.

The fourth chapter turns to just the sort of differentiated institutional structure that best realizes political rights as human rights. It is possible to determine this structures's principles of design from an ongoing experiment in transnational political integration and polity building: the European Union. Although there are several forms of constitutionalism beyond the nation-state—including the United Nations, the World Trade Organization, and other institutions that seek to bind their members through self-governance—the EU is distinct in its political goals and democratic ambitions. In particular, the EU is not simply an aggregate of peoples governed by a minimal overlapping consensus, but a political community, and as such it does not "merely replicate on a larger scale the typical modern political form."[13] Given that states must be democratic to become members, the European Union is a polity of *dêmoi*, a "people of others" (in Joseph Weiler's terms).[14] This suggests some general principles of institutional design: namely, a principle of institutional differentiation that includes both distinct institutions at the transnational level and iterated institutions, with the same competences but distributed at different levels, both of which secure robust nondomination. This creates parallel and intersecting forms of deliberation, as can be seen in various novel forms of deliberation in the EU. The second task of this reconstruction of the EU institutions is to consider the conditions necessary for its further democratization and to conceive of its democratic reform, with the benefit of the will of the people in the standard sense that includes their constituent powers. Such a shift requires a new constitutionalism, especially given the problem of legal domination or juridification that is the biggest source of the EU's democratic deficit— that is, its perceived lack of democratic legitimacy when compared with member states. The problem of legitimacy, I argue, is more specific than an overly generalized democratic deficit. It is rather a deliberative deficit, a deficit in the reflexive capacity of citizens to initiate democratic reform. The problem of constitutionalism is not to create a European *dêmos*, but to create in the EU's institutional structure the democratic capacity to initiate legitimate democratic reform, which is required if it is to become something more like a transnational republic.

The conclusion brings these arguments together by raising the fundamental issue facing many forms of cosmopolitanism: global justice. Here I argue that democracy and justice are mutually dependent terms and that one cannot be achieved in any secure way without the other. Two examples that are important for global justice illustrate this dependence. The first is the problem of borders, which liberal democratic theory treats simply as a given. I argue instead that to the extent that borders and jurisdictions set the terms of democratic arrangements, they must be open to democratic deliberation. In multiunit polities, this requires that both citizens and noncitizens have the ability to place an item on the political agenda in order to ensure that such a power is not democratically arbitrary. Second, I argue that transnational democracy is also instrumental in producing peace and security in addition to creating the capacity to avoid other great human evils such as famine and extreme destitution. In particular, we can see this from the failure of the democratic peace hypothesis, when it is turned into public policy. Democracy promotes peace only if there is a positive feedback relationship between democracy within states and the international system. Indeed, it is only when some supranational institutions exist to make these states more rather than less democratic that such values are best secured. In other words, peace requires not democracies, but democratization at positively interacting levels.

If this cumulative argument succeeds in each of its steps, I will have shown that the republican conception of nondomination provides the normative warrant for democracy that is generally lacking in more liberal versions of political cosmopolitanism. Cosmopolitan democracy makes more sense in republican terms, for without freedom as nondomination it can address neither the political problems of complexity and interdependence nor check its own potential for democratic domination and juridification. Perhaps some might argue that a commitment to a more minimal form of democracy at the international level, based on demands of transparency, would be more feasible and less ambitious than the democratic project of establishing a political community of *dêmoi*. While perhaps enabling some reforms, such a minimal form of democracy does not achieve the necessary conditions for democratization and is insufficiently republican to solve the fundamental problem of domination. It may indeed be possible to have some universal human rights without a democratic cosmopolitan political community, but then such human rights could not include political and civil rights against domination and tyranny. If we want to be true to our commitment to both rights and democracy, then we must also be committed to establishing an international political community that is entailed both by human rights as political rights and by political rights as human rights. Republicanism tells us that we cannot institute these norms except in a properly organized political community. Cosmopolitan republicanism adds that freedom from domination cannot be achieved without transforming our fundamental democratic conceptions and ultimately embedding our democratic institutions within a transnational polity.

This argument is able to fulfill Dewey's two main desiderata for democratic theory in a period of transformation. First, it returns to the fundamental requirements of democracy and asks how they can best be fulfilled under the new political circumstances. Second, it takes its principles of institutional design from the innovative forms that have already developed in various settings, from international regimes to the European Union, to show that transnational democracy is a realistic extension of political possibilities. The ideal of democracy does not merely apply to the international arena and its institutions, but rather elaborates the conditions for the legitimacy of any modern democracy committed to human rights. In this sense, Kant and other transnational republicans were right when they contended that the achievement of a democracy of *dêmoi* is now a fundamental demand of political justice and an obligation of humanity to construct.

1

From *Dêmos* to *Dêmoi*: The Conceptual Foundations of Transnational Democracy

Debates in democratic theory are often presented as recurring struggles among great schools or "isms," such as between liberalism and republicanism. This mode of presentation often obscures the differing assumptions that underlie many theoretical disputes, especially when they take place during periods of historical change and uncertainty. Ours is such a period. For example, while announcements about the end of the nation-state may well be premature, there is good social scientific evidence to suggest that the democratic character of this political form may well be declining, or is at least at risk. If the changes taking place are great enough, the difficulty in making such assessments may be in part conceptual. In the case of democracy, one particular conception has been so historically dominant that it underlies many different and even opposing mainstream theories, from contractualism to liberalism to deliberative democracy. Perhaps it is not democracy as such that is threatened, but rather the practical viability of this particular and historically contingent interpretation of its ideals. Indeed, the assumptions we make about democracy are often far more historically specific than we realize; the bourgeoning discussion of cosmopolitan, supranational, and transnational alternatives to the nation-state has again revealed just how difficult it is to talk about a transformation in democracy without implicitly assuming too much of our inherited conceptual framework.

Disputes about the future of democracy within and beyond the state, especially the question of whether we have already experienced its historically best realization, depend less on differences in diagnoses of its current problems than on normative issues involving debates about differing interpretations of the meaning of democracy in the global era. However much they differ in their theoretical justifications and institutional proposals, those who argue for the need for greater democracy at the global level must ultimately share very similar diagnoses of the problems with the current international system. Given that democracies have worked together to produce the international system as it currently exists, the prior question is: more of what *sort* of democracy?

This question has brought forth two responses. In describing them I employ David Held's useful terms "gradualist" and "transformationalist," while departing from Held in applying them not to accounts of globalization and its impacts, but to various practical interpretations of global democracy. The prospects for democracy now depend upon different conceptions of the subject. In this regard, the key issue is whether the conception of democracy first articulated in the founding democratic constitutions and theories of the eighteenth century must be sustained or transformed. On the one hand, gradualists seek to find the proper way to extend the democratic ideal given the new factors of pluralism, complexity, and globalization. For gradualists, it is the *form* of democracy that is transformed, not its substance, basic conceptions, or norms. On the other hand, some see these challenges as requiring a much deeper and more structural transformation of democracy, down to the conception of the *dêmos* that gradualists take to be constitutive of the very idea of democracy. To distinguish this position from overly strong hyperglobalist interpretations of the global market order without political institutions, David Held has called this group "transformationalists"—those who see the current institutional order as undergoing a structural transformation that continues rather than ends the modern social institutions. Contrary to his intent, however, on central issues of democratic theory Held may not number among the transformationalists after all. According to the transformative model, democracy is indeed undergoing as fundamental a transformation now as it did when representative democracy emerged in the early modern city-state.[1] At that time, many citizens and philosophers argued that this new institutional form violated the basic democratic principle of self-rule. As a result, the new ideal equated democracy with self-legislation, as the act of the people giving itself laws through the elected legislature that expresses the popular will. As can be shown in the work of Held and Habermas, however, this monism cannot provide a theory of democracy consistent with the pluralization of authority and the disaggregation of sovereignty implied in the core transformationalist thesis.[2]

For theorists who think beyond the state form of democracy and its conception of the legislating will, the problem that democratic theory needs to solve is not how to preserve democracy as it is now or how even to promote more of the same democracy, but rather how to establish a different *type* of democracy. Similar to the transition from the freedom of the ancients based on self-rule to the freedom of the moderns based on consent and representation manifested in the legislative process, transformationalists think that the different kind of democracy required may sometimes seem like *less* democracy. Others think that such a transition demands the return to a more robust and direct ideal of self-rule in new institutional forms. "Given the limits and possibilities of our world," Dahl asks, "is a third transformation of democracy a realistic possibility?"[3] This transformation is, I shall argue, a realistic possibility if it is fundamentally a transition from a singular to a plural subject, from *dêmos* to *dêmoi*. Democracy must now not only change its institutional form, it must also rethink its political subject. In the full form I am defending here, transformationalism must analyze not just institutional forms but also the normative basis of basic democratic conceptions. If this is correct, then most transformationalists, including cosmopolitans such as David Held, do not go far enough.

My discussion of this double—normative and institutional—transformation of democracy has three steps. First, I consider the extent to which globalization and the forms of interdependence that result from it are sufficient to require this double transformation. Contrary to the dominant transformationalist argument, I contend that the empirical fact of the increasing scope of interaction and interdependence is not sufficient to decide the issue between gradualists and transformationalists. Rather, these facts give rise to a problem for democracy to solve, no matter what form it may eventually take: the problem of the increasing vulnerability of persons to domination, particularly with the emergence of incompletely defined forms of international political authority that are no longer contained within any political community.

Second, with this analysis of global political circumstances in mind, I develop an exhaustive typology of the conceptual space of feasible theories of democracy beyond the nation-state. The central issue of these theories is whether the modern conception of the self-legislating *dêmos* and its representative institutions is sufficient to solve the problem of domination in the global era. I consider four major accounts that, taken together, provide the basis for a complete typology of the main theories. The current discussion can be reconstructed on four main axes: political or social, institutional or noninstitutional, democratic or nondemocratic, and transnational or cosmopolitan. Allen Buchanan and Jürgen Habermas develop two broadly gradualist accounts that are incomplete in important respects. While John Dryzek and David Held present the fullest of the available accounts, each fails in a crucial respect in developing their democratic theories. An adequate theory lines up along the first member of each of these axes: it must be political, institutional, democratic, and transnational. Finally, I begin the positive argument in favor of this alternative with a conception of the democratic minimum, the starting point for a transnational theory of a democracy of *dêmoi*.

Globalization, Freedom, and Interdependence

While debates about the political consequences of globalization have often focused on the constraints it imposes on policy options, global interdependence goes beyond these impacts and refers more fundamentally to the unprecedented extent, intensity, and speed of social interactions across borders, encompassing such diverse dimensions as trade, cultural exchange, and migration.[4] Whether states can maintain specific policies—such as the social rights of the social democratic welfare state—is largely an empirical question. While the demise of the nation-state has been greatly exaggerated, the political difficulties posed by globalization are more properly normative than functional. In order to maintain control over their boundaries, states have to heighten executive powers, and in this regard they often delegate such authority to international institutions such as the World Trade Organization and the International Monetary Fund. Thus, even if states maintain important regulatory functions, and even if membership in a state continues to have significant benefits and protections, states cannot both solve pressing transnational problems and maintain their undivided sovereignty and traditional monopoly powers.[5]

Certain functional tasks of political and legal integration, once solely the jurisdiction of states, are no longer as subject to democratic control and accountability. At the very least, standard conceptions of liberal constitutional democracy are deficient: given the ways in which interdependence has disaggregated political organization and membership, rights founded in citizenship are much less effective in addressing the domination of anonymous members of modern societies. Granting that this description of the greater potential for domination is true, what follows for political cosmopolitanism—that is, for the view that some political institutions are required to secure the freedom and life prospects of persons as free and equal citizens?

Domination and the New Circumstances of Politics

For some cosmopolitans, the greater the global interdependence that can be established at the empirical level, the greater the normative support globalization lends to cosmopolitan governance. The connection of the one to the other, however, is not so clear. In this regard, Kant was much clearer than many contemporary cosmopolitans in that he argued both empirically and normatively, both in terms of the fact of increasing interdependence across communities and polities and in terms of the new political obligation to create a "cosmopolitan public law." Given the value of freedom and the empirical consequences of robust interdependence, Kant argued that a basic political obligation emerges: that we *ought* then to enter into a "cosmopolitan political condition subject to cosmopolitan right" or law.[6] Such a political condition reflects the fact that "the peoples of the earth have to various degrees entered into a universal community, and it has developed to the point that a violation of rights in one part of the world is felt everywhere."[7] This political condition is not established de facto through mere economic interdependence or by mutual influence on each other's interests,[8] but rather solely with regard to the relationships among autonomous persons "insofar as they are regarded as free."[9] The question then becomes, what sort of freedom is relevant for the political obligation to form a universal community?

As an alternative to Kant's emphasis on freedom, proponents of the most straightforward route to cosmopolitanism argue that simple interdependence establishes the scope of obligations of justice. "Dwelling together" means to live in a complex chain of causal and institutional interaction and interdependence, the scope of which establishes both the bounds of justice and of community.[10] Those obligations need not be political, however, and political obligations do not always require such a strong form of interdependence. Rather than a common space or a singular and uniform condition, global interdependence is more often than not highly stratified, with "differential interconnectedness in different domains."[11] Thus, even if globalization enlarges the ways in which we live together in political space and time, it does not follow that we all share the same fate within it (although such convergence may apply to specific global problems, such as global warming).

The more common phenomenon of differential rather than shared consequences means globalization does not produce a shared social space. Instead it is experienced in different ways by different peoples or political communities, with markedly different impacts at different locations. Indeed, as Dobson puts it, many of the associated social activities and processes "cross boundaries in one direction only."[12] In some domains, such as global financial markets, globalization is profoundly uneven and reinforces already-existing hierarchies. Inequalities in political access to international rule-making institutions or in the ability to control globalization processes may reflect older patterns of subordination and order, even while the process excludes some communities from financial markets entirely and makes others more vulnerable to its increased volatility.[13]

Once the convergent picture of globalization is rejected, a normative theory is better served by seeing how global activities do not necessarily affect everyone, or even the majority of people, in the same way. Rather, the sort of social activities in question affect an *indefinite* number of people. Such activities are indefinite in the sense that they include spatially and temporally dispersed groups "whom we cannot individuate but can specify."[14] The actions of a large multinational corporation or of institutions that regulate financial markets influence the life possibilities of indefinite others—as when, for example, decisions in China affect workers in many, but not all, locations. Whether they intend to or not, in these cases authoritative agents "make potent assumptions about the lives that will be available to distant contemporaries and remote successors."[15] But since these others cannot be individuated, they may be part of some agents' plans without having freely given their cooperation or consent. Under these conditions, a cooperative scheme is not best understood as a "basic structure"[16] of a single society writ large or as a founding of a social contract. Given such differences in affectedness, these notions are too counterfactual to be of use in creating a just global order. Instead of a "common world" or "dwelling together" situation, as is presupposed in both of these notions, indefinite social activities and the organizations that plan and carry them out create something more akin to what Albert Weale calls the "circumstances of politics."[17]

If social actions are indefinite in this way, then we cannot choose those with whom we must cooperate, and in the absence of such a choice, the existing scheme of cooperation must be open for negotiation and deliberation. Interdependence via indefinite social activity thus establishes the scope of political obligation precisely because the circumstances of global politics emerge through nonvoluntary inclusion in indefinite cooperative schemes. Inclusion in such schemes, often created by agents who are acting for specific principals (such as the shareholders of some corporation or the citizens of another state), is itself a form of domination.

Nondomination as a Primary Political Good

Because of this indefinite extension of conflict (and, correlatively, possible cooperation), the problem of domination can no longer be solved according to the old republican formula that "to be free is to be a citizen of a free state." Because of the problem of nonindividuated activity, one aim of global democratic politics should be to permit those affected to give their voluntary (but ultimately counterfactual) consent. Instead of creating a social contract that makes the terms of cooperation definite, indefinite activities require a new form of membership and citizenship that permits the ongoing negotiation of conflicts and sufficient cooperation to secure human rights against domination across borders.[18] In more political terms, nondomination would require the creation of a political community in which citizens are able to challenge and reconstitute those institutions that enable globalization to occur. Indeed, the possibility of establishing such a community has empirical support, including the emergence of transnational civil society as well as global public spheres in which political terms of cooperation imposed by various corporate and political institutional actors (from corporations to the World Bank) may be challenged and contested.

In order to see the difference that nondomination makes, consider the alternative conception of cosmopolitan democracy based on freedom as self-determination. According to this view, "the idea of democracy derives its power and significance from the notion that the members of the political community—citizens—should be able to choose freely the conditions of their own association."[19] An ideal of freedom as self-determination suggests that the task of cosmopolitan democracy is to use the binding power of positive law to introduce political control beyond the nation-state, where it is now absent.[20] Yet the sorts of transformations of social conditions that could democratically achieve such control remain largely unspecified. Most importantly, it is unclear how a community could be internally democratic without first recognizing the commitment to the nondomination of the communities it is linked with in indefinite social interaction. Given these difficulties, political relationships under these conditions would be as indefinite as other forms of social and economic interdependence, and as a result freedom as control over conditions of association would supply no normative guidance for solving problems of cooperation and conflict among nonindividuated actors. How does such an appeal to nondomination avoid this indeterminacy?

Rawls's theory of justice offers Pettit one republican answer to this question: in democratic communities, nondomination as a primary good provides the basis for the fair value of political liberty as well as the social basis of respect.[21] The argument here is that any agent qua

rational with a life plan would want more and more secure nondomination as a condition for being able to plan one's life at all. Since
nondomination is a comparative status—where some people are
more vulnerable to domination than others—a difference principle
of this sort must apply in the form of an indexed minimum of statuses and powers necessary to secure it.[22]

Compelling as it is with regard to individual planning, Pettit's account of nondomination as a primary good does not go far enough.
The powers necessary for nondomination fundamentally derive from a
status, primarily one that comes with being a member or citizen of a
free political community and is thus a good within an already established scheme of social cooperation. Because of this, Walzer is correct
in arguing that rights of membership are basic, or, as he puts it, "the
first social good" to be distributed, and thus the basis for the recognition of further entitlements and of participation in social life.[23]
However, to think about nondomination as a good to be distributed is
misleading; membership is rather a basic freedom, the most basic with
respect to freedom from domination. Nondomination is in fact more
basic than any such good, primary or otherwise, since to be part of a
cooperative scheme is already to have legitimate expectations concerning one's status with respect to others in that scheme. Thus, we can see
nondomination as a fundamental condition for participation in projects that are common only to the extent that, qua member, one can
influence the terms of cooperation with others and not be ruled by
them. Consequently any well-ordered cooperative scheme would have
to secure this most basic status, and with this status would come certain
powers and capabilities. Only because such a status is connected to normative powers can we say that its bearers are "very powerful indeed."[24]
Pettit's modal powers are normative powers, including the capacity to
"obey oneself" by creating and regulating one's own obligations and
duties rather than "being prescribed to by others" (as Rousseau put it
in *The Social Contract*[25]). A main issue for transformationalists is then
the question of what relevant normative powers are necessary for citizens to secure freedom from domination across borders.

In periods of social change, democracy has provided citizens and
noncitizens alike with the means to make claims of justice and freedom. But it has not always done so. On the contrary, democracies

have historically also promoted domination, as when a group of citizens dominates noncitizens within their borders. Indeed, Western liberal democracies have acted together to construct the current system that enables the global economy to operate. This has created a general problem that democratic theory cannot ignore, especially if it is concerned with democracy as a path to global justice. Under circumstances as unjust as the current international system, the instrumental use of strong versions of democratic principles faces a potentially vicious circularity: "for democracy to promote justice, it must already be just."[26] This does not yet describe the circularity fully enough: to the extent that democracy is also necessary for justice, they can only be realized together. Democracy can be justified instrumentally as a means to justice, but to the extent that it realizes justice it is also justified intrinsically. This makes it a challenge to realize democratic ideals through democratic procedures (such as majority rule) under unjust circumstances.

While it can never be said to disappear, this mutual dependence between democracy and justice at the normative level can be expressed through the concept of the democratic minimum: the achievement of a normative status sufficient for citizens to exercise their creative powers to reshape democracy itself according to the demands of justice. The rights, equality, and freedoms that are constitutive of the democratic ideal are substantively related to various ends of justice, including self-development, peace and self-rule.[27] For my purposes here, however, the constitutive elements of justice have greater prominence; a practice is just only if it treats participants as free and equal, and unjust to the extent that it does not. Ultimately, democracy promotes justice precisely because it enables citizens to *demand* to be treated justly. I take it as uncontroversial that the current global system, characterized by extreme destitution, sweatshops, and other forms of tyranny and domination, is neither fully just nor fully democratic nor able to realize basic human freedoms.

From *Dêmos* to *Dêmoi*: Democracy beyond the State

Gradualists typically tell us a compelling historical narrative that brings out the universal character of the democratic ideal as expressed in its radical form in the French Revolution. According to this story, the democratic inclusion of all those who are subject to the law was intended to lead to the recognition of all those affected by laws as citizens, even beyond the borders of states. Nationalism then emerged in the nineteenth century to distort this universal core of democratic freedom and equality by tying it to a particular territory and to a particular form of shared collective identity taken to be the source of solidarity. With the recent emergence of human rights, including civil and political rights, the emphasis on universal inclusion returns, so that, for example, in a constitutional democracy, rights are extended to all persons, whether they are formal citizens or not. In most democracies, some restricted set of rights (such as free speech and due process) applies to noncitizens. The idea is that universal rights create a dynamic whose *telos* is universal inclusion, even if de facto democracies remain Eurocentric and thus part of a global system of domination of non-Europeans. Here democratization in the international sphere continues the dynamics of citizenship and solidarity already at work in its original sphere of the nation-state, and aims at an ever more inclusive *dêmos*, ultimately encompassing all those subject to the law. The goal of such inclusion is to establish ideal congruence between citizens as subjects and those who actually exercise power as authors of the law. It is this fundamental gap in any real democracy that gradualists claim can only be closed counterfactually in the human right to democracy.

While this historical reconstruction points to a deep consistency between human rights and the idea of a universal political community, it does not do justice to the more political dimension of democratic autonomy. The idea of a self-legislating *dêmos*, of citizens ruling and being ruled in return, requires a delimited political community of citizens, consisting of all those and *only* those who are full citizens and thus *both* authors *and* subjects of the law. The gradualist history of the modern state optimistically asserts that once the connection between universal human rights and the principle of democracy is made, only effective international law and its enforcement stands in the way of the solution to the gap in the scope of democracy. But this claim neglects the fundamental tension between universality and particularity that is built into the constitutions of modern states, especially those parts that concern universal human political rights.

Even this tension fails to give us the full picture of the limits of universality inherent in modern democracies. As Habermas puts it, the natural law theory espoused by most founders of modern constitutional orders requires that the political community consists of "a determinate group of persons, united by the decision to grant to each other precisely those rights that are necessary for the legitimate ordering of their collective existence by means of positive law."[28] The delimitation of political community is thus not a result of the de facto limits on current democracy, but of the democratic ideal in the constitutional version that links it to the creation of positive law: a democratic ideal that normatively demands a social limitation of the relevant community, which is then combined de facto with the centralized authority and the territorial limitations of the nation-state. If human rights are the moral rights of the *subjects* of the law, then political rights to the law's authorship require membership not in humanity but in the self-legislating *dêmos*. Thus, using the fundamental difference between the status of being a citizen *within* a political community and the negative status of being a bearer of human rights as an alternative basis for claims *against* the political community does not solve the problem so much as name it, by showing the gap between self-legislation as an ideal and human rights as universal. Legal cosmopolitans such as Kant sought to extend the juridical status, seeing the creation of a global legal community as the solution to the problem of interdependence. But this solution only goes so far, creating institutions that see human rights as juridical statuses that supplement political membership in a state. But these statuses are not sufficient for nondomination, whatever the achievements of the current human rights regime. This juridical status lacks the specific powers necessary to ensure that a regime does not simply prescribe norms that its subjects cannot shape. Without an accompanying political status, the real possibility of legal domination cannot be avoided. Within a political community, such legal statuses add to the powers of free and equal individuals; they have a right to petition a court to hear their claims, just as they have various rights that make it possible for these same petitioners to initiate deliberation about the fairness of these procedures.

Once the problem of global political inclusion is so described, its solution is not to establish a global legal community, but rather to create the conditions of political nondomination under the current circumstances of politics. In order to understand the problem a democratic community is supposed to solve, it is first necessary to transform the conception of democracy itself as the *dêmos* changes. According to Habermas, "decentering" is the operation by which democratic theory is rid of the metaphysical assumption that there is a "people" whose "collective will" is genuinely expressed if and only if democratic norms are fully implemented.[29] In order for democracy to be applicable to large-scale, complex, and pluralistic societies, a similar assumption of the need for a single deliberative forum must also be abandoned. As Iris Young puts it, a singular democratic subject such as the state cannot apply to the "context of large and complex social processes, the whole of which cannot come into view, let alone under decision-making control."[30] If federalism is a good indication, most enduring solutions to the problems of size and complexity require differentiation between the sites and powers of deliberation and authority. Given that a certain level of differentiation and complexity has been attained in most modern state-organized societies, democracy has adapted to these social facts by decentering institutionally along two dimensions: the microdimension that encompasses the sort of processes that constitute decision making, and the macrodimension that encompasses interlocking levels of governance from cities to regions to global society, levels that do not resolve themselves into some higher-order convergence or hierarchy.

Other democratic conceptions can be similarly decentered, including the normative ideal of a democratic public sphere. It is not at all clear that there are any global public spheres, weak or strong, in the sense used with regard to national public spheres. The contrast between weak and strong public spheres makes sense only against the background of a particular set of political institutions, the function of which is to enable the expression of the legislative will of the people. Those that are connected to the core parliamentary complex are strong public spheres; those that are not so connected are by contrast weak. In light of this set of conceptual distinctions, the problem of democracy is to transform weak publics into strong ones. It is simply a conceptual mistake, however, to assume that global public spheres are weak when it is quite possible that they take a qualitatively new form, and are thus neither weak nor strong in this sense. Rather than somehow seeking to constitute a unified global public by analogy to the national case, transformationalists argue that the public sphere is undergoing a structural transformation, which opens up new and innovative possibilities for the formation of deliberative publics that cross political, cultural, and even linguistic borders into a distributive public sphere.

Decentered publics are different in kind, not just in scope. By "distributive," I mean that the new form of publicity decenters the public sphere; it becomes a public of publics that are not unified in an encompassing public sphere where all communicators participate. Rather than simply offering a new and larger version of the existing public sphere, a decentered social space becomes a public sphere only through the work of agents who engage in reflexive and democratic activity. Participants in such a space, who take themselves to be responsible to those who address them, must first actively constitute it as a public sphere. Even as such new possibilities emerge with different forms of technological and institutional mediation, it is unlikely that a distributive public can be transformed into a convergent strong public whose decisions constitute a single legislative will. To do so would require a public at the same global scale; but this public would lack the interactive dimension of mutual claim making that makes public communication an essential feature of democracy.

While gradualists often recognize the role of electronic media in the construction of cosmopolitan public spheres, they continue to see the contrast between weak publics (that merely form opinions) and strong publics (that form a collective will) as identical across various transformations, from print to computer-assisted communication and from national to transnational interaction. For Sunstein, the emphasis on strong public spheres leads to skepticism about the democratic potential of the Internet.[31] The difficulty disappears, however, when we recognize that the concept of a public sphere is not univocal across social circumstances, and that the goal of such decentered distributive public communication is to create forms of interaction and inquiry that enhance deliberation across _dêmoi,_ a role that public spheres have historically played in the emergence of complex forms of social differentiation.

Similar considerations apply to the ideal of democratic self-rule in a dispersed and multilevel polity. In such a polity, good governance demands that democracy be organized into multiple units, from cities to states to national institutions, each with powers of self-government and each with its own interacting publics. The difficulty of reconciling the potential conflicts among the *dêmoi* emerges whenever there is more than one political unit that is already organized democratically. Call this the *dêmoi problem*. Indeed, global democracy is not a search for lost congruence between the politically organized space of the authors of the law on the one hand, and the nonpolitical space of the subjects and addressees of those laws on the other. If this were the case, the solution would be to find the proper and authoritative *dêmos*. Indeed, according to this conception, the larger the *dêmos*, the more democratic authority it has to act as the voice of the people. Rather, the problem of *dêmoi* becomes acute when the issue of sovereignty is raised: does democracy then require that one of the many units or *dêmoi* is sovereign so that it "has control over all the others"?[32] Along with most other democratic theories, gradualism answers that the largest and most inclusive *dêmos* is always democratically superior. As in the case of borders and jurisdiction more generally, these issues are taken to be settled or parametric, leaving little room to develop a normative vocabulary capable of answering such questions. Externalizing such claims as exogenous to the polity explains the lack of fit between much of democratic theory and a transnational polity such as the European Union (EU): while categories of modern democratic theory revolve around the state and "typically presuppose the existence of a *dêmos*,"[33] the transnational polity consists of *dêmoi*.[34]

This shift is already apparent in states, many of which are now federal and have multiple groups that might be able to make a legitimate claim to legislative sovereignty as a people entitled to self-determination. The developed and complex modern state is in Dahl's terms much more "polyarchical" than the simple notion of rule "by the people" can capture. This lack of a core institutional complex of power in the state shifts the judgment of its democratic potential to a different level, precisely because the rulers in the state seem to be "a heterogeneous aggregate of relatively autonomous groups," including groups that lay claim to the authority of expert knowledge.[35]

Indeed, the internationalization of political authority is the continuation of such heterogeneous and indirectly democratic authority, but at a higher level of disaggregation and with much less transparency. However, neither of these forms of political authority exercises real control over the complex social processes they seek to promote and regulate. In cases of both too much centralization and too much decentralization, democracy creates the potential for domination and thus may need emancipatory social movements to act in place of the people. In actual democracies, different institutional and non-institutional actors play the decisive role in various constitutional moments in which the basic democratic framework changes. By such means distributed across the entire structure, the people take various guises and emerge in novel ways, even in purportedly singular polities.

There are many other related problems of institutional design in established democracies, given that democratic state institutions have over time promoted and successfully entrenched conditions of ever-increasing pluralism, complexity, and interdependence. Under these circumstances, it may be the case that some members, in their status as citizens in one or more heterogeneous units, have lost the full range of their constituent power to initiate deliberation about the conditions under which they exercise their democratic powers. It is widely recognized that democratic states may dominate one another in some particular respect, as is the case in various international financial institutions with weighted voting indexed to contribution; but political domination is also common within states as either a consequence of centralization or as the domination of one unit by another. It emerges wherever multiple units are necessary for good governance, and yet these units possess a unitary institutional design that is still guided by the principle that democracy is popular sovereignty, or political control by a singular *dêmos*. A good example of this problem is the legal powerlessness of cities in the United States as units and the troubling and persistent injustices this lack causes for those who live in them. Residents of cities lack the normative powers to put these injustices on the deliberative agenda.

This example serves to illustrate the conditions under which a transnational democracy of democracies could promote conditions of justice across borders. As many have suspected, positive law does not necessarily help to address such matters, since the coercive aspect of law brings with it the potential for *juridification*, that is, the effective use of law as an integrating and regulatory instrument, but with a potential for domination under nonideal democratic conditions. This is certainly a great danger for the EU. This and other examples I discuss later show that the proper antidote for domination is not the inflated notion of sovereignty, but rather a nonunitary form of popular control that employs the normative powers that accrue to citizens and members of publics across borders.

As opposed to the sovereignty of the people in either its Lockean or Rousseauian versions, there is an alternative democratic tradition that recognizes the possibility of distributed or shared sovereignty across *dêmoi*. I have already mentioned a nearly forgotten form of federalism that emerged from the federalists' rejection of the antiquated form of the centralized empire. For many republicans (including Price, Diderot, and Turgot, among many others) federalism had the suitable dispersion of power necessary to overcome the increasingly coercive domination of colonies by the center.[36] Given that the transnational political problem to be solved was (and remains) domination, republicans rejected the idea that the size of the polity was the decisive consideration. Indeed, neither hypothetical nor real contractualism, based on counterfactual agreement or actual consent, is enough to overcome the potential for domination built into sovereignty as hierarchical authority. Nor did they regard decentralization by itself as the solution: it is in virtue of being part of a larger, well-ordered republic that the lower units may effectively govern themselves and be responsive to minority demands. The problem should be thought of in different terms—not in terms of a maximalist conception of democracy that would secure nondomination robustly, but in terms of a minimum—a minimum set of powers and conditions that would make it possible for citizens to not be dominated and thus be free to make claims to justice in unjust circumstances.[37] It would be easier to see how this conception of a minimum of effective freedom, as opposed to the achievement of popular sovereignty in the sense of the final say over each and every decision, could be realized under the circumstances of interdependence among a plurality of

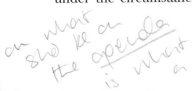
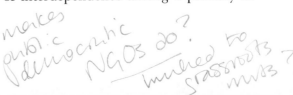

dêmoi. Distributive publics could contribute to such a conception of freedom as nondomination in ways that are not conceivable under the alternative conception of freedom as self-legislation.

While many civic republicans see like-mindedness or a common identity (political or prepolitical) as a condition of political freedom, cosmopolitan and federalist republicans think that, in fact, deliberation is more likely to be responsive to claims against domination when the citizenry is large and diverse. The regime characterized by institutionalized interaction among overlapping *dêmoi* does not require that all must participate in the same set of institutions at the same time or suffer the consequences of a uniform policy, but rather that all should be able to participate in a polity qua members of empowered institutions that redefine the relationships among the local, the national, and the supranational levels in terms of an authority that goes beyond positive law. This sort of distribution of normative powers, including the fundamental power to initiate deliberation, offers a better way to specify the democratic minimum.

The transformationalist hypothesis should not be based on an overly specific theory of an ideal democracy, but rather in a theory of *democratization*, of creating the reflexive conditions necessary for enhancing democracy through more democracy. Transnational democracy must do so in a way consistent with citizenship in multiple *dêmoi*. In order to develop a specific account of the democratic minimum, let me return to the core dispute in theories of cosmopolitan democracy, the dispute between the two forms of political cosmopolitanism. Neither provides an adequate theory of democratization under the current circumstances of globalization. In order to develop the particular alternative that I favor, I first develop an exhaustive typology of the main theories, which can be associated with two opposed pairs of thinkers: Buchanan and Habermas on the one hand, and Held and Dryzek on the other. As I have noted, the current discussion can be reconstructed on four main axes: political or social, institutional or noninstitutional, democratic or nondemocratic, and transnational or cosmopolitan. After considering the arguments of Buchanan, Habermas, Held, and Dryzek as the best representatives of particular positions, I develop my own political, institutional, democratic, and transnational account.

Cosmopolitanism and Democracy: Classifying the Theoretical Alternatives

In this section I consider the problems of current cosmopolitan and transnational theories in developing an adequate account of democracy beyond the nation-state. My main claim is that none of these four positions represents a plausible transformationalist position that provides the right sort of institutional mechanisms to convert the outcomes of democratic political processes into political power. While substantively opposed to each other, each of these theories fails for complementary reasons. An alternative account can be developed that incorporates the strengths of each while overcoming their fundamental weaknesses. These theories are informed by background assumptions about the scope of cosmopolitanism: whether it is moral to the extent that it is concerned with individuals and their life opportunities, social to the extent that it makes associations and institutions central, or political to the extent that it focuses on specifically legal and political institutions, including citizenship.

The best place to begin is the most minimalist account of international democracy, which is offered by Allen Buchanan. This minimalist impulse informs Rawls's work, so much so that he is best thought of as a social rather than a political cosmopolitan. Rawls proposes that we should determine the basic structure of institutions that peoples would agree to in the "second" original position, while tempering the scope of these institutions through the toleration required by the fact of pluralism. The result leaves no room for genuinely political and democratic institutions outside of states that organize peoples, given Rawls's Millian arguments that politics depends on "common sentiments," and his Kantian argument about the limits of size for legislation. Buchanan endorses this moral minimalism about basic rights, but disagrees about "how minimal this minimum is."[38] The next step for Buchanan is to accept a minimal justification of democracy on the instrumental grounds that democracy protects "basic" human rights through the "right combination" of representative institutions; these institutions are said to "most reliably achieve the accountability necessary for protecting basic human rights," understood as basic interests that are essential to leading a decent human life.[39] Thus, Buchanan is a political cosmopolitan who endorses political rights and democratic institutions as necessary for the accountability of any institution, including international ones.

Such an instrumental justification is insufficient on its own terms. If among human rights we include political rights and the right to democracy itself, as Buchanan suggests, then democracy is not merely a means of realizing human rights, but constitutive of them. Such an instrumental justification cannot justify the full democratic entitlement typically recognized in international law to the extent that it permits, as Buchanan admits, tradeoffs in the international system between "the capacity to protect basic human rights and building its capacity for democratic governance."[40] If democracy were indeed a basic human right, then these tradeoffs would be contradictory. Moreover, even the most minimal democracy presupposes the very rights that it is supposed to protect. As even Schumpeter admits, for example, free competitive elections "presuppose a considerable amount of freedom of discussion *for all.*"[41] On the same grounds, the instrumental justification of democracy as protecting human rights cannot be sufficient, since democracy also instantiates political rights, such as rights of association, participation, and expression, among many others. The justification of democracy in terms of human rights is thus unavoidably intrinsic as well as instrumental; as in the case of justice and democracy, one cannot be realized without the other.

Given the intrinsic justification of democracy and the constitutive features of citizenship that are necessary for accountability, democratic minimalism fails to provide a sufficiently robust conception of democracy, leaving the institutional and political bases of accountability unexplored. The central feature of democratic accountability enabled by political rights is a distinctive form of reflexivity. Reflexivity does not directly ensure that citizens are protected and that institutions act according to their basic interests, but rather that they are jointly empowered to refashion the terms and rules of democratic governance itself. Indeed, social scientific generalizations about the protective effects of democracy in the case of famines or wars point not to the efficacy of representative institutions or even to the rule of law, but to the creation of the conditions for an active citizenry with robust powers and entitlements to secure accountability through better democratic practice.

The second conception is associated with the work of Habermas and is more strongly democratic, to the extent that it is guided by a particular ideal of a self-determining people who govern themselves by acts of legislation. Democracy on the nation-state model connects three central ideas: that the proper political community is a bounded one; that it possesses ultimate political authority; and that this authority enables political autonomy, so that the members of the *dêmos* may "choose freely the conditions of their own association."[42] The normative core of this conception of democracy is the conception of freedom articulated in the third condition: that the subject of the constraints of law is free precisely in being the author of the law. Earlier I introduced Habermas's argument for "decentering" democracy under the conditions of pluralism and complexity. If this applies to the modern state, then it would seem that cosmopolitan democracy would take this trend even further. Yet, when discussing postnational legitimacy, Habermas clearly makes self-determination by a singular *dêmos* the fundamental normative core of the democratic ideal.

In both *The Postnational Constellation* and more recent essays on the EU, Habermas seeks to accommodate wider institutional pluralism.[43] Still, he cannot have it both ways. When considering various disaggregated and distributed forms of transnational political order, he describes them in nondemocratic terms as a "negotiating system" governed by fair bargaining.[44] This is because he clearly and indeed surprisingly accepts that self-determination through legislation is the deciding criterion of democracy, leaving negotiation among democracies as the fundamental form of political activity at the transnational level. Even given that this *dêmos* is at best a civic one, he nonetheless links the possibility of a "postnational democracy" to a shared and therefore particular political identity, without which, he contends, we are left with mere "moral" rather than "civic" solidarity. According to Habermas, even if such a political community is based on the universal principles of a democratic constitution, "it still forms a collective identity, in the sense that it interprets and realizes these principles in light of its history and in the context of its own particular form of life."[45] Without a common ethical basis, institutions beyond the state must look to a "less demanding basis for legitimacy in the organizational forms of an international negotiation system," the deliberative processes of which will be accessible to various publics and to organizations in international civil society.[46]

More recently, Habermas argues that regulatory political institutions at the global level could only be effective if they would take on features of governance without government, even if human rights as juridical statuses must be constitutionalized in the international system.[47] As in the case of Buchanan's minimalism, this less-demanding standard of legitimacy does not include the capacity to deliberate about the terms governing the political authority of the negotiation system itself. This position is transnational, but ultimately nondemocratic, primarily because it restricts its overly robust deliberative democracy to the nation-state level. The stronger criteria for democracy are not applied outside the nation-state, where governance is only indirectly democratic and left to negotiations and policy networks. Furthermore, the commitment to human rights as legal statuses pushes him in the direction of David Held's fundamentally legal form of political cosmopolitanism.

David Held's work on cosmopolitan democracy provides a more complete account than the previous two minimalist democratic positions. It is also more closely tied to an empirical examination of the impacts of globalization than are Habermas's conceptual claims, and thus does not so easily take over the metaphysical assumptions of social contract theory. Not only does Held show how international society is already thickly institutionalized well beyond the systems of negotiation that Habermas makes central, he further recognizes that "individuals increasingly have complex and multilayered identities, corresponding to the globalization of economic forces and the reconfiguration of political power."[48] Such potentially overlapping identities are the basis for participation in global civil society, in nongovernmental organizations (NGOs), and in other transnational civil associations, movements, and agencies that create opportunities for political participation at the global level. The enormous advantage of Held's approach over the other two approaches is thus threefold: an emphasis on a variety of institutions, a multiplicity of levels and sites for common democratic activity, and a focus on the need for organized political actors in international civil society to play an important role in a system of global democracy. For all these benefits, the self-legislating *dêmos* reappears in Held's explicitly Lockean insistence that "the artificial person at the center of the modern state must be reconceived in terms of cosmopolitan public law."[49]

When does this artificial person become a *dêmos* with supreme power? In Held's view this political subject becomes more abstract. It is not manifested in individual legislative acts, but in making the global political framework itself the subject of the popular will and consent. Once legitimated, this political subject emerges within a common structure for political action that enables individuals and groups to pursue their individual and collective projects. The framework itself functions as a would-be sovereign rather than a distributed process of will formation, since sovereignty now becomes simply an attribute of democratic public law itself. In order to reconstitute the community as sovereign, Held argues that the *dêmoi* must submit to the will of the global *dêmos*: "cosmopolitan law demands the subordination of regional, national and local sovereignties to an overarching legal framework."[50]

That this framework is both legal and overarching raises a potential democratic dilemma for such a global *dêmos*. In order to be overarching, the framework must instantiate a hierarchy of authority. In order to be democratic, the common framework will have to pass through the collective will and reason of its citizens, thereby recreating at the global level the contractual moment of a determinate people granting each other their mutual rights. In willing the general framework, the exact character of the rights and obligations necessarily entailed by the common structure of political action cannot be fully determined. At the same time, however, in order to be enforceable, these rights and duties must be specified in some way by an authoritative institution with the competence to do so, and thus it must act both legislatively and judicially. The dilemma can be put this way: if it acts judicially, it seems undemocratic; yet, if it acts legislatively, it has no special democratic status over other legitimately constituted legislative wills.

Held's demand for democratic control over "the overarching general legal framework" creates a fundamental continuity between democracy within and democracy beyond the nation-state. But it does so at a high price. Second-order questions about the nature of democracy itself are thereby removed from the international political agenda. As constituting the global *dêmos*, higher-level international politics are thus adjudicative rather than deliberative. This introduces a fundamental disanalogy with other cases of democratic self-determination: no such separation exists in a constitutional democracy that institutionalizes reflexivity through its openness to revision and amendment. At best, this legal framework recreates the weakness of the state within a dispersed international society, centering rather than decentering it and dispersing its democratic authority. Even if such a body were to exist, and even if it were somehow adequately representative, its judgments would always be made in terms of the particular modes of institutionalized representation that abstract from the relations and networks that make up international society. Such a dispersed and diverse polity requires a much more differentiated democratic structure, as it cannot exercise the power of the *dêmos* without being a potential dominator. Although Held has more recently (in *The Global Covenant*) emphasized multilevel and polycentric governance as necessary in the short- and medium-term, much more so than global parliamentary institutions, he still employs the same conception of cosmopolitan self-legislation as fundamental to a long-term global democratic order. In a word, in a period when even democracy in the state is disaggregated and decentered, the cosmopolitan conception of democracy is not sufficiently transformed and thus risks increasing rather than decreasing the problems of domination. I return to this theme below when discussing the European Union.

The fourth and final position can be called transnational rather than cosmopolitan precisely because it rejects the traditional state model in favor of a bottom-up strategy that promotes a robust transnational civil society as the nonjuridical basis for an alternative to the subordination of citizens to a common framework of public law. This account rejects the analogy to democracy in the nation-state *tout court*, seeing its development as one of an ever-declining democracy rather than a threshold to be met by international institutions. According to John Dryzek, its leading proponent, "there are imperatives that all states must meet" that are located in the core areas of their functioning, including economic growth, social control, and legitimation. These imperatives impose "structural limitations" on the state's public orientation in policy matters.[51] Among these are the structural limitations of capital on redistributive policies, now exacerbated by the mobility of capital in globalization. In the international arena, Dryzek's approach is further supported by the increasing importance of NGOs and the emergence of transnational public spheres consisting primarily of informal networks of association and communication.[52] It is also supported by the emergence of various international "regimes," that is, agreements about the rules and decision-making procedures that regulate specific activities or domains, including commercial whaling, the rights of children, nuclear accidents, and so on.

As with Held's insistence on an "overarching framework," this shift to informal networks and weak publics comes at a high price for democracy. The complementary weakness to Held's juridical model derives from the fact that on Dryzek's account transnational democracy can only be "contestatory." Dryzek thus ends up with a kind of institutional minimalism that also omits the dimension of active and empowered citizenship. This is most evident in the following sort of claim that is central to this approach: "Most of the government that does exist (in the form of organizations such as the UN, WTO, or the EU) is not at all democratic, which suggests that transnational democrats might usefully focus their efforts on governance," in which civil society already has a large contestatory and discursive role.[53] But why should we call this mixture of formal and informal institutions democratic even in some minimal sense? What is the alternative means by which those who suffer injustice in the current system can convert their claims into effective political power? Lacking any clear account of such successes or how the powerless are able to entrench their claims institutionally, contestation is not what the dominated require. The same is true of Held's more maximalist account, since the kind of institutional framework he develops, while differentiated and multileveled, does not address the issue of *which* active powers of citizenship are sufficient for democratization in the international sphere. The minimum here must be sufficient to contain within it not only the constitutive features of democratic citizenship, but also the necessary conditions for nondomination.

These criticisms of the range of possible theories of democracy beyond the state suggest a fifth, more adequate alternative: it must be institutional, political, democratic, and transnational. The first two features are necessary for the theory to be of the appropriate type, minimal or not. The question is, then: should these institutions be comopolitan or transnational in scope? Cosmopolitan democracy is insufficiently transformationalist, precisely because its top-down account of fundamentally legal global institutions requires a new global *dêmos*, not a democracy of *dêmoi*. In this respect, transnational democracy is the preferred alternative. At the same time, Dryzek's bottom-up version does not provide any basis for an institutional elaboration of the context of transnational citizenship. A normatively richer alternative is to reject both bottom-up and top-down approaches in favor of an approach that emphasizes vigorous interactions between publics and institutions as the ongoing source of democratic change and institutional innovation. Here deliberation replaces contestation as the proper democratizing activity. An adequate theory must in this respect be more like Held's cosmopolitanism with its well-articulated multi-leveled institutional structure. While I defend a different way of developing this basic sort of institutional structure, it is hard to see how any conception of transnational democracy can avoid using its general structural features. In this way, the account of transnational democracy offered here will preserve the best features of these other conceptions while overcoming their fundamental weaknesses.

Such an interactive and deliberative approach can also appeal to some actually existing institutions in order to test for feasibility and adequacy. Indeed, the European Union exhibits this basic structure well, and includes novel ways of organizing public deliberation across borders. In particular, Sabel and others have discussed interactions between publics and institutions that facilitate citizens' influence over dispersed but empowered decision-making processes, such as the Open Method of Coordination (OMC) in the EU. Novel deliberative institutions such as the EU committees that coordinate the OMC can act as institutionalized intermediaries that facilitate interaction, communication, and the exchange of information across sites and levels in a complex and iterated decision-making process. Even if such processes are still in need of further democratization, they exhibit two core institutional features lacking in Dryzek's transnational conception: they are both deliberative and reflexive. Given these two features, they can make dimensions of decision making, such as agenda setting or the normative framework that empowers the public, open to democratic control. Such possible democratizing processes embody just the sorts of interactions among publics and institutions that are able to recast existing political forms.

The next step of the argument is to develop the distinctively republican justification for this conception of transnational democracy. To do so, it is first necessary to offer an alternative both to cosmopolitan self-legislation and to transnational network contestation that makes nondomination the basic democratic ideal. The core of this conception is the democratic minimum, which provides an interpretation of the most basic statuses and powers necessary for citizenship. It answers the question, "but is it democratic?" by showing how democratic institutions can function reflexively as both the space to create new publics and as a means of achieving justice. A deliberative approach to the democratic minimum also helps us see the interactive relationship between the powers of citizens to initiate deliberation and the accountability of institutional actors. Such interaction and accountability promote not only democratic justice but also institutional stability.

The Democratic Minimum: A Republican Cosmopolitan Interpretation

Before developing this institutional and transnational account further, it is perhaps best to restate my working definition of democracy. Democracy is that set of institutions and procedures by which individuals are empowered as free and equal citizens to form and change the terms of their common life together, including democracy itself. In this sense, democracy is reflexive and consists in procedures by which rules and practices are subject to the deliberation of citizens themselves. Democracy is thus an ideal of self-determination in that the terms of self-rule are made by citizens and not by others. The democratic minimum serves to designate just those necessary conditions of nondomination necessary for democratization—that is, for citizens to be able to form and change the terms of their common life. The same conception could be expressed in terms of basic human rights, but these would have to include political rights as well as rights of membership, such as the internationally recognized right to nationality. Existing democracies often use human rights standards to deliberate about the adequacy of the community's established practices. When these deliberative practices are part of the international system, human rights are the main currency of evaluation. But much like the democratic ideal itself, the content of human rights is often historically specific, as, for example, when international treaties argue for rights to vote and even for highly specific liberal conceptions of self-determination. Moreover, rights are often cast only in terms of juridical protections, leaving aside political rights that are equally basic freedoms. Any full account of human rights must include reference to those statuses that are implied by rights against tyranny and domination, which form the republican core of the basic freedoms that are central to human rights.

For this reason, the democratic minimum must be expressed in terms that go beyond the usual set of minimum protective rights and negative liberties. Indeed, the United Nations Universal Declaration of Human Rights includes not only political and civil rights, but also a fundamental entitlement to an institutional system that fully realizes the whole range of human rights.[54] The democratic entitlement that has become part of international law is justified precisely because of the recognition that democracy is necessary in order to realize human rights. The argument in the next few chapters also shows that human rights require a transnational political community with some institutions that are global in scope, that is, an appropriately structured democracy of *dêmoi* in which such rights are multiply and robustly realized. Promoting human rights requires, in Dewey's terms, not merely more of the same democracy, but a new and better form of democracy interacting with new publics.

Why does the realization of human rights require democracy? If human rights include political rights, they can only be realized where there is meaningful political activity. Such activity may not yet be present in transnational contexts, but it is a constitutive condition for the exercise of these rights, as are certain kinds of statuses and powers that make it possible for citizens to address claims to each other. The democratic minimum permits meaningful political activity to emerge, since it attributes to each citizen the capacity to initiate deliberation and thus to take up the common activity of deliberating about common concerns, including the agenda of political institutions and the rules which guide political activity within them. These normative powers represent a minimum sense of self-governance that does not presuppose any particular conception of democracy, but instead can be realized in a variety of practices and procedures. At the same time, some institutions that are regarded as democratic in the broad sense do not realize human rights sufficiently; their citizens can use their normative powers to demand that their institutions and practices be deepened or expanded in some way in response to claims of justice. These rights thus require that practices of meaningful political activity be established.

The fact that human rights require actual democracy in some minimal sense has potentially troubling consequences for their realization. Since some particular form of democracy is necessary for the realization of human rights, a potential circularity ensues: human rights require democracy in order to be exercised, but democracy requires human rights in order to be self-correcting and nontyrannical, and thus minimally just. Only under ideal conditions would democracy realize justice and rights; in nonideal conditions, democracy might promote the continued existence of unjust circumstances (as the long history of the acceptance of slavery and then segregation in the United States shows). An existing democracy could fail in two respects: it could either fail instrumentally to be a means to justice, or it could fail constitutively to embody sufficiently deep or extensive democratic norms in its institutions. Both are failures of existing political rights and entitlements to promote justice.

According to such an account, democracy is related to justice in at least two different ways, and these complex relationships help give rise to what I call "the democratic circle." This circularity leads Rawls to distinguish between ideal and nonideal normative theory, where nonideal democratic conditions are defined in terms of the likelihood of noncompliance with fair normative expectations. This further leads Rawls to distinguish domains of applicability of the theory of justice: international relations or relations among peoples are part of nonideal theory, in which the requirements of political justice within societies must be weakened for the sake of toleration among peoples.[55] An alternative to this diagnosis might be that the indeterminacy of human rights requires some reference to procedural justice in political institutions. Understood in terms of the theory of democracy, the methodological distinction between ideal and nonideal theory simply assumes that the democratic circle cannot be broken. As part of a theory of democracy, an account of democratization should be supplemented by practical distinctions among various sorts of nonideal conditions. Rather than paint all nonideal conditions with the same gray, it is better to distinguish them in terms of those conditions that produce vicious democratic circles and those that are nonideal but still potentially virtuous. It could then be argued that in the latter nonideal cases, the adage still holds that the solution to the problems of democracy is more democracy. Ideal theory thus still has a role in providing the regulative ideal toward which virtuous circles aim.

Since ideal conditions are by definition never empirically real, virtuous circles must always operate under nonideal, but not entirely unjust, conditions. Tyranny provides the contrast class of entirely unjust conditions. Domination is possible without the total absence of justice, namely in mixed circumstances in which institutions may provide for some, but not all, of the conditions instrumental to justice. Determining how such democratic circles become more fruitful under less than just conditions is the problem of the democratic minimum. Once delineated more precisely, it can then be argued that the democratic minimum is not specific to particular domains or institutions. This democratic minimum, or threshold, may or may not be present in any given transnational and international institution, just as it may or may not be present within constitutional states.

The failure to meet even a minimal democratic threshold is particularly apparent in the lack of transparency in many intergovernmental negotiations, as well as in rules and frameworks that permit only the more powerful stakeholders to take part in most bargaining situations. Of course, not all bargaining or negotiation must be democratic, since such processes depend on the actors' implicit authority to reach a stable equilibrium. Whenever a variety of subunits are needed to govern the polity well, the democratic minimum may be unevenly distributed. The institutions that organize the polity into subunits with their own *dêmoi* may be currently unable to provide their members with the opportunities for the self-development requisite for the full use of their rights of membership. In these cases, membership may not provide statuses, powers, or entitlements sufficient to break the democratic circle, so these must then be acquired through other political relationships.

The purpose of the conception of the democratic minimum is thus to describe the necessary but not sufficient conditions for democratic arrangements to be a means of realizing justice under appropriate nonideal conditions. However, even if all of these conditions were realized, a democracy will not necessarily be just in all its dealings. It may, for example, be unjust in some domains, such as in relation to noncitizens affected by its decisions. To the extent that the democratic minimum is a matter of degree, it can be specified along a number of dimensions and in a variety of procedures. But once this minimum is met, a democracy cannot become more just without also becoming more democratic, and vice versa. This is so in the first instance because certain features of democracy are constitutive of justice—in particular, the treatment of citizens as free and equal. Part of the egalitarian democratic ideal is not simply that individuals are free from interference, but rather that they are free in the sense of possessing certain normative powers, the powers needed to assign and modify duties and obligations. The converse is also true. When citizens become less free with regard to their judgments or in considering the claims of others, their polity becomes less just and less democratic. Just as it holds among units of a democratic polity, the minimum must have application *across* polities as well; indeed, one polity may undermine the democratic minimum of another by ignoring its normative statuses and powers as a *dêmos*. But human rights do not apply merely to the members of the *dêmos*, and if there is a strong connection between democracy and human rights, then democracies that violate these rights, both of citizens of other *dêmoi* outside their borders and of noncitizens within them, are thereby also less democratic.

Democracies that recognize the political rights of the citizens of other democracies and of all the citizens in their own subunits have obligations to assure a whole variety of minima. These minima would apply to various locations, modes, and avenues for the exercise of influence over decisions. Just as citizens within a polity may disagree with one another as to whether or not they are violating the democratic minimum, so too may citizens of different polities. The issue in both cases is one of normative statuses and powers: that is, whether or not someone has the normative power to make a claim that others will genuinely deliberate about. The only way the minimum would be met in these cases is for the various citizens to deliberate together in some way. If other citizens have equal political rights as human rights, then the specific obligation to avoid the domination of nonmembers is much the same as that which we now recognize for our fellow citizens. Otherwise, nonmembers lack the power to make claims, the recognition of which is a minimal requirement of democratic citizenship. Here important empirical considerations of interdependence have their proper normative significance. Even if our obligations to members are often more extensive in this regard, we are nonetheless involved with many nonmembers in a web of social and political relationships that extend the potential for domination. The democratic circle suggests that duties to noncitizens are thus not distinct in kind, but rather in degree. The democratic circle in this case is a transnational one for any democracy that claims to be just and to honor commitments to human rights.

The democratic minimum is not solely concerned with the distribution of minimally necessary normative powers to enable citizens to influence the distributions of rights and duties. A democracy could promote justice by other means than these institutional statuses or powers, for example, by the development of wider, more effective, and better-informed ways of solving problems. A democracy may also promote justice in virtue of its cooperative mode of inquiry, making available a full range of information, or in the creativity and effectiveness of its collaborative problem solving. As a means to knowledge, democracy may promote justice outside of formal institutions, as associative and expressive freedoms spill over into the broader political domain over the long term. It could also be effective both in securing compliance to rules that promote beneficial consequences related to claims of justice and in developing citizens' political capabilities in virtue of their participation with others. These are not the only benefits of a transnational democracy, a democracy of *dêmoi*. More specifically, such a democracy must also enable the robust realization of human rights sufficient for nondomination. Democratization is thus political inclusion in the specific sense of the development of powers, statuses, and freedoms of citizens; this is its core task in any domain, including the domain of global justice.

However, these instrumental benefits need not necessarily occur, even under propitious circumstances. In light of the epistemic values promoted by democracy, a good case can be made that these benefits are not merely contingent by-products, but the result of reducing deliberative bias through the availability of all relevant perspectives, which is due to democracy's normative commitments to cooperative deliberation and open discussion. These benefits accrue, however, only if institutions already meet the democratic minimum. Problems may be solved effectively only if they are on the agenda; cooperation and compliance are enhanced only if those affected are able to participate effectively. Here is the result of a general maximin principle applied to freedom from domination: there are no increases in freedom overall (say, those stemming from gains in institutional efficacy) that do not also decrease the extent and intensity of domination. Many international institutions fail to meet this minimum and thus may increase domination by increasing efficacy and efficiency.

Given its goals, the theory of the democratic minimum requires thinking about democracy and the capacities of its institutions in new ways. Institutions need not be ideally just to achieve the democratic minimum, but rather may need to equip citizens with certain powers. The obvious place to begin developing the democratic minimum is in terms of the republican account of those human rights that contribute to individuals having the status of a free and equal citizen. I argue later that the absence of tyranny that is entailed by membership in humanity is a basic condition of any just polity. Nonetheless, this absence of tyranny may not reach the democratic minimum, although it certainly reaches something more fundamental in cases of extreme injustice. While the conditions necessary for nontyranny are part of nondomination, it is also the case that democracies in settler societies that continue to act tyrannically toward aboriginal peoples have not yet met all their obligations to realize human political rights.

In the standard liberal view, this nontyranny condition could be fulfilled by simple noninterference, thus making rights against tyranny a very plausible political means of realizing more justice. But this argument falls victim to the democratic circle in presupposing that the conditions of justice already hold. Nontyranny is insufficient to establish the potential reflexivity about normative powers necessary for rectifying injustice. For example, even if protection against the worst injustices were secured by mechanisms of consultation in a Rawlsian decent hierarchical society, the terms of justice and the framework for assigning normative powers would not thereby be made part of the democratically open agenda. A consultation hierarchy promotes a particular conception of the common good by defining only certain reasons as relevant, such as those in accord with a specific interpretation of a specific religious tradition. In this way the framework for deliberation is prescribed, and only those members who formulate their reasons accordingly will be consulted. This means that members of such societies do not have the power to initiate deliberation, but rather are merely consulted on terms they cannot alter. However decent, consultation alone cannot create the conditions for public inquiry that would be effective in securing the democratic minimum.

Another important aspect of democratic theory transformed by the focus on the democratic minimum concerns the requirements for legitimate authority. To grant only powers of consultation and contestation falls well short of democratization, as is shown in the republican contrast between citizen and slave. Unlike the slave, a citizen has the ability *to initiate deliberation,* which Arendt calls "the supreme human freedom."[56] By contrast, whatever freedoms are granted the slave, she remains dominated and thus lacks any intrinsic normative authority even over herself; at best, she may only follow the initiatives of others. The capacity to begin indicates a fundamental authority—what Rawls calls a self-initiating source of claims. But such claims are addressed to another such source, and thus take place within a community of persons with such authorization. The capacity to begin deliberation, rather than existing for the achievement of greater or lesser available liberties, thus provides the basic measure for the statuses of persons required for democratization. It should also be noted that extreme destitution creates conditions that are functionally equivalent to tyranny and the absence of political rights and other basic freedoms.[57]

In the last section I discussed Buchanan's instrumentalist conception of minimal democracy and argued that it could not account for the intrinsic and constitutive aspects of active citizenship. Buchanan's argument leaves open just *why* representative democratic institutions succeed in protecting basic rights. The empirical literature suggests that they succeed to the extent that they promote active citizenship. I turn now to Pettit's similarly consequentialist arguments for democracy, based on a specific dimension of active citizenship: contestation within a deliberative republic. According to Pettit, republican institutions must be constructed in such a way that as a matter of fact the policies and laws they produce will "track" the common good. In order that such institutions do not produce domination, nonmastering interference for the sake of realizing the common good is nonarbitrary to the extent that it takes into account the interests and opinions of citizens from their own point of view.[58] But how will this be possible? Here Pettit develops something akin to the democratic minimum, since tracking requires that citizens have a certain shared power: the power to engage in effective contestation. Citizens are accordingly free from domination only if they are "able effectively to contest any interference" that does not answer to their relevant interests and ideas.[59] But is contestation what makes nondomination possible?

According to Pettit, in order to be effective, contestation must occur within deliberative institutions, in which public decisions are responsive to reasons because they are made in a "deliberative way."[60] Pettit's analysis seems to have it exactly backward, since he embraces deliberative democracy only insofar as it makes decisions contestable. If citizens' intrinsic power to contest decisions depends on their more basic power to participate in deliberation effectively, then it follows that contestation is based on the even more fundamental power to *initiate* new deliberation. Otherwise, citizens will merely be consulted, and thus unable to introduce new points of view and new relevant interests and opinions. For this reason, this deliberative capacity is constitutive of, and not merely instrumental to, nondomination. In the next chapter I more fully develop the argument that this shift from contestation to deliberation requires rethinking the idea of non-domination in terms of normative powers rather than as freedom from arbitrary interference.

The consequentialist justifications offered by Pettit and Buchanan for minimal democracy fail. Since democracy enacts basic political rights, it is intrinsically justified to the extent that it is constitutive of human political rights and nondomination, and not merely the means to attain these goals. Without such constitutive features, it would be hard to see how it is that democracy could be reflexive and capable of democratization and novel self-transformation in a way that is more than simply a better means to certain given ends. The initiation of deliberation is thus generative of political power in a way in which con-testatory tracking and post hoc disapproval are not. When faced with cases of injustice, it is this dynamic and creative interaction between freedom of initiation and democratic accountability that makes it pos-sible for citizens to make their democracies more just and more accountable. This dynamic is lacking in any purely contestatory con-ception of democracy aimed at changing discourses. While one might number this capacity among the democratic powers, contestation that receives any institutional response that may be transformed into a decision must take the form of deliberation addressed to a public of citizens. Even more specifically, such institutions must be organized to respond not just to citizens' reasons, but also to their deliberative ini-tiatives. Many institutions' actors are quite powerful but lack the fun-damental normative power to initiate. While judges may refuse to hear particular cases, they cannot initiate them and instead must rely on citizens to do so. Indeed, judges lack final control over the agenda precisely so that they do not come to dominate citizens.

With a deliberative democratic minimum in mind, we can now diag-nose the complementary weaknesses of current cosmopolitan and transnational approaches. On the one hand, transnational approaches that emphasize contestation are unable to generate a coherent account of how nondomination would arise without effective deliberative in-stitutions to transform such public opinions into political power. Cosmopolitan approaches cannot identify a feasible process by which international institutions could be democratized, allowing the global *dêmos* to act autonomously through public law. In taking the framework of global order to be constitutive of deliberation, it leaves out the reflexive task of democratization. In order to develop the virtues of a more republican account, the democratic threshold of freedom as the capacity to begin must be a fundamental political right. This right can then be further operationalized in two ways: first, in terms of the capacity of citizens to initiate deliberation in order to amend the basic normative framework; and, second, in terms of the capacity to set an item on an open agenda and thus to initiate joint public deliberation. How and in what sense this basic democratic capability can be constitutionalized is thus a fundamental question for a transnational polity, since the democratic minimum requires this kind of reflexive order. It would also require that such reflexivity could be exercised across a highly differentiated institutional structure such as the one developed in the EU.

These sorts of institutions permit the expansion of membership and jurisdiction; under the proper circumstances of justice, their deliberative boundaries are porous. A polity that closes this open space created for the initiation of deliberation on injustice may fail to meet the democratic minimum. Even if democratic in some respects, such a polity lacks the requisite resources for deepening and extending democracy. Such an arrangement may fail to produce justice due to democratic domination through law, that is, through the democratically arbitrary character of membership in a single *dêmos*. If nondomination is to be realized transnationally, borders must be included in the open agenda through which citizens are able to reorder the existing order and change the terms of democracy itself.

Conclusion: Democratizing the Transnational Polity

Should we be optimistic about the potential for democratization under current conditions of globalization? The world in which we live is now more complex, interdependent, and highly uneven than ever with regard to the distribution of power and resources. For the last two centuries, from the Chartist movement for universal suffrage onward, democracy has been seen as a means to achieve more justice. Under current conditions, however, it can do so only if it is organized transnationally, as a democracy of many *dêmoi* that crosses the borders between them and organizes inquiry into and deliberation on the conditions for ongoing cooperation and collaborative problem solving. If we ask ourselves whether democratically organized societies are likely to become more rather than less interdependent, pluralistic, and complex, it is clear that they will to the extent that democracy entrenches such conditions, even as these conditions interact back upon such institutions and often require their transformation. These very conditions that cut across borders can promote injustice and possibly even turn a virtuous democratic circle into a vicious one. In that case, democratization is required at various levels at once, and to do this requires that citizens initiate new and experimental forms of deliberation in new contexts.

My argument has been both normative and empirical. It has been normative to the extent that it shows the superiority of a particular sort of reflexive democracy over other nonstate-oriented possibilities, such as transnational contestation from below or public legal frameworks from above. It has been empirical, because it has considered the political realities of increasing interdependence and its consequent potential for domination: given the limits of current realizations of human rights and democratic capabilities. The next step in the argument is to show that such a democracy of *dêmoi* is sustainable. While this argument cannot be developed fully in this chapter, the general principles of institutional design suggest the line of inquiry I shall pursue in the next two chapters. If justice is best realized among dispersed *dêmoi* in a multiunit polity, then its stability relies not on the centralized power of some sovereign, but on robust connections across diverse *dêmoi* and institutional locations. For example, directly deliberative designs in the EU rely on institutional actors to collect information, compare the success of various decisions on policy, and mediate communication and deliberation at various levels. Other institutional actors, such as officeholders and representatives, can act as intermediaries among various *dêmoi* if these representatives see themselves as citizens.

In the cases outlined above, nondomination across polities requires a thickly institutionalized space that includes various publics and civil associations that interact and communicate across units as well as various intermediate institutions that promote interaction across borders and levels. One of the insights of transnational republicanism has been precisely to show that properly organized democratic institutions can function as intermediaries and promote public interaction and nondomination across borders. In so doing, they can be thought of as part of a long-term project to extend the democratic minimum across democracies. In the next chapter, I turn to the task of developing some of the positive preconditions of transnational democratization, taking as a starting point the emergence of new sorts of publics and forms of network interaction that might be required to initiate and sustain such a process, one in which citizens mutually constitute those communicative powers that are a condition of democratic change across borders. In order to develop such an account, it will be necessary to reconsider the republican concept of nondomination in a more normative direction if it is to be useful for transnational politics.

2

Transforming the Public Sphere: Communicative Freedom and Transnational Publics

In the last chapter I examined the ways in which most cosmopolitan theories of democracy are guided by deep and unanalyzed assumptions about the circumstances and location of democratic politics. As they inform standard democratic theories, I argued that cosmopolitan theories generally rely on a singular conception of the *dêmos* as the will of the people, expressed as self-legislation within a relatively unified nation-state. Elaborating this conceptual archeology had a positive aim: to help identify feasible alternatives that are not as strongly connected to state structures and institutions. While Henry Richardson, Frank Michelman, and Cass Sunstein have developed republican theories of deliberative democracy, they have done so with constitutional states in mind.[1] The republican tradition, with its emphasis on nondomination, is a largely untapped resource for alternative interpretations of cosmopolitan and transnational democracy. According to the republican form of transnational democracy that I have been developing, freedom and citizenship are understood in terms of the normative powers established and distributed within a framework of institutions. So long as such a framework is able to create and sustain democratic rights and obligations, then the specific properties tied to the modern state are not required. Given the impact of the current uneven process of globalization and its form of political authority, one of the main challenges for republicanism is to develop the international dimensions that have long been part of its theoretical and practical legacy.[2]

The republican tradition has long been suspicious of the world state. Because of the deeply undemocratic character of current international political authority, many democratically minded cosmopolitans have turned to transnational civil society in order to challenge the emerging globalized forms of domination. However important transnational associations and movements have been to many social struggles, they do not always promote the conditions for democracy; and when they do, they provide only one dimension of the processes of democratization. In this chapter I argue that publics are more central to achieving the conditions for the possibility of democracy across borders precisely because they enable the emergence of communicative freedom that is central to challenging potentially dominating forms of authority. Ultimately, the task of democracy is to connect communicative freedom to institutionally realized and distributed normative powers.

The aim of this chapter is to take the first steps toward a positive theory of democratization by looking at the ways in which its fundamental preconditions have been transformed by global interconnectedness and by certain relatively recent technological phenomena. First and foremost, I have in mind two relatively uncontroversial social conditions that have long been widely identified across many different modern theories of democracy: namely, the need for a rich associative life of civil society, and the need for a communicative infrastructure of the public sphere that permits the expression and diffusion of public opinion. I use the term "public sphere" in a technical sense that begins with Kant and is developed further by Habermas.[3] A public sphere does not simply consist of the *res publica* of the institutions of government, but is rather a sphere of a particular sort of communication characterized by three necessary conditions. First, the public sphere is a type of forum in which the participants are "a public"—that is, a social space in which speakers may express their views to others who in turn respond to them and raise their own opinions and concerns. There may be a variety of publics, including literary, scientific, and democratic, as well as subaltern publics. Second, such communication must manifest the commitment of participants to freedom and equality. Third, rather than simple face-to-face interaction, this communication must address an indefinite audience. Communication is then public if it is directed at an indefinite audience with the expectation of a response. Publics can deliberate together with or without any strong connections to institutional decision making. At the very least, such public deliberation can add to and change the pool of reasons available to deliberation. Along with many other complex factors, the rights of communication and the democratization of state authority have historically emerged hand in hand. With the advent of new forms of political authority that directly influence the structure of communication across borders, new forms of publicity have also emerged, and with them new public spheres. Given the role of initiation and claim making I emphasized in the last chapter, such public spheres establish crucial deliberative conditions for the democratic minimum.

If new forms of communication and structures of publicity have indeed come into existence across borders, this would give special salience to deliberation as an important basis for democratization, as well as for transnational institutional design. Given the differences between democratic arrangements that presuppose a singular *dêmos* and decentered ones that organize *dêmoi*, we should not expect that all democracies have exactly the same communicative infrastructure. This means that transnational civil society and public spheres face different difficulties with regard to independently constituted political authority than do strong or public spheres connected to powerful state institutions. In the case of the state, publics provide access to influence over the state's sovereign power by mediating public opinion through the collective deliberation of the *dêmos*. In transnational polities, by contrast, the democratizing effect of publics consists in the creation of communicative networks that are as dispersed and distributed as the authority with which they interact. The issue explored in this chapter is, as John Dewey put it, how to elaborate "those conditions under which the inchoate public may function democratically."[4]

In the case of transnational politics, the inchoate publics under consideration are plural, and that makes a great deal of difference as to how we are to conceive of their emergence and contribution to global democratization. Such an account is decentered insofar as it takes a whole array of transnational publics as necessary in order to enable such freedom, and insofar as these publics need not collect themselves into a single global public sphere in the same way that citizens formed national publics that aimed at restricting the centralized authority of the early modern state as it infringed upon their communicative freedom through censorship.

The current situation is different in another respect as well. Democracy is now an explicitly avowed goal of many different formal international institutions and nongovernmental organizations. Current transnational publics do not always understand themselves as contributors to the overall democratization of the international system. In the absence of responsive institutions, most transnational associations take contestation rather than popular control as their fundamental political purpose. The first concern of many transnational networks and movements is simply to resist domination, and success is measured by whether or not they actually attain some degree of influence over decisions. One way they may do so is by constituting those affected by such decisions into publics. Indeed, many of these authorities are in fact agents of states and other large-scale organizations such as multinational corporations. While contestation is certainly an important feature of democratic politics in any context, publics can do more as initiators of democratization. In this role, they are able to attempt to shift authority away from states and the agents who govern them back to the principals themselves, who are capable of exercising popular control and accountability. This task is admittedly made difficult by the way in which transnational publics are formed, without the benefit of a unifying forum in which they might constitute themselves as a democratic will.

Besides the emergence of international human rights law after the Nuremberg Trials, one of the most striking features of international society in the last twenty years is the deepening and broadening of transnational civil society and of the public spheres surrounding many issues of common concern. This fact might suggest that we need look no further than this increasingly vibrant public sphere and civil society to find the potential for democratization. But while these publics offer hope for transnational democracy, they are only necessary and not sufficient conditions. We ought not overlook the deep differences between international and national public spheres and civil society, most of which concern the ways in which publics interact with institutions. Given that formal international political organizations such as the WTO do not interact directly with political publics, oppositional counterpublics form around them to exercise influence indirectly by mobilizing popular opinion. To the extent that transnational associations help to form such counterpublics, they contribute to the capacity of international society to democratize its relations of power and authority. However, counterpublics do not rule; and even if they did, we should not take this as a sign of an emerging global public that speaks for the collective will of humanity (or even one that speaks for multilingual Europe).[5] If a unitary global public sphere or world public opinion so formed seem to be unlikely prospects even in the long term, what is the alternative? And how might new public spheres contribute to increasing the extent and intensity of nondomination in the international arena?

Since publics and institutions constitute each other in their mutual interaction, any good theory of transnational democratization must treat both at the same time. Good exemplars of this process can be seen in the European Union and in the ways in which certain institutional practices organize deliberation across borders and networks. First, I provide an analysis of new forms of political authority and new public spheres, precisely because they provide a useful structural analogue that could help solve the difficult problems of the structural transformation of the conditions of democracy. Whether in institutions or in publics, the transformation is from a unitary to a disaggregated or distributive form. In the case of authority, the unitary state form has already been disaggregated into a multiplicity of principal/agent relations. In the case of the public sphere, the transformation is from a unitary forum to a *distributive* public of the type best exemplified in computer-mediated network forms of communication. If this analysis is successful, such a transformation of the pulic sphere might provide a structural analogue for the kind of empirical and conceptual changes necessary to develop any theory of genuinely transnational democracy. Second, I describe the sort of institutionalized authority in light of which such publics were formed and with which they interact as well as attempt to influence. It is important here to understand the exact nature of global political authority and the ways publics form by resisting the influence of such authority in the communicative domain. The third step is to develop the particular contribution that transnational public spheres make to the democratization of international society. Developing such public spaces for the exercise of communicative freedom is an essential requirement of nondomination. When communicatively free participants in the public sphere interact with empowered institutions, they acquire and extend their normative powers to secure and transform their own statuses as citizens affected by such institutions.

The effects of these interactions can be illustrated through a variety of examples taken from various international institutions, most especially from the European Union. These institutional forms of deliberation help us understand the task of democracy: how to overcome the reversal of agency typical of the new forms of authority in such a way as to make democratization possible. Democratization itself requires a further transformation, one in the understanding of the global political subject of democracy that I undertake in the subsequent chapter. In this chapter, I am concerned primarily with two questions. First, what sort of public spheres are appropriate for realizing communicative freedom under these new conditions of political authority? And how can emerging transnational publics interact with the forms of political authority typical of powerful international institutions? I turn first to the transformation of political authority in the global era, the consequences of which are as significant as the emergence of modern state power.

Publics, Principals, and Agents: The Transformation of Political Authority

Some conceptions of democracy demand that the people be able to control most decisions directly, however that might be achieved. In modern representative democracies, however, "the people" speak only intermittently and at best only indirectly influence those who control the levers of power. As applied to present-day democracies, a crucial challenge to the idea of the will of the people is the institutional complexity of those regimes. Arguably, then, a necessary move in rehabilitating the idea of the will of the people in modern times is to conceive of it in an institutionally distributed fashion. By the same token, the will of the people cannot be defined in abstraction from actual institutions and their operations (as some attempt to do when they think of it in terms of preference aggregation). Because of the indirect character of the popular legitimation of authority, citizens must be able to influence the authority exercised within such institutions at least in those cases in which they object to its unresponsive manner of operation.

What makes contestation so salient in the context of current international institutions? Contestation has typically emerged in periods of large-scale institutional shifts in the distribution of political authority, as was historically the case, for example, with the rise of the mercantilist state, and now recurs with the emergence of powerful international institutions. More often than not, these shifts in political authority beyond the state have been pursued as a matter of policy by states themselves, mostly through denationalization, and thus by the delegation of authority to international bodies and institutions that act as agents through which they may achieve their own interests. These policies have especially been pursued with regard to economic integration and the protection of markets from financial volatility, with some groups more than others bearing the costs of such policies.[6] Even apart from the emergence of fully supranational polities such as the European Union, such institutional strategies disperse political authority widely and at a variety of levels.

Without regularized channels of political influence (such as elections and representation) in the international sphere, challenge and contestation by the broader public sphere of international public opinion seem to be the only ways to exercise indirect influence over decision making. In the absence of formal democratic institutions, the public sphere is the only place in which informal nongovernmental organizations (NGOs) can challenge political decisions and attempt to organize public opinion around matters of common concern across borders. When successful, they may become integrated into a "regime" instituted to monitor the performance of various international institutions, as is the case, for example, with environmental groups who both monitor compliance to pollution and to whaling regimes and represent environmental interests in discussions and negotiations of their relevant rules and policies.[7] In this

way, NGOs now often act as surrogate publics and expand the scope of those who can influence decision making and implementation in public institutions.

This sort of indirect public influence has some legitimizing force, but it does not by itself make such regimes democratic, nor does it solve the problem of domination inherent in the relatively independent operation of their quasi-legal powers. Although participation in NGO-mediated regimes may indeed increase the number of actors who participate in decision making, it does not solve the basic difficulty: the widening gap between those who govern and define the terms of cooperation and those who are governed and thus still remain outside of civil society.[8]

By comparison, state-oriented public spheres have had significantly different features. Even when citizens do not influence decisions directly, they are able to exercise certain normative powers. In participating in free and fair elections, citizens have the normative power to change representatives and officeholders and to express their consent to being governed. Given this channel for influence, citizens may be said to at least have electoral sovereignty. This normative power of the collective will of the citizenry is dependent on the role of citizens within an institutional framework that allows for a distributed system of normative powers. In the event that political authority strays outside of the available means to exert democratic influence, citizens can also exercise accountability through the contestatory sovereignty of the *dêmos,* as when the voice of the people becomes salient in periods of constitutional crisis or reform.[9] In a democracy, the location of sovereignty becomes an issue when the people find their institutions and those who exercise authority through them unresponsive. Often authority is unresponsive not because citizens as a collective body are disempowered, but because these democratic institutions were constructed for a public that is different from the one that currently exists. Similarly, in the international arena, many powerful institutions, such as the International Monetary Fund or the World Bank, lack any mechanism for creating public influence over their agendas.

Viewed in terms of opportunities for public influence, international institutions introduce a further problem regarding their interaction with the public. To the extent that they are organized into a plurality of levels, international institutions amplify the heterogeneous polyarchy of political authority that is already characteristic of contemporary democracies. In so doing, they may sometimes extend the antidemocratic tensions within the modern administrative state, particularly those based on the modern phenomenon of "agency," a form of authority that is meant to solve the problem of social control for central and hierarchical authority. These new types of hierarchical relationships have been pervasive in modern economies organized around the firm as the unit of production.[10] They are hierarchical because they are based on asymmetrical information: the principal delegates authority to the agent to act in his or her interest precisely because the principal does not possess the resources, information, or expertise necessary to perform the relevant tasks. Given that the principals may not be in a position to monitor their agents even when given the opportunity, the division of epistemic labor creates pervasive asymmetries in competence and access to information.

These asymmetries are accentuated when they operate in highly uneven and asymmetrical social relations created by globalization and its indefinite social activity. One might even claim that the presence of economic actors such as corporations make the term "exploitation" descriptively more accurate. However, exploitation does not identify the distinctly normative character of these forms of authority. As large-scale organizations, often with vast resources, corporations operate more as nascent political authorities in that they are quite successful in imposing statuses and duties in the terms of cooperation, even upon states. While not employing simple coercion, such organizations act as dominators by devaluing citizenship and by being able to change important statuses and powers necessary for democracy.

Such pervasive asymmetries are yet more pervasive insofar as they have filtered into many situations in ordinary life, from stepping on an elevator to taking prescription drugs. The problem is not only in access to information, but also in the ability to interpret it, since most of us, for example, are "unable to render medical diagnoses, to test the purity of food and drugs before ingesting them, to conduct structural tests of skyscrapers before entering them, or to make safety checks of elevators, automobiles, or airplanes before embarking on them."[11] To this list we can now add "unable to assess the myriad of global financial markets and instruments." Such relationships of epistemic dependence and asymmetrical information define the specific relations of agency, in which one person (the agent) is dealing with others (third parties) on behalf of another or others (the principals). This epistemic asymmetry is a practical challenge to democracy.[12] As Karl Llewellyn already pointed out, the very idea of self-government is eroded by agency relationships to the degree that principals find "it is repeatedly necessary to give agents powers wider than those they are normally expected to use."[13] What interests me here is not the full economic theory motivating this analysis, but the incompletely defined normative powers that are entailed by the principal/agent relationship. The demand for self-government is not the solution, since it would attempt to assert the form of political authority that necessitated agency relations in the first place: that of a singular self-legislating *dêmos*. The issue as I see it is to constitute a democratic form of dispersed authority rather than to recreate a form of legitimation that cannot solve the problem of new forms of domination.

How precisely does the pervasiveness of such hierarchies potentially undermine the possibility of democracy, either at the nation-state or cosmopolitan level? The problem lies in the specific character of the principal/agent relationship that has replaced formal political authority. Unlike many forms of the principal/agent relationship in economic life, the new global agents are acting in a more general regulatory capacity, concerned primarily with the very political authorities for which they are agents. Moreover, the lack of any legal framework through which to check private forms of international regulatory regimes accentuates the hierarchical features of agency as directly imported from economic contexts. In these contexts, hierarchy may be defined as "the asymmetric and *incompletely defined* authority of one actor to direct the activities of another within certain bounds."[14] Such authority may transform a scheme based on cooperation into one of nonvoluntary inclusion. It is not simply that new international regimes are coercive as such (as Pogge and many others have argued), but rather that they are based on a form of incompletely defined authority as a failed solution to a problem of political control.[15] By calling the current global regime coercive, we implicitly appeal to a model of tyranny or exploitation rather than domination, and thus suggest a remedy to an entirely different problem. A new self-legislating *dêmos* would only repeat the same problem since it is precisely the limits of political control by such a mechanism that leads to the need for an agent in the first place. Such a *dêmos* would then only act as an agent for other *dêmoi*, and in this way also as a potential dominator.

Unlike the minimal political accountability of the Federal Reserve, the purpose of these neo-liberal regulatory hierarchies is not to bind popular passion; rather, concerned with deregulation, they mark shifts in the structure of accountability away from political authority. This shift does not create a vacuum, but rather a new type of authority. No longer are the agents accountable to states, much less to the political public spheres that operate in order to influence state authority; rather, after denationalizing many aspects of market relations, the states are accountable to the financial markets. To put it more precisely, states are accountable to particular agents in the regulatory regime—that is, to those "nationally registered statistical agencies" that formulate specific standards used to rate loans to governments and firms, and in that way specify the sort of financial conditions that structurally restrain state influence on economic distribution.[16] Once authority is delegated in an ascending chain, the exercise of political power by the agent is separated from the generation of political power among the principals, and thus from principals' deliberative judgments about the legitimacy of the obligations that the agents may impose.

In analyzing new forms of international authority, it is crucial that agency relations are not seen as "losing control," as Sassen has suggested.[17] By delegating authority to the agent, the principal seeks to *extend* the scope of his or her control and to procure specialized knowledge and skills that would otherwise be costly to acquire. In this way, in the face of pressures from globalizing economies, states in the world's developed regions have sought to extend their national-level authority where it could not otherwise go by denationalizing administrative and legal authority to agents, who then exercise it in the state's interest. However, this sort of delegation creates asymmetrical information as a byproduct of specialization, and

* the perennial problem of bureaucracy
— also endemic in national
context?

with it the phenomenon of the reversal of control. An example of such a reversal can be found in the evolution of business intermediary roles such as factor and banker, roles that often require the introduction of new "legislative control in the interests of scattered and unorganized principals."[18] If democracy is the goal, then this reversal must be undone, and it can be undone only with a minimal level of popular influence sufficient to make representatives more than another type of agent.

How can such a reversal be avoided and authority democratized? Civil society remains too disaggregated to provide any political solution, however appealing and inherently democratic the bottom-up strategy seems. Practices of empowerment by NGOs may have paradoxes built into them, such as when less well-off civil society organizations become accountable to better-off organizations in exchange for resources and assistance.[19] Similarly, powerful institutions may co-opt and capture the NGOs monitoring them, especially if they have a say in the composition of an NGO's consultative body, and in this fashion exercise control over the public that influences them. New groups aggregated so as to function as the *dêmos* for all those affected simply create a new, higher-level *dêmos*, which is at best a heterogeneous aggregate. Absent from this picture of democratization is the distinctive infrastructure of communicative power that may act to reshape such social relations and their hierarchies. One activity that reflects the distinctive kind of communication that goes on in the public sphere is the ability to raise topics or express concerns that cut across social spheres. This not only circulates information about the state and the economy, but it also establishes a forum for criticism in which the boundaries of these spheres can be crossed and challenged, primarily in response to citizens' demands for accountability and influence.

Putting the public sphere back into the political structure leads to a very different understanding of deliberative political activity, one that does not automatically consider the entitlements of participants in terms of the relationship of those who govern to those who are governed. The public sphere is not only necessary as a theoretical term in order to explain why these structures are so interconnected in democratic societies; it also suggests that democratic politics provides the forum in which publics act as intermediaries between civil society, markets, and formal political institutions. This intermediate structure is necessary in global politics, where top-down institutions remain remote from citizens and civil society organizations cannot provide the basis for translating bottom-up deliberation into political power. Such strategies fail because they ignore conditions necessary for the success of both democracy and empowerment, conditions found in the proper relations among responsive institutions, in a vibrant civil society, and in robust communication across public spheres. John Dewey seems to have come closest to developing the proper transnational alternative strategy of democratization when he responded to Walter Lippmann's criticism of the "phantom" public in modern complex societies: instead of regarding them as separate spheres, he argued for the ongoing interaction between institutions and the publics that constitute them.[20] The capabilities of citizens may sometimes outstrip the institutions that frame their normative powers, as happens when the public for whom they were created no longer exists (as was the case for the rural and agrarian public of early American democracy). Given complex and overlapping interdependence, many citizens now see the need for new institutions that are more transparent, inclusive, responsive, and cosmopolitan.[21]

Even when authority is disaggregated, citizens still may exercise certain powers through the public sphere simply by defining themselves as a public and interacting with institutions accordingly. In the first instance, a public sphere institutionalizes a particular kind of relationship between persons. As members of a public, persons can regard each other as having at the very least the capacity and standing to address and to be addressed by one another. Call this the communicative freedom of publics, a form of freedom that may take on a constructive role in which members grant each other rights and duties as participants in the public sphere. This freedom emerges from the interaction between the communicative power of participants in the public sphere and those more limited normative powers that they may have in their roles within various institutions. By acquiring such communicative freedom beyond the control of even a disaggregated authority, membership in a public uses the creative and constructive powers of communication and public opinion to reshape the operations of authority delegated to an agent from the obligations of officeholders into those of citizens. One way that such a public can effect a reversal of control is to see its emergence as recapturing the constituent power of the people, now in a dispersed form, when their constitutive power as citizens has failed.

This gap between public spheres and institutions creates an open question for citizens—has the authority of their institutions been legitimately exercised? The beginnings of popular control, and thus the preconditions for democratization, are not to be found in the moment of original authorization by either the sovereign or the unified *dêmos*, but in something that is more spatially, temporally, and institutionally dispersed. In the next section I want to develop an alternative normative conception of the power of publics and citizens and of the role of communicatively generated power in the achievement of nondomination and legitimate political authority. This account will help us to see what the transnational public sphere contributes to nondomination, where freedom from domination is manifested in the exercise of distinctly normative powers. Democratization, I argue, is best thought of as the creative interaction between communicative freedom and the exercise of normative powers, the powers that one and the same group of people may have in their roles as citizens and participants in public spheres.

Before I turn to the public sphere as a location for the emergence and exercise of communicative freedom, let me address an issue that is in some sense both prior and fundamental to the difficulty of obtaining a foothold for democratization. What sort of public sphere is appropriate for challenging and reconstructing relations of political authority, especially ones lying outside the boundaries of the nation-state? Such transnational public spheres cannot be the same as the ones that emerged to help democratize the state. They will not be unified, but distributed. This will allow us to ask the question of popular control or the will of the people in a different way so that it is not a phantom public but something more akin to Mead's generalized other. Or, as Aristotle put it, "'all' can be said in a variety of ways" in the corporate sense, or in the distributive sense of each and every one.[22] In order to become political again, the public sphere is undergoing a transformation from a corporate to a distributive

form. With this change, the possibilities for popular control are disaggregated into the constituent power of dispersed publics to initiate
democratization.

Publics and the Public Sphere: Some Conceptual Issues

In order to adopt this transformationalist approach, it is first necessary to set aside some misleading assumptions that guide most
thinking about the public sphere and complicate any discussion of
transnational democratization.[23] These assumptions are normatively
significant precisely because they directly establish the connection
between the public sphere and the democratic ideal of deliberation
among free and equal citizens. They can be misleading when the suggested connection between them is overly specific and leaves out two
essential conditions for the existence of a public sphere in large and
highly differentiated modern societies, conditions crucial to understanding what sort of public sphere transnational polities might
require. The first is the necessity in modern societies of a technological mediation of public communication so that a realizable public
sphere can no longer be thought of as just a forum for face-to-face
communication. There are other ways to realize the public forum
and its multiple forms of exchange that are also more appropriate to
modern forms of popular control and democratic public influence,
such as print or visual media, which temporally defer the audience
response. The second feature is historical: technologically mediated
public spheres have emerged through challenging political authority, specifically the state's authority to censor communication. In this
respect, sustaining a sphere of free communication has been crucial
to the expansion of emerging normative powers and freedoms of
citizens.

If this account of the necessary features of public communication
is correct, then the very existence of the public sphere is always
dependent on some form of communications technology, to the
extent that it requires the expansion of dialogue beyond face-to-face
encounters. Writing first served to open up this sort of indefinite
social space of possibilities with the spatial extension of the audience and the temporal extension of possible responses. Taking the

potential of writing further, the printed word produced a new form of communication based on a one-to-many form of interaction. Television and radio did not essentially alter this one-to-many extension of communicative interaction, even as they eased the entry requirement of literacy and raised the costs of adopting the speaker role to a mass audience.

Perhaps more controversially, computer-mediated communication—especially on the Internet—further extends the public forum by providing a new unbounded space for communicative interaction. But its innovative potential lies not just in its speed and scale, but also in its new form of address or interaction. As a many-to-many mode of communication, it has radically lowered the cost of interacting with an indefinite and potentially large audience, especially with regard to adopting the speaker role without assuming the costs of mass media. Moreover, many-to-many communication holds the promise of capturing the features of dialogue and communication more robustly than print. This network-based extension of dialogue suggests the possibility of re-embedding the public sphere in a new and potentially larger set of institutions. At present, there is a lack of congruity between existing political institutions and these expanded forms of public communicative interaction. Hence, the nature of the public or publics is changing, along with the nature of the authority with which it interacts.

Before leaping from innovative possibilities to an unwarranted optimism about the Internet's contribution to global democracy, it is first necessary to look more closely at the requirements of publicity and how the Internet might fulfill them. The sheer potential of the Internet to become a public sphere is insufficient to establish democracy at this scale for two reasons. First, this mediated many-to-many communication may increase interactivity without preserving the essential features of dialogue, such as responsive uptake. And second, the Internet may be embedded in institutions that do not help in transforming its communicative space into a public sphere. Even if it is a free and open space, the Internet could simply be a marketplace or a commons, as Lessig and others have argued.[24] However, even if this were so, actors could still transform such communicative resources and embed them within institutions that seek to extend dialogue and sustain deliberation. What would make it a "public sphere"?

Consider first the normative features of communicative public interaction. Publicity at the level of social action is most basic, in the sense that all other forms of publicity presuppose it. Social acts are public only if they meet two basic requirements. First, they must not only be directed to an indefinite audience, but must also be offered with some expectation of a response, especially with regard to interpretability and justifiability. The description of the second general feature of publicity is dominated by spatial metaphors: public actions constitute a common and open space for interaction with indefinite others—or, as Habermas puts it, publicity in this broadest sense is simply "the social space generated by communicative action."[25] This is where the agency and creativity of participants becomes significant, to the extent that such normative expectations and social space can be created by participants' attitudes toward each other and their communicative activities. But how did the public sphere historically extend beyond concern with public opinion and the publicity of communication to ultimately acquire political functions?

In his *Structural Transformation of the Public Sphere*, Habermas gives a historical account of the creation of the distinctly modern public sphere that depends upon just such a free exercise of the creative powers of communication. In contrast to the representative public of the aristocracy, for whom nonparticipants are regarded as spectators, participation in a democratic public is fundamentally open. "The issues discussed became 'general,' not merely in their significance but also in their accessibility: everyone had to be able to participate."[26] Even when the public was in fact a group of people holding a discussion in a salon or newspaper, it was also interested in its own adherence to norms of publicity and regarded itself as a public within a larger public. Because the public sphere of this sort required such universal access, participants in the public sphere resisted any restrictions or censorship imposed by state interests. In England these restrictions were placed precisely on information related to transnational trade, thought to violate the state's interest in maintaining control over the colonies. This conflict with authority was so great that, at least in England, the development of the public sphere was marked by continual confrontation between the authority of the Crown and Parliament and the press, particularly with regard to attempts to assert political authority over the public sphere itself.[27] For participants in the public sphere, such censorship threatened to undermine the openness and freedom of public communication and thus the status of being a member of the public. This status was one of fundamental equality, of being able to address one another and be addressed by them in turn, an equality that outside authority and status could not alter.

This specifically egalitarian expansion of the public sphere requires a more elaborate institutional structure to support it (such as that achieved by the modern democratic state, but not identical to it), as the social contexts of communication are enlarged with the number of relevant speakers and audience. In public spheres there is a demand for the inclusion of all those who participate and recognize each other as participants; this inclusion is not merely a matter of literal size or scope but of mutually granted equal standing. Contrary to misleading analogies to the national public sphere, such a development hardly demands that the public sphere be "integrated with media systems of matching scale that occupy the same social space as that over which economic and political decisions will have an impact."[28] But if the only effective way to create a public sphere across a differentiated social space is through multiple communicative networks rather than with an encompassing mass media, then the global public sphere should not be expected to mirror the cultural unity and spatial congruence of the national public sphere; as a public of publics, it permits a decentered public sphere with many different levels. Disaggregated networks must always be embedded in some other set of social institutions rather than in an assumed unified national public sphere. Once we examine the potential ways in which the Internet can expand the features of communicative interaction using such distributive and network forms, the issue of whether or not the Internet can support public spheres changes in character. Whether the Internet is a public sphere depends on the political agency of those concerned with its public character.

The main lesson to be drawn from these preliminaries is that discussions of the democratic potential of any form or medium of communication cannot be satisfied by listing its positive or intrinsic features, for example, its speed, its scale, its anarchic nature, its ability to facilitate resistance to centralized control as a network of networks, and so on. The same is true for its negative effects or consequences, such as its well-known disaggregative character or its anonymity. Taken together, both these types of considerations tell against regarding the Internet as a variation of existing print and national public spheres. Rather, the space opened up by computer-mediated communication supports a new sort of distributive rather than unified public sphere, with new forms of interaction. By "distributive," I mean a form of communication that decenters the public sphere; it is a public of publics rather than a distinctively unified and encompassing public sphere in which all communicators participate. Here there is also a clear analogy to current thinking on human cognition. The conception of rationality employed in most traditional theories tends to favor hierarchical structures, where reason is a higher-order executive function. One might argue that this is the only real possibility, given that collective reasoning can only be organized hierarchically in a process where authority resides at only one highest level. There is no empirical evidence that human reasoning occurs only in this way, however. As Susan Hurley points out, much of cognitive science has rejected such a view of a central cognitive process and its "vertical modularity," and has replaced it with one of "leaky boundaries" and "horizontal modularity" in which "each layer or horizontal module is dynamic" and extends "from input through output and back to input in various feedback loops."[29] By analogy (and by analogy only), this kind of recursive structure is best organized in social settings through dynamically overlapping and interacting units rather than in distinct units related to a central unit of deliberation exercising executive control. In complex operations, such as guiding a large vessel into harbor, no one person possesses sufficient knowledge to fulfill the task. Errors can only be determined post hoc. Given that most polities do not exhibit such a unitary structure, the escalation of power in attempts to assert central control not only has antidemocratic consequences, but it also serves to undermine gains in rationality.

Rather than simply offering a new version of the existing print-mediated public sphere, the Internet becomes a public sphere only through agents who engage in reflexive and democratic activity. In other words, for the Internet to create a new form of publicity beyond the mere aggregate of all its users, it must first be *constituted* as a public sphere by those people whose interactions exhibit the features of dialogue and who are concerned with its publicity. In order to support a public sphere and technologically mediate the appropriate norms, the network form must become a viable means of expanding the possibilities of dialogue and the deliberative, second-order features of communicative interaction. These features are indeed not the same as manifested in previous political public spheres (such as the bourgeois public sphere of private persons), but they can nonetheless give rise to such higher-order and reflexive forms of publicity.

In the next section I argue that it is precisely such a distributive public sphere that can respond to the new, post-Westphalian world of politics that is in very significant ways located beyond the state. With the emergence of new distributive publics, the dispersed and denationalized authority of agents could once again become the subject of public debate, even if the consequences of such authority are not uniformly felt. The most obvious example is the exercise of corporate power over the Internet and the attempt to control universal access so as to create the functional equivalent of censorship without centralized public authority. Such a concern with publicity also creates attitudes of common public concern, as illustrated below by the role of dispersed publics who sought to reverse the reversal of agency in the disputes about the Multilateral Agreement on Investment (MAI). This example shows the potential democratizing power of new distributive publics in their relation to the signature form of global political authority. It is no accident that this authority is exercised precisely within a structurally similar but new historical setting with the potential to undermine the public sphere. This provides a possibility of freedom from domination that is not only a matter of being a citizen in a free state, but now also depends on the ability to become a participant in a public sphere embedded in other public spheres.

Communicative Freedom and the Distributive Public Sphere

As I have discussed thus far, communicative freedom typically operates in a generic modern public sphere, that is, one that combines
both face-to-face and mediated communication. The forms of such
mediation now seem inadequate for a public sphere writ large
enough to operate on the global level. And even if this were possible,
it would hardly create the conditions for communicative freedom
necessary for democracy. Two problems are now emerging: the first
concerns the issue of a feasible form of mediation and the possibilities for communicative freedom within it. The second takes up the
possibility of new formal and institutional forms that could interact
and mediate such preconditions transnationally, as well as have the
potential for interaction between the normative powers of institutional roles such as citizen and officeholder and the communicative
freedom of members of publics created by interacting publics. The
first issue concerns informal network forms of communication such
as the Internet, while the second concerns new forms of highly dispersed deliberation such as those emerging in certain practices and
institutions of the European Union, primarily at the level of policy
formation. Both permit the exercise of new forms of political agency
while at the same time demanding the agency of those who might
otherwise suffer a reversal of agency, both as users and as principals.

If Internet communication has no intrinsic features, it is because,
like writing, it holds out many different possibilities for transforming
the public sphere. At the same time the Internet does have certain
structural features that are relevant to issues of agency and control.
Here it is useful to distinguish between hardware and software. As
hardware, the World Wide Web is a network of networks with technical properties that enable the conveyance of information over great
distances with near simultaneity. This hardware can be used for different purposes, as embodied in software that configures participants
as "users." Indeed, as Lessig notes, "an extraordinary amount of control can be built into the environment that people know in cyberspace," perhaps even without their knowledge.[30] Such computer
programs depend on software in a much broader sense: software not
only includes the variety of programs available, but also shapes the

ways in which people improvise and collaborate to create new possibilities for interaction. Software in the latter sense includes both the modes of social organization mediated through the network and the institutions in which such communication is embedded. For example, the indeterminacy of the addressees of an anonymous message can be settled by reconfiguring the Internet into an intranet, creating a private space that excludes others and defines the audience. This is indeed how most corporations use the Web today, creating inaccessible and commercial spaces within networks through the use of firewalls and other devices that protect commercial and monetary interactions between corporations and anonymous consumers. The Web thus enables political and social power to be distributed in civil society, but it also permits such power to be manifested less in the capacity to interfere with others than in the capacity to exclude them from interaction and constrain the freedom and openness of the Internet as a public space. For the Internet to be a public space, users can reflexively configure themselves as agents and intermediaries, and thus as a public.

Given that what is needed in order to secure various public spaces are alternatives to the current set of intermediaries rather than their absence, civil society organizations have distinctive advantages in taking on such a responsibility for publicity in cyberspace. They have organizational identities so that they are no longer anonymous. They also take over the responsibility for responsiveness that remains indeterminate in many-to-many communication. Most of all, they employ the Internet, but not as users; they create their own spaces, promote interactions, conduct deliberation, make information available, and so on. As I mentioned above, a variety of organizations created a forum for debate on the Multilateral Agreement on Investment, an issue that hardly registered in the national media. Not only did these organizations make the MAI widely available, they also held detailed online discussions of the merits of its various provisions.[31] As a tool for various forms of activism, the Internet promotes a vibrant civil society; it extends the public sphere of civil society, but does not necessarily transform it. The point is not simply to create a Web site or to convey information. The Internet becomes something more only when sites are created as public spaces in which free, open, and responsive dialogue occurs. This sort of project is not uncommon and includes experiments among neighborhood groups, NGOs, and others. The civil society organization acts as an intermediary in a different and public-regarding way: not as an expert communicator, but rather as the creator and facilitator of institutional software that socializes the commons and makes it a public space.

As long as there are actors who will create and maintain transnational communication, this sort of serial and distributed public sphere is potentially global in scope. Its unity is to be found in the general conditions for the formation of publics themselves, and in the actions of those who see themselves as constituting a public against this background. Membership in these shifting publics is to be found in civil society in both formal and informal organizations that emerge to discuss and deliberate on the issues of the day. The creation of publics is a matter of communicators becoming concerned with and acting to create the general conditions that make such a process possible. Once such agents are present, it is a matter for formal institutionalization, just as sustaining the conditions for the national public sphere is a central concern of the citizens of democratic nation-states. In the case of such shifting and potentially transnational publics, the institutions that sustain publicity and become the focus of the self-referential activity of civil society must also be innovative if they are to have their communicative basis in dispersed and decentered forms of publicity. At the same time, these institutions must be deliberative and democratic. The public must itself be embedded in an institutional context, not only to secure the conditions of publicity, but also to promote the interaction among publics that is required for deliberative democracy. Thus, both network forms of communication and the publics formed in them must be embedded in a larger institutional and political context if they are to be transformed into public spheres in which citizens can make claims and expect an appropriate response. In much the same way that they have responded to censorship, publics interact with institutions in order to shape them and to secure their own communicative freedom. In so doing, they expand their normative powers as citizens: powers which shape the conditions of communication rather than simply demand immunity from interference.

There are several reasons to think that current democratic institutions are insufficient for this task. States have promoted the privatization of various media spaces for communication, including not only the Internet but also broadcast frequencies. Even if the Internet is not intrinsically anarchistic, and even if states were willing to do more by protecting the public character of cyberspace, it remains an open question whether this form of communication can escape the state's monopoly powers over political space and time, including public space and the temporality of deliberation. It is precisely the Internet's potentially aterritorial character that makes it difficult to square with centralized forms of authority over a delimited territory. This process of deterritorialization, however, does not produce common benefits for all, especially since Internet use may reflect inequalities in access to rule-making institutions as well as older patterns of subordination at the international level. It is also true that people do not as yet have patterns of communication sufficient to identify with each other on cosmopolitan terms. Nonetheless, the new opportunities the Internet affords for deliberation and the access to influence it provides in its distributive and network forms do not require such strong preconditions in order to open up new forms of democratization.

It is certainly not the case that states have been entirely ineffective in sustaining these conditions, nor is it true that national public spheres are so culturally limited that they serve no democratic purpose. Rather, what is at stake is whether such public spheres will cease to be as politically important. If the Internet escapes territoriality, then there will be no analogue at the institutional level for the particular connections and feedback relations between the national public sphere and the democratic state. Whatever the institutions that are able to promote and protect such a dispersed and disaggregated public sphere, they will represent a novel political possibility as long as they do not "merely replicate on a larger scale the typical modern political form."[32] This access to political influence through mediated communication will not be attained once and for all, as it was in the unified public sphere of nation-states in which citizens gained influence through the complex of parliamentary or representative institutions. Currently, Internet publics are "weak" publics, which generally exert influence over decision-making institutions through public opinion. But they may become "strong" publics when they are able to exercise influence through institutionalized decision procedures with regularized opportunities for input. One necessary condition for transnational institutions to be democratic is that they promote access to influence distributively across various domains and levels, rather than merely aggregatively in the summative public sphere of all citizens. Because there is no single institution to which strong publics are connected, the contrast between weak and strong publics is much more fluid than the current usage presupposes.

Before turning to the question of how public spheres may be institutionalized transnationally, let me consider an objection put forth by Will Kymlicka, if only to show the specific difference that transnational publics make as preconditions for democratization. Because the political institutions of democracy must be territorially congruent with the available forms of publicity, the difficulties posed by the disunity of a global public sphere cut much deeper for the idea of deliberative democracy. As Kymlicka has pointed out, territoriality continues to survive by other means, particularly since "language is increasingly important in defining the boundaries of political communities and the identities of the actors."[33] For this reason, Kymlicka argues, national communities "remain the primary forum for participatory democratic debates." Whereas international forums are dominated by elites, national public spheres are more likely to be spaces for egalitarian mass participation in vernacular languages, and are thus the only forums that guarantee "genuine" democratic participation and influence. Moreover, Kymlicka argues that since deliberation depends on common cultural frameworks (such as newspapers and political parties), the scope of a deliberative community must be limited to those who share a political culture. Without such a culture democracy cannot be participatory and deliberative, and perhaps not even genuinely democratic at all.[34] This argument is particularly challenging to the view defended here, since it employs the same idea of a dialogical public sphere within a deliberative democracy in order to reach the *opposite* conclusion. Can mediated communication and the extension of dialogue go beyond a territorial, self-governing linguistic community?

Without a single location of public power, the unified public sphere that Kymlicka makes a necessary condition of democracy becomes an impediment to rather than an enabling condition for mass participation in decisions at a single location of authority. The minimal criterion of participatory adequacy is that even with the diffusion of authority, participants in the public sphere would have to be sufficiently empowered to create opportunities to access influence over transnational decision making. Currently such publics are weak in the sense that they exert influence only through general public opinion. Or, as in the case of NGOs with respect to human rights, publics may rely heavily on supranational judicial institutions, adjudication boards, and other already constituted and authoritative bodies. For publics to use their communicative freedom to transform normative powers, they need not ever become strong publics in the national sense of being connected to a particular set of parliamentary or representative institutions.[35] However, even strong publics do not rule. That is because strong publics can be regularized through the entrenched connection between the public opinion formed in them and a particular sort of legislatively empowered collective will. While this mechanism is inadequate for situations in which the dispersed institutional distribution of processes form a popular will, transnational institutions would still have to permit agents to influence deliberation and decisions through the exercise of their communicative freedom across various domains and levels.

Rather than look for a single axis on which to connect emerging publics to decision-making processes in international and transnational institutions, it will be more useful to consider a variety of possible forms of communication given the various ways connections can be made between communicative freedom and normative powers in the public sphere. While the Internet provides a paradigmatic case of a distributive public sphere, the European Union provides the fullest and most exemplary case. Given that I provide a much fuller account of the European Union's institutional structure in chapter 4, I will consider only one aspect of the debate here: proposals that are suggestive of how a polycentric form of publicity might permit rather different forms of democratic deliberative influence than the standard model of a national public formed around parliamentary debate.

While the full range of its possible forms of institutionalization cannot be considered here, the European Union is transnational and as such obviously lacks the unitary and linguistic features of previous public spheres. I will consider only one aspect of the interaction between transnational publics and political institutions: the practices of decision making that are suggestive of how a polycentric form of publicity would allow for a more rather than a less directly deliberative form of governance (once we abandon the assumption that there must be a unified public sphere connected to a single set of state-like authority structures that impose uniform policies over its entire territory). As Charles Sabel has argued, a "directly deliberative" design in many ways incorporates epistemic innovations and increased capabilities of economic organizations, in the same way the regulatory institutions of the New Deal followed the innovative patterns of industrial organization in the centralized mass production they attempted to administer and regulate.[36] Roughly, such a form of organization uses nested and collaborative forms of decision-making based on highly dispersed collaborative processes for jointly defining problems and setting goals already typical of many large firms with dispersed sites of production. One such process is found in the use of the Open Method of Coordination (OMC) for many different policies (such as unemployment or poverty reduction) within the EU, and is best described as "a decentralized specification of standards, disciplined by systematic comparison."[37] In this process, citizens in France, Greece, and elsewhere deliberate as publics simultaneously with other EU citizens at different locations, thereby diffusing Kymlicka's objections to transnational deliberation. Why would such a design not produce something quite similar to the agency problem, to the extent that authoritative decisions made by some replace deliberation by all?

The features of the deliberative process promoted by the OMC are quite different from simple delegation. First, decisions so produced do not take the form of a uniform policy that governs all. Nonetheless, the OMC promotes a great deal of interaction, both within EU organizations and across sites and locations, so that solutions to problems generated by other deliberators can provide alternatives or can be used as premises for the deliberation of others. Second, a shared normative framework established by initial goals and benchmarks structures the deliberation at each site and level, and the process of their application requires new deliberations at various levels of scale. At all levels, citizens can introduce concerns and issues based on local knowledge of problems, even as they are informed by the diverse solutions and outcomes of other planning and design bodies. This sort of distributive process concerns the deliberative division of labor, which takes advantage of the diverse circumstances and competences of various groups. Thus, while these publics are highly dispersed and distributed, various levels of deliberation permit public testing and correction even if they do not hierarchically override decisions at lower levels. Such a collaborative process of setting goals and defining problems produces a shared body of knowledge and common goals, even if the solutions need not be uniform across or within various organizations and locations. Sabel calls this "learning by monitoring," and proposes ways in which administrative agencies could employ such distributive processes even while evaluating performance at lower levels by systematic comparisons across sites.[38] Furthermore, innovative solutions are not handed down from the top, since collective learning does not assume that the higher levels are epistemically superior.

From this brief description, it is possible to see how the OMC provides a space for ongoing reflection on agendas and problems, as well as promotes an interest in inclusiveness and diversity of perspectives. These enabling conditions for democracy can take advantage of intensified interaction across borders, a by-product of the thickening of the communicative infrastructure across state borders. This sort of federalism provides for modes of accountability within the process itself, even while allowing for local variations that go beyond the assumption of the uniformity of policy over a single bounded territory that is typical of nation-state regulation. Sabel and Cohen argue that the European Union already has features of a directly deliberative polyarchy in its implementation of the OMC in its economic, industrial, and educational standards. The advantage of such deliberative methods is that the interaction at different levels of decision making promotes robust accountability—accountability that operates upward, downward, and laterally, and in this way cuts across the typical distinction of vertical and horizontal accountability.[39] Thus, directly deliberative polyarchy describes a method of decision making, used in institutions across various levels and with plural authority structures, that makes use of distributive publics.

Nonetheless, even in this best possible interpretation, committees currently function as forums for political processes and as coordinating bodies across various levels of governance; even with the OMC, such forums are deficient as argumentative forums to the extent that they are only semi-public and relate primarily to networks of administrative agencies and private policy experts.[40] Such a procedure, however deliberative, retains the weaknesses of the hierarchical relations of experts, officials, and citizens within which it is embedded. One possibility for correcting this deficit is to organize deliberation self-consciously by convening and empowering "minipublics."[41] Whether chosen randomly or as representatives of the body of citizens as a whole, such procedures aim to avoid the problem of self-selection typically found in NGOs and other civil society organizations. Minipublics offer a strategy for getting beyond the dilemma of insider consultation and outsider contestation that is a structural feature of civil society activity in currently existing international institutions that rely on expert authority and knowledge as the basis for their legitimacy. Since minipublics are self-consciously created and seek either to include all the relevant stakeholders or to convene a representative body of citizens, they do not directly rely on representation as their mode of communicating interests. For example, bodies of citizens have been empowered as minipublics to propose electoral reform in British Columbia, adjudicate environmental disputes in Australia and other places, and much more. Minipublics provide opportunities for empowered participation where groups of citizens, not experts, are given specific normative powers to deliberate and form opinions and to make recommendations and decisions. The advantage is that such smaller publics are able to deliberate within specific institutional, functional, and temporal constraints in ways that the public at large cannot.

Rather than simply a form of consultation, this form of influence requires that an institution transfer some of its authority to the minipublic whose deliberation it empowers, opening up a directly deliberative process within the institution that includes as many perspectives as possible and can be repeated when necessary. This transfer of authority requires formal or constitutional legitimacy—the delegation of some power usually assigned to other locations in the constitutional structure—and thus depends on further decentering of institutional power. A minipublic is thus an institutionally constructed intermediary in popular will formation, although it could act in such a way as to become an agent for the creation of a larger public with normative powers. This step would require broadening the democratic agenda-setting powers of bodies outside the Commission, which would then have the normative power to convene such publics and set their objectives. This would also make institutionalized deliberation more responsive by virtue of strengthening and shortening the feedback loops necessary for implementation and learning in decentered decision making.

The possible institutional designs of a minipublic are varied depending on the democratic values and institutional goals they seek to fulfill as well as the subject and scope of deliberation. Collaboration and problem solving, innovation and creativity, civic education and engagement, and the assessment of policies all provide opportunities for the less powerful to have a voice. Minipublics are not simply made out of preexisting social partners, but are constructed so as to enable more open-ended processes of participation and the empowerment of those affected by a policy. A directly deliberative process cannot simply wait to collect responses from the spontaneous and diffuse general public sphere, but rather must ongoingly and iteratively construct the public or publics with which it interacts and which it empowers to make decisions and to change its procedures. By contrast, minipublics rely on experimental efforts to convene citizens and create self-consciously organized publics. National public spheres only appear to be less constructed because they have lost the traces of their historical development in nation building over centuries.

By interacting with deliberative institutions at various levels, members of minipublics also interact with each other, thereby beginning a process of deepening democracy over which the delegating institution has no direct control. As empowered members of various polities and of the EU itself, such participants can make claims to other publics and to other institutions as they exercise their political rights as members of the European polity. The emergence of such transnational publics in effective democratic governance does not depend directly on whether or not a "European public sphere" emerges.[42] Highly differentiated and dispersed public spheres that sometimes overlap and intersect would be sufficient for the requisite interaction between institutions and publics. While such processes would go well beyond the current use of committees and the OMC, these structures might well permit the emergence of wider and deeper forms of deliberative interaction across institutions and *dêmoi* than has been realized thus far.

The question still remains: at the level of democratic experimentation and implementation in directly deliberative processes, who is the public at large? Sabel and Cohen provide no clear answer to this question, asserting only that the process must be open to the public.[43] The problem for the institutional design of directly deliberative democracy is how to create precisely the appropriate feedback relations between disaggregated publics and a polycentric decision-making process. As my discussion of the Internet shows, there is a technology through which distributive publicity is produced and which expands and maintains the deliberative potential of dialogue. Thus, at least in some of its decision-making processes, the EU could seek to marry directly deliberative decision making to computer-assisted, mediated, and distributive forms of publicity. Most of all, implementing this design would require experimentation to reconcile the dispersed form of many-to-many communication with the demands of the forum. Rather than providing an institutional blueprint, such direct and vigorous interaction among dispersed publics at various levels of decision making creates new forums and publics around locations at which various sorts of decisions are debated and discussed. This sort of Internet counterpublic sphere is potentially transnational, as is the case with the public that formed around the Multilateral Agreement on Investment. Hence, appropriately designed decision-making processes such as those in the EU, combined with the existence of a suitable form of publicity, at least show how dialogue could be technologically and institutionally extended and democratically empowered in a transnational context.

NGOs and other actors in international civil society are often able to gain influence through consultation and contestation, sometimes involving public processes of deliberation. In most international organizations, this influence comes not only from internal norms of transparency and accountability, but also via the mechanisms of various adjudicative and judicial institutions that empower individual citizens with rights of appeal. This sort of institutional architecture promotes deliberation through accountability and monitoring and works particularly well with regard to national authorities and their normative commitments. Such adjudicative bodies also expand the possibilities of contestatory influence in the international context, in the same way that civil rights law in the United States or various sorts of antidiscrimination laws in many different countries produce compliance. This sort of judicial influence may also work, as Andrew Moravcsik has suggested, as moral pressures without the backing of real sanctions: "The decisive causal links lie in civil society: international pressure works when it can work through free and influential public opinion and an independent judiciary."[44] As the EU case shows, these uses of communicative freedom and the normative powers created by recognizing the status of free and equal members of a public need not then be understood as only applying to adjudicative institutions. While highly dispersed and distributed, various levels of deliberation permit testing and correction across a variety of mutually informative criteria. This method, with its diverse institutional structure, takes advantage of the enabling conditions of the public sphere, which have produced the thickening of the communicative infrastructure needed for deliberation across state borders.

These examples of transnational public spheres bear out the significance of an interactive approach to the democratization of new social conditions suggested by Dewey in "The Public and Its Problems." In response to Lippmann's insistence that the influence of experts replaces that of the public, Dewey conceded that "existing political practice, with its complete ignoring of occupational groups and the organized knowledge and purposes that are involved in the existence of such groups, manifests a dependence upon a summation of individuals quantitatively."[45] In response to Lippmann's elitist view of majority rule, Dewey holds on to the possibility and feasibility of democratic participation by the well-informed citizen, but only if democracy creatively reshapes its institutions to fit "a scattered, mobile and manifold public" as well as interdependent communities that have yet to recognize themselves as publics and form their own distinct common interests. Thus, the solution is a transformation both of what it is to be a public and of the institutions with which the public interacts. Such interaction will provide the basis for determining how the functions of the new form of political organization will be limited and expanded, the scope of which is "something to be critically and experimentally determined"[46] in democracy as a mode of practical inquiry (such as that exemplified in the OMC method of problem solving). Therefore, it is Dewey's conception of the interaction of public and institutions that is responsible not only for their democratic character, but also for the mechanism of their structural transformation.

This approach to the transformation of the public's role in a democracy has three implications for democratizing international society. First, neither bottom-up nor top-down strategies are sufficient to take advantage of communicative power, nor are contestation and consultation alone sufficient for nondomination. Rather, as my argument for the democratic minimum suggests, the capacity to initiate deliberation is essential. Beyond the minimum, the full potential for transnational democracy requires a constant interaction among institutions and publics—indeed, one that is fully reciprocal and co-constitutive. A condition of democracy in the reflexive sense, as I have defined it, requires that publics be able to shape the very institutions that in turn shape their freedoms and powers.

Second, as the EU examples show, democracy and nondomination at this level of aggregation are more likely to be promoted by a highly differentiated institutional structure with multiple levels and domains, as well as multiple communities and publics, rather than just through consultation in a single institutionalized decision-making process. In these transnational contexts, communicative freedom in a public sphere remains a minimal requirement of nondominating institutions, since the existence of many domains and levels permits citizens to address others and be addressed by them in multiple ways and to employ the resources of multiple jurisdictions and overlapping memberships against structures of domination.

Third, such freedom will require a structure with both interrelated local and cosmopolitan dimensions, each with their own normative powers. This interactive, polyarchic, and multilevel strategy is elaborated here in order to develop a transnational form of democracy and constitutionalism consistent with nondomination. When publics shape institutions and in turn are shaped by them, democracy emerges as the fruitful interaction between the openness of communicative freedom and the institutional recognition of normative statuses and powers.

The Democratic Role of Distributive Publics: Nondomination, Communicative Freedom, and Normative Powers

The proliferation of principal/agent relations is part of the context of globalization, in which various international organizations and administrative officeholders act as agents for their principals, national governments (whether democratic or not). The problem they solve is the typical agency problem of networked social relations and activities that cut across many types of political borders. As I suggested in the first chapter, these sorts of social activities in question now affect an indefinite number of people and thus have a distributive character in the sense that I have been using the term. Inclusion in such schemes is a form of domination. Still, by virtue of being affected by these activities in a variety of ways, those persons make up a potential public of sorts, "whom we cannot individuate but can specify."[47] They could become a public in the way Dewey describes in "The Public and Its Problems": when those affected by the consequences of social activities begin to communicate with each other and become aware of their common affectedness. In this way, such a public not only consists of definite individuals, but also each individual, in becoming part of a public, acquires the freedom that stems from their common commitments to each other and to the norms of publicity.

In order to face the problem of domination inherent in such processes, it would seem that more than communicative freedom is required, namely, the freedom generated by the mutual recognition of others as participants in public spheres. It might seem that in additions to such freedom, a fair scheme of cooperation across borders is required—perhaps as Rawls suggests, a "law of peoples" that makes possible "a relation of fair equality with all other societies."[48] Similarly, cosmopolitan democracy asks for the protection of freedoms that depend on membership in a specific political community or over-lapping set of communities. As Held puts it, as "members of the political community citizens should be able to choose freely the conditions of their own association."[49] Both approaches share with my view an emphasis on the importance of membership, of having normative statuses and powers that come from membership in a specific political community. They also point to the recognition that communicative freedom is only one way in which nondomination is secured. More is required, and many different views of democracy see this freedom as derived from political membership. Modern democratic theory has seen membership as a condition for the exercise of autonomy—for the capacity of people to control the circumstances of their lives. The difficulty here is that autonomy, or self-determination, is either too broad or too indeterminate. If it is thought of broadly, then it requires independence rather than interdependence, as is the case with the law of peoples or of states. When it is not tied to specific political communities, however, as is the case with most cosmopolitan theories, it becomes too indeterminate. The difficulty is then to see that what is demanded is not self-determination as such, but normative powers, the powers that citizens have to protect and change their normative statuses and powers. Democracy is then an ideal of freedom and equality, of the exercise of communicative freedom in interaction with such normative powers and statuses secured as rights.

How does an appeal to nondomination avoid this indeterminacy and fulfill these two conditions as the aim of democratization? In democratic communities nondomination is manifested in the ability of each member of such a scheme to avoid having his terms set by others. But the only way in which each can have this ability is if all have it and enjoy their cooperation as a product of their common liberty. Cooperation is nondominating only if it meets two conditions: communicative freedom, and the democratic minimum of the shared ability to initiate deliberation about the content of the scheme. Cooperation is free from domination to the extent that no one is excluded from publicly challenging the rules of cooperation, and these rules establish the legitimate mutual expectations for influence that are the basis for effective action and common projects among cooperators (whether indefinite or definite in their form of activity). Thus, cooperation is always against the background of normative expectations that provide the basis for the joint exercise of common liberty.

In order to develop these possibilities further and suggest the appropriate remedy, it is first necessary to develop an appropriate conception of nondomination itself. This conception should do justice to the democratic minimum as well as take into account the ways in which institutions and public spheres are the means of developing such powers and freedoms. Central to such a minimum is that one's statuses, rights, and duties cannot be changed arbitrarily without deliberation. Since Rawls sees nondomination as related to "reasonable" agreement, it might seem that the underlying requirement is that all obligations among peoples must be voluntary and thus subject to explicit consent. Such a requirement is not feasible, however, given the indefiniteness of social actions and cooperation under conditions of interdependence. Following Pettit's view of domination as arbitrary interference, we may instead think that the indefiniteness of social action allows new and wider opportunities for others to arbitrarily interfere in our lives, whereas those who are dominated have no effective legal means of resisting such interference. Pettit includes among potentially arbitrary influences "financial clout, political authority, social connections, communal standing, informational access, ideological positions, cultural legitimation and the like."[50] In Pettit's conception, such arbitrary influences have to do with properties of agents, who are able to exercise their will arbitrarily to achieve their freedom at the cost of others' interests.

But what makes such interference arbitrary cannot be determined simply by reference to the affected parties' interests. Arbitrariness as a predicate makes sense only on the normative background of rights, duties, roles, and institutions that actors take for granted in their social action, including various legal and political rights. For this reasons, Henry Richardson has criticized Pettit's republicanism for giving a "nonnormative definition of domination" that concedes too much to liberal noninterference.[51] Richardson argues instead that domination and nondomination are inherently normative notions, that "the purported exercise of a normative power—the power to modify the rights and duties of others—is essential to the idea of domination."[52] Domination is thus not just the capacity to interfere arbitrarily in one's life, but also the capacity to make use of distinctly normative power that operates against this institutionalized background of legitimate norms; it is the ability to impose obligations and duties arbitrarily. The key here is then to recast the important term "arbitrary" in terms of the use of normative powers to purport to impose duties on others.

What is it to use normative powers arbitrarily with respect to duties and statuses? If we follow Richardson here, it would seem that instances of domination must somehow violate norms and statuses or the expectations that norms and statuses produce. Indeed, when we are secure from domination we can count on our statuses to entail certain powers, but if someone dominates us they can change our statuses and violate our expectations. To be fully dominated is to have no normative expectations at all, to be reduced to the status of a slave subject to the arbitrary will of a tyrant and thus no longer a genuine participant in their common life. Thus, dominators stand in some normative relation to the dominated, as father, or king, or colonial administrator, who exercises the normative power of authority to arbitrarily change the dominated's normative statuses. However, the "rational" administrator may well decide rationally and impartially to impose new duties for the sake of the common good and even in conformity with general legal rules that are publicly known. Would this still be domination?

As these examples show, domination is not merely the violation of settled expectations in social roles and relationships, especially if these expectations are themselves unjust. As such, domination does not require that a power be used arbitrarily in the sense of its being a violation of a rule or norm. If this were so, then certainly many cases of social exclusion would not be considered forms of domination. Something more is required than the violation of a settled expectation: namely, the use of normative powers without recourse or remedy—without any effective opportunity to influence that use. In this way, "citizenship is a status that exists of necessity, in a suitable legal regime"[53] that is sufficient for nondomination, so long as this normative status is independent of the good will of others. The stability of normative expectations (or justice as regularity, in Rawls's terms), is too weak to capture the normative powers of citizens.

With respect to the content of particular obligations, the requisite sort of political freedom might then be thought of as antipower. According to Pettit, antipower is "the capacity to command noninterference as a power."[54] As in the case of domination, Pettit's emphasis on the will leaves out the essential normative features of antipower: rather than the capacity to control others and resist having obligations imposed by another's will, it must be the power over the content of one's obligations and statuses. That is, the most basic normative power necessary for nondomination is the positive and creative power to interpret, shape, and reform those very normative powers as possessed by agents who seek to impose obligations and duties on others, but without allowing themselves to be addressed by others. As Habermas puts it, because the public use of communicative freedom is constructive and can thus create new obligations among speakers and hearers who accept the content of particular utterances, "such acceptance creates a new social fact."[55] Thus when two speakers promise each other that they will meet at a certain place and time tomorrow on the condition that the other will do the same, they have together freely imposed a new obligation that binds them both. In chess, however, as Hollis notes, the goals "are defined by the rules" so that "no player can doubt that a move that delivers mate is the best move."[56] But in the social world we may also doubt that existing rules constitute the best way to govern ourselves, and we may even doubt that we should do what is considered "rational," such as maximize profits according to the demands of instrumental rationality.

Here Rawls's distinction between natural duties and voluntary obligations might be helpful in clarifying the specificity of institutional normative powers. Natural duties, if they exist, are obligations that we have irrespective of institutional relationships; they are thus moral and apply to all persons. By contrast, in the institutional case, even if obligations are entered into voluntarily, "the content of obligations is defined by an institution or practice the rules of which specify what it is that one is required to do."[57] In this way specifically normative powers regulate social relationships and powers not merely by constraining them through rules or norms, but by making creatures who possess social and natural powers able to produce novel possibilities of thought and expression.

In no other role or location than as citizens in democratic institutions do members of modern societies exercise their normative power to change obligations and statuses under the condition of common liberty. In this case obligations are not imposed, but are the product of the joint exercise of normative powers and the communicative freedom that shapes them. Certainly, in modern societies other forms of authority exist that would also make it possible for these statuses and obligations to change without popular influence or the discursive control of citizens. Democracy itself is then the joint exercise of these powers and capacities so that they are not under the control of any given individual or group of citizens, but are jointly exercised by all. The central precondition for such nondomination is the existence of the public sphere, a space for the exercise of common communicative freedom. This space must now be transnational, as well as be a new kind of public sphere, with new forms of technological and institutional mediation. Without this open structure of publics, the overlapping and crosscutting dimensions of interactions across various political communities could not secure the freedom that is sufficient for nondomination.

Conclusion

My argument here has been two-sided. On the one hand I have developed an account of the potential of the new distributive form of the public sphere to create certain preconditions for democracy, specifically, the conditions necessary for communicative freedom, which emerge from the mutual recognition of participants in the public sphere and their struggles to maintain the public sphere against censorship and other arbitrary forms of dominating political authority. On the other hand, I have argued that such freedoms can be secured only through innovative institutions in which the democratic minimum becomes entrenched in various basic rights. In each case, new circumstances suggest rethinking both democracy and the public sphere outside the limits of their previous historical forms. Rethinking publicity allows us to see that some critical diagnoses of the problems of new forms of communication and publics for democracy are short-circuited by a failure to think beyond what is politically familiar. If my argument is correct that distributive publics are able to preserve and extend the dialogical character of the public sphere in a potentially cosmopolitan form, then a deliberative transnational democracy can be considered a "realistic utopia" in Rawls's sense; these new public spheres extend the range of political possibilities for a deliberative democracy across borders.

If the obligation-constituting elements of dialogue are preserved and extended within the new form of a deliberative public sphere, then a further essential democratic element is also possible: that the public sphere can serve as a source of agency and social criticism. In either adopting the role of the critic or in taking up such criticism in the public sphere, speakers adopt the standpoint of the generalized other, the relevant critical perspective that opens up the potential standpoint of a free and more inclusive community. As Mead put it: "The question of whether we belong to a larger community is answered in terms of whether our own actions call out a response in this wider community, and whether its response is reflected back into our own conduct."[58] This deliberatively responsive community requires a democracy that is able to accommodate many different perspectives. On the question of the applicability of such norms and institutions internationally, Mead is quite optimistic: "Could a conversation be conducted internationally? The question is a question of social organization." Organization requires agency, and the democratic reorganization of technological mediation begins with the interventions of democratic agents and intermediaries, both of which require publics.

This generalized other may also be the political subject of a new form of democracy. In the next chapter I argue that this is one role of humanity when humanity constitutes itself as a political community and sees its communicative freedom and normative powers as the core of any conception of human rights. Developing a normative conception of humanity as the subject of transnational democracy also allows us to begin to talk about its institutional features and the normative powers that are necessary for it to realize basic human freedom. In a transnational democracy, being a member of humanity brings with it certain normative statuses and powers that are themselves conditions for democratization, normative powers that Hannah Arendt has called "the right to have rights." A democracy that meets this condition will have to incorporate the perspective of humanity into its practices of justification. In this respect, as Mead suggests, the republican emphasis on freedom from domination and normative powers as based in human rights is inherently cosmopolitan.

3

Constituting Humanity: The Human Right to Membership

In the previous chapter I analyzed some of the practical presuppositions necessary for lessening the potential for domination within the new structure of global political authority. If the expansion of principal/agent hierarchies is a consequence of new forms of indefinite activity characteristic of globalization, then the social conditions created by a vibrant civil society and public sphere are necessary for creating new forms of popular control and influence. Analysis of the distributive publics provided not only the means by which to transform the normative conception of the public sphere beyond the presuppositions of the print medium and a national political culture, it also identified the powers exercised within them that are important for creating social relations based on nondomination. Among these powers is the capability to initiate communicative and social relationships that form the social basis for democratization. But in order to see why the public sphere is necessary for nondomination, the communicative freedom that comes with participation in the public sphere has to interact with institutionalized normative powers, in particular the power to shape and reshape those very institutions that assign rights and obligations. The distinctly creative and generative side of public communication is a feature of robust nondomination that goes beyond the more narrow power to make legitimate claims only within some particular framework or according to terms defined by others. As such, freedom of communication and participation in the public sphere are necessary conditions for a global democratic minimum.

The particular political conception of justice that I am defending
has now been articulated sufficiently to give it a name: it is "republican
cosmopolitanism." Contrary to the dominant civic republican interpretation, republicanism is neither inherently anticosmopolitan nor
inseparable from the nation-state, and this holds despite the classic
republican adage that "to be free is to be a citizen of a free state." My
aim here is to show that in fact the opposite is the case; namely, that
republicanism provides the best interpretation of the basic claim
that there is an obligation to form a political community beyond the
nation-state. Critics of liberal democracy, including civic republicans
and participatory democrats, often think that even the national context is too large for robust democracy. These views often inspire criticisms of globalization as undermining democratic self-determination
and as increasing the scope of nondemocratic political authority typical of international institutions. Republican cosmopolitans turn these
democratically motivated arguments around and argue that political
rights aimed at freedom from domination supply the normative warrant for democracy generally lacking in more liberal versions of political cosmopolitanism. Not only does cosmopolitan democracy make
more sense in republican terms, but also, without freedom as nondomination as its aim, cosmopolitan democracy cannot address the
political problems of globalization. The next step in the argument
moves from transnational publics toward a political community in
which human rights and democracy are realized at the transnational
level. This step introduces human rights as the normative basis of a
political community that constitutes humanity as the addressee of
claims to justice.

My purpose here is not to offer a full theory of human rights, but
rather to see the place of democracy as constitutive of and instrumental to their realization. Human rights are often considered to be
grounded in basic interests. As my discussion of primary goods has
shown, I understand human rights to be basic freedoms, including
rights against tyranny and domination. These basic freedoms are justified negatively and positively as necessary conditions for avoiding
great harms such as domination and destitution, on the one hand,
and for living a worthwhile human life on the other. For both, membership in humanity is basic, understood as the right to have rights

and thus the most basic of the basic human freedoms. For an initial clarification of this idea we can do no better than to quote from the *Universal Declaration of Human Rights*: "Everyone is entitled to a social and international order in which the rights and freedoms set forth in this Declaration can be fully realized."[1] The political community of humanity developed in this chapter offers a philosophical interpretation of this right to have rights, the right to membership in the most fundamental sense.

Democracy and human rights have long been strongly connected in international covenants. In documents such as the 1948 United Nations Universal Declaration of Human Rights and the 1966 International Covenant of Civil and Political Rights, democracy is justified both intrinsically, in terms of popular sovereignty, and instrumentally, as the best way to "foster the full realization of all human rights."[2] Yet, even though they are human and thus universal rights, political rights are often surprisingly specific. In the Covenant, for example, "the right to take part in the conduct of public affairs" is equated with "the right to vote and to be elected."[3] More often than not, the interpretation and implementation of such rights is left to states and their constitutions (as, for example, in the European Convention for the Protection of Human Rights). Political rights have a peculiar status among the typically enumerated human rights, and this difficulty is rooted in deep assumptions about the nature and scope of democracy and political community that remained largely unexamined by the drafters of these important declarations. These same assumptions also make it difficult to determine the precise character of another peculiar but fundamental conception of international law and human rights discourse: the concept of humanity. My purpose here is to argue for a particular interpretation of humanity that makes sense of the universal character of political rights and their relation to the claims of justice made by those who suffer from human rights violations.

The concept of humanity has played a central role in the development of human rights and humanitarian law, as is particularly evident in the important concept of crimes against humanity. As many have remarked, "humanity" has at least two senses. Bernard Williams, for example, claims that it is a name "not merely for a species but for a quality."[4] The distinction here is between humanity as the human species or empirical aggregate of all human beings, and humanity as that moral quality that makes us human. This moral quality might be called "humanness," and it has been given various interpretations— human dignity, rational nature, and so on—that could supply the basis for the attribution of rights.

Rather than accept the usual distinction exemplified by Williams, however, I offer a third conception that combines features of both senses: humanity as *the human political community*. This conception is first and foremost a distinctive interpretation of humanity in terms of a moral property, in this case the status of membership in a political community. Rather than appealing to a specific moral property or status, membership in the human political community has the advantage of including the full range of human capabilities. It also captures humanity in Williams's aggregative sense, since this particular status is membership in a fully inclusive political community. Taken together, these normative conceptions provide the basis for a much richer picture of the nature of political rights, as well as a different account of why a democratic human political community is indeed necessary for the full realization of human rights. Of course, in the absence of various institutions, humanity in this political sense has yet to be fully realized.

My argument for constituting humanity as a political community has five steps. First, after delineating the distinctly political conception of humanity, I consider the nature of political rights as such. I argue that these rights provide citizens with the basic status of membership in humanity—that political community that is the addressee of claims made whenever human rights are violated. This normative status and its powers in turn provide the basis for legitimate claims to justice addressed to this community, as can best be seen by considering the plight of rightless persons, who lack the standing to make such claims to any particular community. Such a status should be taken as *the* basic political right, and hence as a constitutive feature of the democratic minimum. Second, I consider the role of humanity, as an ideal within particular democratically constituted political communities, in claims to political inclusion. In these circumstances, those suffering injustice at the hands of a democratic majority can appeal to the possibility of constitutional revision, based on an inclusive ideal of humanity forming the core of democratic commitments. Third, I argue that humanity for this very reason provides an essential perspective for justification in any democracy that attempts to do justice to others. Both inside and outside any particular community, humanity is for democracies both a practical horizon and a perspective for justification in situations of political injustice, tyranny, and domination. Fourth, these roles suggest that, if it is to realize human rights, humanity must become not only an actual political community, but also one with the particular institutional features of a constitutional order as well as a certain degree of institutional differentiation and complexity. Fifth and finally, these institutions must realize common liberty by various democratic means, including the dispersal of power. This last step establishes a cosmopolitan dimension to transnational democracy.

Humanity and Human Rights: The Rights of Stateless Persons

It is common in the literature on human rights to distinguish between the two senses of humanity operative in international law. In various exchanges with Hannah Arendt concerning the Nuremberg trials, Karl Jaspers notes this distinction between *Menschlichkeit* and *Menschheit*, between humanness and humanity.[5] When Kant in his moral philosophy asks us to "respect the humanity of another," he is referring to the former rather than the latter, to the moral demands of respect owed to persons with their own intrinsic ends or, to use Rawls's phrase, as self-originating sources of claims. As Kant puts it: "A human being regarded as a *person*, that is as the subject of a morally practical reason ... possesses a *dignity* ... by which he demands *respect* for himself from all other rational beings in the world."[6] Dignity is then the specific object of humanness. Indeed, it is a certain moral status or authority that permits one to demand dignity for oneself precisely by reciprocally and freely recognizing it in others.[7] Humanity is then tied to the rational capacities that make persons sources of value.[8] But as his discussion of the capacity to demand respect from others makes clear, Kant thought of the normative property of dignity as a status term, specifically the normative status of being a member of the moral community owed to all rational beings, who as such possess humanity. Notice then that there is a double ambiguity here: not just between humanity and humanness, but also between humanity as tied to a normative capacity to set ends and make claims, and humanity as a normative status that can be rightly demanded even when it is not recognized. We might call humanity as a capacity tied to freedom "first-personal" and humanity as a status "second-personal." It is second-personal in that it is a normative status realized in relations with others who also have this same status. This status is the status of membership in a community.

One dominant understanding of human rights sees them as tied to various, fundamentally first-personal, moral interests such as bodily integrity and security. It is common on this sort of account to distinguish "basic" from "nonbasic" rights, where basic rights are tied to certain negative liberties that ought to be protected. This sort of account often sees political rights as nonbasic and democracy as merely instrumental to protecting more basic rights.[9] In this way political rights are often considered nonbasic because they are justified only as instrumental to achieving some set of more basic rights. This instrumental conception of political freedom severs any intrinsic connection between democracy and human rights. Along these lines, Berlin argues that democracy does not necessarily provide the best protection for negative liberties, "so that it is perfectly conceivable that a liberal-minded despot would allow his subjects a large measure of personal freedom."[10] But even if a despot, or perhaps even a noninterfering slave master, could promote the greatest possible protection of certain basic rights and liberties, and even if he could thereby promote the first-personal aspects of these powers, he could not promote humanity in the sense of the second-personal normative status with respect to others who also possess this status. However enlightened, despots could not achieve for their dependents and slaves the freedom from domination intrinsic to the relations among free persons who share membership status in a political community, and thus share a common liberty with all those who have this status.

The republican adage can then be expressed somewhat differently: "to be free is to be the citizen of a free community." Only in relation to humanity in this second-personal sense do democracy and political rights have intrinsic value. This intrinsic value is present not just in cases of bearers of human rights living in a fully realized democratic political community, but also in the case of rightless persons, of those who have suffered the loss of their status rights in crimes against humanity. The loss of the normative status of membership, of the right to have rights at all, is not only fundamental to all putatively basic rights, but also better explicates the great wrongs done to those who suffer such severe injustices as torture or denationalization. The democratic minimum thus includes this right to have rights in the form of second-personal powers to make claims that initiate deliberation with others who have the same rights and obligations. In recognizing the humanity of persons in just this way, we recognize that they can make claims upon us, and thus we cannot deny them respectful consideration without denying the humanity in ourselves. To be able to claim that this and other wrongs be redressed when they violate the common liberty of humanity is part of the right not to be tortured, the right of all to have a political order that fully realizes human rights.

What aspect of humanity is at stake in crimes against humanity? As Arendt notes, humanity in the first-personal sense is not the status directly at stake in crimes against humanity, even if basic human dignity has been violated; it is rather the second-personal normative status that has been violated when people are made rightless and stateless by organized and systematic acts of violence. People who have lost their membership in some particular political community, whether through acts of violence such as genocide and torture or through explicit acts of denationalization, may appeal to this status of humanity. The calamity of the rightless is not that such people are deprived of life, liberty, and the pursuit of happiness, but "that they no longer belong to any community whatsoever."[11] In other words, *humanity* is at stake because rightless persons have lost more than a specific membership; the systematic violation of their rights undermines their *human* status, which is necessary to demand respect. In Arendt's terms, they have not merely had their specific rights or even human dignity violated, but their "right to have rights" has been denied.

When taken as a second-personal status, humanity captures the strong connection between rights and political status in a just political community called to be responsive to claims of justice and injustice. Crimes against humanity are crimes against *Menschheit*, against those who have recognized the dignity of persons as constitutive of their own ability to demand respect and to have this status when it is shared with others. If they are indeed crimes against humanity, humanity must be a political community rather than a mere aggregate of all individuals who share either the empirical property of being a member of a natural kind or a normative property such as humanness or a rational nature. Violations of human rights are then violations of the conditions of membership in humanity.

There are different ways to argue for conceiving humanity as a moral-political status. Martha Nussbaum attempts to identify humanness with certain central capabilities for functioning that are necessary for living a truly human life.[12] This approach has the advantage of seeing rights as entailed by a range of human powers and capacities, although it does not directly see them as specifically normative powers. Nussbaum notes, however, that rights claims so entailed still require an attitude of respect, so that possessing human capabilities as such grants respect or normative standing. Another way to make this argument is more directly historical in that it might be shown that international society already has a basic structure and thus has the institutions that constitute the necessary conditions for political community. I pursue a different, more clearly normative strategy here that takes rights to be claims addressed to others based on membership status. On this basis, it is possible to see an intrinsic relationship between human rights and democratic political community in which political rights are no longer nonbasic because they are membership rights in humanity as such. In the Universal Declaration of Human Rights, the right to nationality is one such basic political right that complements the more general right to a political order that effectively realizes human rights, especially in the cases of people (such as asylum seekers and refugees) who have no standing in any particular community. Humanity is a political community in the sense that it is the addressee of such claims to justice—indeed, claims that extend beyond the scope of international criminal law to include other claims to basic justice such as the capability failure of severe poverty and deprivation as well as the human rights claims of the disabled.

This account of membership rights yields a particular understanding of universal political rights in which humanity is the addressee of claims having to do with the fundamental normative status of persons. According to this interpretation, human rights are not basic liberties or immunities from interference, but rights of membership. The distinctly republican interpretation of human rights based on nondomination can be summarized as having three components. First, a human right is the basis of a *legitimate* claim against the absence of freedom, that is, against any denial of the status of a member of the human community. Second, the act of making such a claim requires *standing* by which the claimant is recognized as someone who may make such an appeal and to whom others may address a similar appeal. Membership in humanity is then not just a status, but also the normative power to make claims to others that may obligate them. Finally, there is no claim without an *addressee*, a community in which one has membership status. In the case of human rights, the community addressed is not the same as the one in which the violated person has de facto membership, but rather the human community as such.

The right of membership in this community is basic because it is the most fundamental normative status implied by having universal political rights. It is then the most basic normative power to resist the loss of this status in cases of tyranny and domination, while at the same time it creates the community of humanity. Membership in humanity does not only ground claims against tyranny, as important as such claims are in paradigmatic cases of severe human rights violations. Such claims can also be made against any institution that exercises its normative powers to impose duties and obligations arbitrarily, in the sense that it can deny some persons their freedom and fail to secure the political space for the common exercise of their distinctively human normative powers.

Because of the normativity of the concept of humanity I am developing, the concept of crimes against humanity in all of its legal and political dimensions can be used to illustrate the significance of humanity in the sense of the human political community.[13] Instead of appealing, as Kant did, to the fiction of a "state of nature" in which these moral and political second-personal properties are absent, I use this legal concept in order to discover conceptual clues as to what sort of political obligations would constitute a community that is responsive to denials of the status of persons as human beings. These crimes are not distinguished from others due to their particularly horrifying nature, as heinous as they are. They are distinct in that they do not violate only individuals as such, but individuals in what they have in common with all other persons: their humanity, defined politically as their membership in the international community; and indeed, the Rome Treaty establishing the International Criminal Court says of such crimes that they "shock the conscience of humanity." In responding to such abuses, the international community is restoring membership to those persons whose rights are violated, granting them the recognition that their abusers have denied them.

"Humanity" here has two potentially political significances. First of all, crimes against humanity may be attacks against the human status—the value of humanness or dignity—in the same way that we now recognize crimes against peace. In referring to what is violated as the value that all share qua human beings, the concept certainly expresses the depth of the violation at stake and the heinous character of the crime.[14] This does not, however, exhaust the role of humanity in humanitarian law.

While not denying the importance of humanness as a moral status that recognizes intrinsic worth, there is a second and politically more important sense of humanity: it denotes *whom it is* that is addressed and who it is that recognizes the humanity of others, thus constituting humanity as the relevant community beyond any particular community. Criminal trials name a political community as the interested party, as in *Smith v. the State of Massachusetts*. Analogous to civil rights suits brought by "the People of the United States of America," it is humanity as a whole that is "the party of interest."[15] It is to this political community that the victims of crimes against humanity may appeal for recognition of the wrongs done to them; it is this community that holds perpetrators accountable, so that "a violation done to one is a violation to all" (as Hegel put it).[16] The recent institutionalization of crimes against humanity already constitutes the international political community as precisely the party of interest in cases where citizens have no other recourse than to appeal for justice as members of humanity.

In the absence of world government, many have objected that humanity cannot be taken to be a political community, a people, a *dêmos*, or even a collective entity. Indeed, David Luban has recently argued that "to call humanity—humankind—a party of interest is not to regard humanity as a political community but as a set of human individuals."[17] My strategy denies that we can licitly make this direct inference from current facts, but rather requires an intermediate step of seeing human political rights as conferring the membership status in humanity that creates the "interest" of humanity in rights violations. It is the party of interest precisely because what is at stake in such crimes is the very denial of the normative status of membership in humanity, with its complex of rights and powers. But, more importantly, the issue here is what constitutes a political community, and Luban employs a very narrow criterion to insist that international society is only a moral community: "only political communities promulgate law, and for this reason humanity is not a political community."[18] While we may for this reason reject the fiction of laws of humanity, self-legislation is only one aspect of some political communities and is not directly at stake in these cases. Rather, the more general issue is that only a community can confer the kind of general and nonspecific normative powers necessary to secure nondomination. Of course, morality provides the basis for some moral powers manifest in speech acts, such as promising. As a specific normative power, promising creates obligations between persons or groups. But making a promise does not by itself ensure uptake, to the extent that not accepting a particular promise does not in any way violate the moral status of a person. The same cannot be said of citizenship, however, since to bar a person from voting or speaking in a deliberative forum is the same as violating his or her normative status. If humanity is to be able to confer such powers it must in some respect be more than the mere aggregate of all persons. The human rights regime and its institutions thus constitute humanity in the political sense, in the absence of which the normative expectations of the legal punishment of rights violations are insufficient to ensure the human status. Indeed, Luban rightly concludes that such enforcement is based on a "vigilante jurisdiction."

The significance of political rights in conferring this human status is perhaps most clear when they are entirely absent. Consider Hannah Arendt's description of a "rightless person." In the first instance, that person would be stateless, a refugee, a "dislocated person," or even an illegal immigrant. Arendt argues that persons who are stripped of all historical and political features are left with only their "bare humanity," with no place in the world to initiate significant speech and action or to carry them out.[19] To arrive at such a "bare" human status, persons are usually victims of political violence (such as the crime of genocide) depriving them of all rights, statuses, and powers, which together had enabled them to participate in the common world (something true of the systematic domination and degradation of the human status). Such persons are the victims of tyranny, and the absence of civil authority and laws has left them without normative powers; they can then in Locke's memorable phrase only "appeal to heaven."

Having human rights of membership comes with the normative power, or right, to have rights: the power to make claims upon all those who also have human rights (and to be responsive to their claims), and thus to make claims of justice to humanity or the human political community on whose recognition these rights depend. It is the right to have an actual set of institutions in which human rights are fully realized. Article 28 of the Universal Declaration of Human Rights makes sense of Arendt's elliptical phrase, "the right to have rights." Furthermore, international law recognizes a very similar set of claims in the right to nationality as a political right and as the basis of rights of asylum-seekers and refugees as recognized in immigration law. For this reason, the obligations of humanity exceed the list of crimes against humanity as recognized by the International Criminal Court, especially with regard to the statuses that ought to be assigned to all persons as bearers of human rights. The right to nationality is thus not a mere right to protection; it is a positive normative power that includes all the enabling participatory conditions for social and political rights, and it creates political obligations for the international community to all persons lacking membership status or place

in an ongoing or functioning political community. It is not just a right
not to have one's political membership arbitrarily taken away, but the
right to have a status that makes effective social freedom possible
regardless of one's de facto nationality.[20] While it does not yet refer to
the human political community as such, this right to membership is
no longer determined by sovereignty, by the arbitrary choice of those
who are currently members, or by any legislative willing whatsoever. It
is a political obligation of humanity, institutionalized by the United
Nations High Commissioner for Refugees (UNHCR) and other parts
of the international human rights regime that are concerned not
just with crimes such as genocide, but also with violations of the
normative statuses of persons as members of the human political
community. This right demands that we rethink the exclusively juridical understanding of rights that informs the current human rights
regime and much philosophical thinking as well. Habermas, for
example, claims that "rights are juridical by their very nature."[21] At
the same time, this criticism should not lead us to be skeptical about
human rights as such,[22] but only about the prospects for realizing
them in protective and coercive legal institutions independent of a
larger political community of communities. This leads to the final
and decisive step in the argument for a republic of humanity.

This more political argument led many republicans to argue for a
cosmopolitan political order that would realize a common civil condition for all rights bearers rather than merely a legal order simply
based on the coercive protection and enforcement of juridical rights.
For example, Fletcher notes "mankind would be best preserved from
the convolutions of misery if instead of framing laws for a single society" free governments would do so with others in the interests of
their neighbors, and indeed for the common interests of humanity.[23]
A republican transnational trope employed by Madison and Kant (as
well as Fletcher and many others) is the ideal of the Achaean league
of cities, a federation of distinct cities that is not "one vicious and
ungovernable city."[24] Rather, as Kant put it, such a community of
communities realizes the rights of all precisely because it would not
be an order in which every state could "expect to be able to derive its
security and rights from its own power and its own legal judgment,
but solely from this great federation (*Foedus Amphictyonum*)."[25] Just as

we had the obligation "to leave the state of nature and create a civil condition," so too Kant argues that we have the obligation to create a shared cosmopolitan civil condition that establishes freedom from domination as a common liberty. The obligation to create such a political community is an obligation to humanity that is best fulfilled in a joint commitment to democracy and human rights. Certainly, institutions that currently act on behalf of humanity are creating a cosmopolitan legal community that fulfills the obligations of respect demanded by the human moral community. The advantage of a political conception of humanity is that it realizes the civil status necessary for freedom from nondomination as a common liberty, the fundamental advantage of any political community. This obligation demands that at least some of those political institutions constitute a common status with shared powers of citizenship that are global in scope, and to that extent a republic of humanity.

Democracy, Justice, and Political Rights: Humanity and Constitutional Order

I have argued that certain provisions of international law constitute the recognition and enforcement of claims to membership in humanity. Now I ask the question, what are specifically human *political* rights, if human rights confer the status of membership in the human political community? Political human rights confer more than simply the status of being human, as is evidenced by the enumeration of many different human rights, including the right to participation in decision making. In some human rights documents these political rights are quite specific to institutions of representative democracy. Such rights go beyond the institutional practices of specific communities and underwrite claims to the correction of certain injustices that such institutions may perpetuate. Human rights are neither entitlements nor simply standards of legitimacy, but rather have a distinctly justice-making role. Democracy must meet the requirements of human rights if it is to be just. But human rights also require democracy, if we include in them political rights that could only be exercised on the basis of the normative status of being a citizen. Why does the realization of human rights require democracy, the "democratic entitlement" that is widely recognized in many human rights documents and declarations? It is because even a minimal democracy should enable citizens to address claims to justice to the political community and initiate deliberation about them. This minimum does not entail any particular conception of democracy, but instead could be realized in a variety of practices and procedures.

The fact that human rights require democracy even in some minimal sense has some potentially troubling consequences for their realization. Since it seems that democracy is necessary for their realization, an apparent circularity ensues: human rights require democracy in order to be exercised; and democracy requires human rights in order to be self-correcting and nontyrannical, and thus minimally just. Only under ideal conditions would democracy realize justice and rights; in nonideal conditions, democracy might even arguably promote the continued existence of unjust circumstances, as the long history of the acceptance of slavery in the United States shows. Certainly, many reformers appealed to the human status of slaves in order to achieve the eventual international prohibition of the slave trade.

Here we have once again reached the problem of the democratic circle. It might seem that a democracy must be just in order to recognize the humanity of all persons. In this case, we have more than an instrumental failure of institutions to promote justice, but a deeper and more constitutive failure of the current political framework to embody sufficiently deep or extensive democratic norms in its institutions. This constitutes a structural failure to realize human political rights. Such an unjust society is in need of democratization; that is, its democratic norms must be deepened and widened. I have argued that the solution to such vicious circles of injustice is the institution of a democratic minimum. But how can those who suffer from injustice make claims when they are not recognized as persons, much less citizens?

In response to such extreme injustices, the democratic minimum must be deepened and expanded to include humanity as the most basic political status. If others are recognized as having a normative status simply in virtue of being human, humanity is constitutive of the egalitarian democratic ideal, and on that basis regards its own norms and institutions as open to change and revision by claims of justice. This means that a democratic community must be open to claims made by anyone on the basis of their human rights, whether or not that person is a citizen. Openness to such claims means that any democracy must include in its standard of justification the perspective of humanity—the perspective of all potential claimants to justice based on human rights. That is, as a democracy, political community must see itself as a part of humanity in which all persons have political rights to make claims of justice. This is true not just for individuals, but also for communities that constitute themselves as a *dêmos*. For this reason, the democratic minimum must have application across polities as well, since one polity may undermine the democratic minimum of another by ignoring its normative status and powers as a *dêmos*. Just democracies recognize the political rights of the citizens of other democracies as well as their own, as secured in various ways within their institutional structures. As addressees of claims to justice, democracies then have obligations to ensure a whole variety of minima for all bearers of rights and all members of humanity, and a task for international law is to work out the scope of these obligations through adjudicative deliberation. This requires thinking about the democratic basis for such deliberation and the place of adjudicative institutions in transnational democracy.

Deepening and widening the scope of democracy is one response to injustices in the distribution of the powers necessary for the democratic minimum. In such cases deeper or wider democracy may also mean the emergence of new institutions and even new rights, and these may require that the community be able to adopt the perspective of humanity in criticizing and reforming its norms and practices when confronting the normatively arbitrary forms of inclusion and exclusion they sanction. Humanity then plays a role as a perspective of justification, one which unjust democracies cannot expect to address successfully without surrendering some of their current claims to legitimacy. This is the perspective of the generalized other, a perspective not only critical, but also obligation-producing to the extent that it validates previously unrecognized claims to justice.

Consider a case within a particular democratic polity that involves the recognition of new perspectives, reasons, and obligations. The

Canadian Supreme Court recently expanded some standards of justification concerning aboriginal claims by extending legal recognition to the stories of the Gitxsan people as legitimate evidence in land disputes. In discussing this case, Seyla Benhabib follows the standard collective conception of the generalized other and argues that "what lent legitimacy to the Canadian court's decision was precisely its recognition that a specific group's claims are in the best interest of all Canadian citizens."[26] This means that the Gitxsan's perspective becomes a potential source of obligations precisely by being included in the sovereign collective will, the now more impartially constituted "We" of all Canadian citizens rather than the perspective constituted by their individual self-interests. But it is implausible to say that the interests of Canadians can be held constant before and after the decision, as Benhabib's analysis suggests. After the decision, Canadians' best interests have changed, as interests of members of a more multi-perspectival and less dominating polity, just as after *Brown v. Board of Education* the United States became a more multiracial polity than it was before the decision. In both the American and Canadian cases, democracy is self-correcting only to the extent that it is now able to incorporate a new perspective and thus call into question its legitimacy as a collective subject. As such, the *dêmos* is reconstituted as a multi-perspectival community through significant constitutional change that affects the deeper presuppositions concerning the nature of the democratic community.[27] When such change goes deep enough, it often takes several further decisions to make manifest the full membership of excluded persons as citizens by rectifying past injustices and establishing future normative powers and statuses.

The perspective of humanity most often emerges within already constituted democracies in the struggles over status and membership, in claims made by those who might be called quasi-members or denizens, that is, persons who de facto have the dependent status that Kant called "mere auxiliaries to the republic."[28] The role of humanity in these cases is to function as the current addressee of claims to justice that may only be answered by the future democratic community. By exercising their human rights in an effort to constitute this community, the Gitxsan people only now enjoy the democratic minimum. Even though the Gitxsan already formally possessed full citizenship status, it was only through the transformative effect of taking up their claims to justice that Canadian democratic institutions became the potential means of achieving that justice appropriate to human rights. This is true not because the Gitxsan people have now become part of a more fully impartial collective will, or because the Canadian High Court ruled that accepting their claim is in the best interest of all Canadians as free and equal persons. Rather, the issue of justice at stake is more directly constitutional and thus reflexive. A constitutional democracy incorporates humanity when it acts as a political community open to the reinterpretation and revision of its fundamental principles in order to do justice to the claims of humanity.

In discussing this or any other such case of wide-ranging constitutional reform, a systematic ambiguity arises: is such a reform the restoration of genuine popular sovereignty or something much more novel, such as the constitution of a plural subject that *surrenders* rather than exercises sovereignty? Democratic theorists have been interested in a particular subject of collective willing that occupies the first-person plural perspective of "We Canadians," "We Americans," and so on. But there is another sort of plural perspective: the second-person plural "you," the addressee of claims that ask for a response. As these cases of the constitutional reform of democracy show, the second-person plural perspective of democracies cannot be limited *ex ante* to its current citizenry who are its actual members, but must rather be constituted through a more indefinite public with which democratic institutions interact. The reflexive disputability of the scope of any democratic "we" makes any particular limitation always open to the potential objection that its boundaries and jurisdictions are democratically arbitrary and potentially dominating. What then is the perspective of humanity?

In the case of the Gitxsan people, the Court's recognition of the Gitxsan claim to justice opens up a new space for deliberation about the legitimacy of a democratic political community that does not fully manifest the equal status of all its members. In so doing, the Court also initiates public deliberation that may potentially develop into a fusion of horizons, a fundamentally new first-person plural perspective that changes just who constitutes the Canadian people.[29] The encounter with Gitxsan narratives shows the prejudices that are built into the idea of evidence in the court of law, something that induced the Court to see much more than the simple facts of the case and the standard remedies (such as the usual cash payments for loss of land). Once on the terrain of human rights and fundamental justice, the Court saw itself as challenged and addressed by historical claims to justice that transcend the previous normative framework that Canadian institutions had used to justify their past actions. In doing so, Canada became a community of peoples, a transnational polity.

As adjudicative institutions, courts can be addressed by claims of injustice and inhumanity only when who "we" are and what adjudication rules "we" follow are no longer regarded as constitutive of justice, but are open to being challenged by newly recognized historical injustices. Dominated groups such as aboriginal peoples may also appeal to the right to self-determination of colonized people recognized by the United Nations, and argue for shared jurisdiction over land and resources as the remedy for colonization.[30] Because these claims to shared jurisdiction are based in basic human rights (and thus membership in humanity), more is at stake normatively than simply giving equal rights to a first nation or bestowing equal membership status in an existing federation. Rather, the Canadian High Court's decision calls into question the consistency of sovereignty toward human rights, and potentially asks whether the existing Canadian constitution in fact denies to "indigenous people the right to appeal to universal principles of freedom and equality in struggling against injustice."[31] Humanity thus functions as a standpoint of justification by which constitutional orders can be judged as just or unjust to the extent that they permit or deny such claims.

If allowing reflexive questions about the nature and scope of the *dêmos* is a fundamental feature of any democracy based on human rights, then a democracy cannot limit the scope of those by whom it may potentially be addressed. In this case, indigenous peoples have not merely been treated as members of a more inclusive nation, but rather the perspective of humanity has tested and changed the idea of the right to membership. If this is the case, humanity does not seem to be some particularly large or numerous "We" to which we belong. This fact means that for a community to remain democratic, it must adopt a standpoint of justification that is open to the possibility that what "we" decide is unjust, *however much it expresses our collective will.* This requires the perspective of humanity, which occupies the second-personal standpoint of the generalized other in testing the scope and depth of political rights in democratic institutions. In the next section, I turn to democratic theory and argue that the standpoint of the generalized other provides another basis for believing that justice requires thinking of democracy in terms of a plural subject, of *dêmoi* instead of a *dêmos*.

Humanity and the Generalized Other

If we take the realization of human rights as the supreme aim, humanity and democracy seem consistent. But what happens to popular sovereignty once it includes the perspective of humanity? Democracy seems tied to first-personal collective self-determination; these collective subjects are always delimited. But there is another sort of plural perspective. In the second-person plural perspective, the community is an addressee of legitimate rights claims that require an answer. A community in this second-person plural sense cannot exercise sovereignty, even if it is constituted by the democratic distribution of normative powers among its citizens. How might an account of various democratic perspectives help us in understanding the nature of the human political community? What is distinctive about the ideal of the human political community, as the community to whom those who are denied their basic rights can appeal, is that it provides the basis for any claim that any person's basic rights and statuses have been arbitrarily denied by particular delimited political communities. Institutions acting on behalf of humanity can act arbitrarily in other ways, especially if there are no global institutions in which they are nested that might be able to check their operations. One way in which open-textured human political communities can be constructed is by forming publics across existing institutional boundaries, in which members grant to other members the normative power and communicative freedom to address each other and be addressed in turn. This freedom is a self-originating form that is difficult to repress and can cross various social and political boundaries. It requires only that it be realized in some form of communication where each member regards the other as having a particular status as a member of the public sphere. This suggests further that such a status could be grounded in the various human rights of communication and exchange. In this section, I consider how a democratic community might institutionalize this perspective of the generalized other, the perspective of which it is a part and to which it is open when its democratic norms must be deepened and expanded.

Here Mead's conception of the "generalized other" is instructive for its similar normative ambiguity. Mead assigns both collective and distributive meanings to the concept, taking it to be both the perspective of the whole community as a shared "we," and as the many different perspectives of each of its members taken distributively. This difference can be seen in Mead's analogy to games, in which there is both "we the team" and the specific roles and powers of each individual team member that cannot be reduced to simply a part in a whole. Each adopts not merely the perspective of the good of the team or of all the other players on the team, but also a second-person plural perspective in which they all assess the state of play and the expectations and possibilities of members of both teams engaged in play. In the course of interactive and creative play, there is no single authoritative perspective from which to make assessments for the good of the team. Instead, each moves back and forth between perspectives in order to see what it is that one ought to do at any particular time. We might call this interpretive accomplishment "interpersonally wide reflective equilibrium."[32] Thus to be the addressee of such creative and potentially novel play means not only that no player controls the state of play in the game, but also that, taken together, all the players are not even collectively in control of the outcome, since even players on the same team may intend quite different results from each play. The game's course, however, is a matter of all the decisions and assessments that can be made from all the relevant perspectives. Understood in this distributive sense rather than the usual impartial sense, the generalized other is the perspective of "an enlarged mentality." Kant sees such a mentality in a distributive fashion, as thinking and judging from "the standpoint of everyone else."[33] Such reflexivity is part of the ongoing process of realizing a universal ideal compatible with multiple perspectives without dissolving them into a higher unity.

Given that it is distributed in this way, the perspective of the generalized other is potentially fully inclusive of all those who have a perspective. It cannot then itself be a single perspective, but the multiplicity that results from joining normatively relevant perspectives as a reflective accomplishment. The generalized other emerges when participants are able to coordinate various perspectives in the activity of joint deliberation. With the recognition of human rights that include political rights, the perspective of humanity is the generalized other of deliberation and communication in a democratic polity. When deliberation meets these standards, it is conducted in such a way as to fulfill the requirements of constitutional toleration. Such toleration is not just a matter of noninterference, since by extending normative powers to other communities each of them can "be bound by precepts articulated not by 'my people' but by a community composed of distinct political communities."[34] To the extent that this fusion of the horizons of various peoples and *dêmoi* discussed in the Canadian case suggests that the result is the resolution into a new, single, higher perspective, the metaphor is insufficiently pluralist and distributive and thus not fully apt. It is not yet fully transnational, and here we can turn to the jurisprudence of the European Union, which builds the recognition of otherness into the constitutional order.

How might we think of this kind of political subject? Weiler ambiguously describes the EU as a community in first-personal terms as "*a* people," even if he immediately adds "a people, if you wish, of others."[35] Granting that political rights are universal human rights, any "we" is indeed bound by others who are not "our people" precisely because "we" owe "them" a justification as bearers of unique perspectives. In order to understand the requirements of constitutional toleration that would make it possible for us to be obligated politically by someone who is not one of us, the second-personal, distributivist, and plural aspect of the generalized other must also be present. These others are also members of humanity, which relativizes "the people" of Europe as much as Europe relativizes the "peoples" of its member states; each realizes the perspective of humanity and can be judged in these terms. Thus, the requirements of a differentiated institutional structure hold for the same democratic reasons, regardless of the scale of the polity: only in a polity of others, a community of *dêmoi* in which each respects the normative powers of others, can claims to nondomination be seen from a variety of perspectives. To the extent that it seeks justifications that can be endorsed from a variety of perspectives, such a differentiated polity of *dêmoi* is multiperspectival.

In a transnational democracy organized around the political entitlements and obligations of human rights, humanity functions distributively as the generalized other, whose normative attitude we take when addressed by "others" who are also members of the same human political community. These "others" are thus normatively entitled to exercise their communicative powers to change political norms anywhere. As Mead puts it, a "universal society" exists to the extent that "all can enter into relations with others through the medium of communication."[36] In this respect, Mead takes as his starting point the notion that pluralism ensures that any socialized modern individual is "always a member of a larger community" in which her more immediate relations are embedded. By entering into unbounded communication and by engaging in cooperative social activities we can come to see even distant others "as members, as brothers." More generally, critical reflexivity is achieved "only by individuals taking the attitude of the generalized other *toward themselves*" and thus by internal differentiation.[37] As a way to incorporate the perspective of the generalized other in an explicitly distributive rather than collective sense, constitutional toleration ought to be a feature of *any* just democracy. This conception of humanity's role as generalized other requires that the notion of being a member of a political community is much more complex than current understandings of citizenship. Citizenship is often understood to consist in the contrast between viewing a problem from the point of view of the common good and taking a merely self-interested point of view. As we have seen, this does not yet identify the proper normative attitude.

Rather than identify the perspective of the generalized other in justification, impartiality marks the difference between two first-personal perspectives or attitudes—the first-person singular "I" perspective as opposed to the first-person plural "we" perspective that is the source of normativity. By contrast, the generalized other has two rather different functions. In the first instance, it is the source of critical attitudes toward our community and ourselves, and thus of the normative attitude of communicative interaction that permits us to transcend "our" current perspective. In complex, organized, and differentiated societies, membership involves different standpoints: not only do members have the ability to put themselves in other people's places and roles, but each views his membership "from any one of the different standpoints in which he belongs to the community."[38] Institutional differentiation is thus a requirement for promoting the realization of human political rights and for securing the democratic minimum under circumstances that include the complexity and diversity of memberships that now make up the right to have rights.

The critical attitude of the generalized other also points to a second institutional function in democracy: the political order, including its schedule of rights and powers of membership, must be sufficiently democratic to be reflexive and capable of democratic reform. Reflexivity in this sense is required for the particular form of freedom as freedom from domination (as I have already argued), in order that the practices and norms of governance can be tested by democratic means from the perspective of the generalized other. Any well-ordered, democratically organized association should be able to manifest this reflexivity. However, it would have to regularize opportunities for such reflexive reordering and interpret such a power as a fundamental right of all of its members. To do so is already to take a step toward constitutionalization, since such normative expectations require procedures by which to enact reform through deliberation and amendment.[39] Given a certain complexity and internal pluralism among citizens, constitutionalization would further require institutional differentiation so as to ensure that citizens can initiate deliberation and effectively exercise their normative powers in cases where parts of the institutional structure fail to be sufficiently reflexive. This includes the power of amendment, which enables the "reordering the order itself."[40] Taken together, institutional differentiation and normative reflexivity are necessary conditions for nondomination. To the extent that they are realized, democracy can be a means to justice, where justice is not restricted to a particular subject of self-legislation or collective self-determination.

These institutional requirements can be illustrated by considering the role of human rights in the European Union. Here we might ask how institutions in the European Union have developed a transnational order able to promote democratization and resist democratic closure. That is, how does the EU embody the perspective of humanity in its constitutional practices concerning human rights? As a transnational polity, the EU has begun to address the tyranny of citizens over noncitizens practiced by some European states with their policy of "guest workers," immigrants, and cultural minorities. It is clear that with respect to these gaps in human rights between citizens and noncitizens, the EU has been a catalyst for democratization, fulfilling the democratic minimum for the first time for many residents of Europe who lack citizenship in any member state.[41] Indeed, it might be thought that these rights are matters for individual states to decide (perhaps as a task for the principle of subsidiarity). However, EU-level courts recognize the supremacy of the rights listed in the Fundamental Charter of Rights, which are the basis for immigrants' direct rights of appeal to the European Human Rights Court. Indeed, the European Convention on Human Rights already entitles foreigners without nationality in any EU member state to appeal to the European Human Rights Court and the EU Court of Justice for the ongoing juridical recognition of their rights, creating adjudicative institutions that build upon the constitutional traditions of member states even as they are extended to noncitizens.[42] In addition to the normative powers contained in the legal status of EU citizenship, the multiplication of institutions whose task it is to preserve the conditions of nondomination makes such powers and statuses more robust. EU-level institutions can thus "serve to make these states more democratic."[43] The extension of human rights in the EU to even noncitizens without naturalization shows the advantages of multiply realizing human rights in differentiated institutions that incorporate the perspective of humanity.

The purpose of a transnational constitutionalism is to create just such a reflexive, deliberative, and dispersed order with the minimally democratic feature that basic rights, political liberties, and their implementation must pass through the public deliberation of its citizens. In recognizing humanity, transnational democracy is inherently decentered. How might democracy be decentered? As expressed by Habermas, the goal is achieved by ridding democratic theory of some of the metaphysical assumptions it inherited from eighteenth-century voluntarism about the collective will of "the people" controlling social processes.[44] In deliberative democracy, these same assumptions lead to privileging face-to-face interaction in a single forum in which citizens mutually and simultaneously accept decisions. Given a certain level of differentiation and complexity in state-organized societies, democracy has already been decentered institutionally along two dimensions: in the microdimension, in the sheer variety of mechanisms and processes that constitute political decision making; and in the macrodimension, in the multiplicity of interlocking levels of governance from cities to federal states to regions and global society. Such decentering can further be found in democratic theory's lack of an adequate vocabulary to describe various emerging supranational polities such as the European Union.[45] Decentering is thus part of the shift from *dêmos* to *dêmoi*, where the normative status terms are conferred by humanity as a political community of *dêmoi*.

Incorporating humanity as a political community and as an end of justice requires a new sort of political community of others, one whose democratic contours are different enough that many fail to see how humanity can be a political subject at all—or if they do, it is as a dominator, a nation-state writ large. Deliberative democracy, to give just one example, is a theory of democracy that does not require that its community be linked to a state, and thus it may be applied in a broad array of decision-making processes that may decenter or even suspend one or all of these institutional and normative assumptions of the modern state in order to reinterpret its proper place in a larger, differentiated structure. This is the best way to interpret Article 28 of the Universal Declaration of Human Rights: "everyone is entitled to a social and institutional order in which the rights to freedom set forth in this Declaration can be fully realized." If this is itself to be understood as a human right, then under current circumstances we should add that everyone is entitled to a variety of social and institutional orders in which freedom from tyranny and domination can be fully realized across borders. My argument is that the normative powers one has by virtue of being a member of the human political community are sufficient to achieve the democratic minimum, the most basic requirement of these institutional orders. In the next section, I take this argument one step further and argue that a republic of humanity is necessary to achieve the common liberty required for nondomination. I suggest that arguments about the despotic character of cosmopolitan arrangements can be turned on their heads.

The Republic of Humanity: Common Liberty, Security, and the Dispersal of Power

Once again, it might be objected that particular democratic communities are sufficient to realize human rights so long as they incorporate either the perspective of humanity in their deliberative practices or basic human rights into their constitutions. In order to justify the obligation to establish a republic of humanity, the general institutional requirements for nondomination need to be considered, in particular as found in the republican analogy between justifications for federations and for transnational institutions. One of the great benefits of federal arrangements is their ability to deal with questions of complexity and size. Furthermore, contrary to the state demand for exclusive sovereignty and the monopoly of certain powers, federal institutions are based upon an antidomination principle that Pettit calls the "dispersion of power condition," the purpose of which is to counteract the tendency toward the centralization and localization of state power.[46] Once we accept the force of this argument, there is no reason to stop at states if we can disperse potentially dominating powers more thoroughly in a transnational federation. In this way, the dispersion of power condition is best seen as historically variable. Given that some executive powers of the state have already been delegated to international bodies, such as the World Trade Organization, and to transnational bodies, such as NAFTA adjudication boards, the dispersal of power condition has a new range of applications.

The dispersal of power in multiple levels thus provides a means of achieving robust nondomination. Some have argued that deliberative legitimacy is local, rising to no higher level than that of the nation-state.[47] Properly organized with dispersed power, however, large and numerous units also have deliberative advantages. At least some existing EU practices employ institutional structures of cooperation to take advantage of the dispersal of power and deliberation in multileveled and polycentric polities. Contrary to classical modern sovereignty, transnational institutions governed by republican principles ought to further disaggregate state monopolies of powers and functions into a variety of institutional levels and locations by disaggregating centralized transnational powers and redistributing them to citizens, thereby opening them up to public deliberation. Multiple juridical and political institutions achieve the dispersal of power by multiplying locations for the exercise of differentiated citizenship. Such overlapping differentiated and polyarchical structures permit greater realization of these rights and their claims against domination, as citizens exercise the various entitlements gained from their overlapping memberships. This feature of the EU can be generalized and cannot be captured by its current use of the concept of subsidiarity, which is typically the requirement that decision making be made at the *lowest* possible level. Rather, in order to create common liberty it is necessary to have many different levels—both higher and lower—in which to distribute power. This includes the highest possible level, the republic of humanity, which includes the need for at least some global political institutions to secure nondomination.

How do multiple levels and sites promote the powers of democratic citizenship, and especially the central normative power to initiate deliberation about claims to justice? We can answer this question in two ways. One way is to see how the EU's institutional design and practices could be used to promote this fundamental normative power, a power basic to the right to have rights. The EU could do so by providing a variety of locations and sites for deliberation in which publics interact with institutional powers and authorities. This division of powers could not be exclusively territorial or else it would be indistinguishable from a large nation-state. The second way to promote deliberation follows from these features. To achieve more robust interaction across various levels and diverse locales and to promote citizens' capacity to initiate deliberation at multiple levels, large federal institutions require a written constitution. In order to become legitimate enough to reform itself democratically, the EU not only has to promote European citizenship as a status, but must also create those institutional contexts in which such a status is linked to normative powers of deliberation. This same understanding of nondomination suggests that such normative powers should be extended to all human beings, as a right to membership in the human political community.

Here the republican argument for transnationalism has its greatest force. Without common liberty, the security of one's freedom from domination is tied to a particular community's capacity to protect its citizens, leaving those in weak or failed states with only the capacity to appeal to stronger states to act on behalf of humanity. Indeed, even in cases of functioning states, the capacity to secure the common liberty of its members may be limited by the larger world around them. In an insecure world, security-minded democracies often end up restricting the liberties of their own citizens. This negative feedback relationship between nondomination as realized in democratic states and the anarchy and insecurity of the current international system is thus self-defeating for internal democracy. It is also self-defeating externally in securing nondomination by threat and force. If some communities are dominated for the sake of the security of other communities, then all may be dominated under the right circumstances. The only way to realize secure nondomination is through common liberty, and in this case such freedom from domination requires that all are free, and not merely as a result of the power exercised by a particular democratically arbitrary community. Shared common liberty not only explains the peace among democracies, but also why some increasingly warlike democracies are unable to achieve their security without sacrificing their own commitments to democratic ideals. Moreover, the heightening of executive, military, and police power also undermines common liberty at home, just as colonialism did in earlier periods. Peace and security are instrumental benefits of liberty as well as goods that are undermined when they are taken to be final ends.

Transforming the EU's method of inquiry into the effects of policies on human rights and normative powers also depends on incorporating a cosmopolitan perspective of the generalized other into its public judgments and practices of assessment. The duties of EU citizens to the large numbers of noncitizens residing in the EU include granting them some power to influence deliberative processes so that these remain democratically legitimate. With their commitments to human rights as contained in the Charter of Fundamental Rights explicitly constitutionalized, a more democratic EU would have greater constitutionally based obligations toward nonmembers, those obligations that already exist in virtue of all European residents having the normative powers that emerge from the commitments of a democracy of *dêmoi*. This cosmopolitan perspective may also provide the impetus for ongoing collective learning at the constitutional level to go beyond some of the limits of the EU as a bounded community. For human political rights to be realized, the EU must be a community within a larger political community, a collection of *dêmoi* integrated as a larger democratic community. This transforms the problem of boundaries from an external to an internal one. With the recognition of the full range of human rights of all persons within a complex and differentiated institutional structure, the EU shifts from a regional to a cosmopolitan polity.

If they seek not to be dominators, democracies have obligations to create a republic of humanity for two main reasons. First, they cannot ignore these claims to common liberty without becoming dominators and thereby undermining the conditions for democracy. Second, democratic communities that honor the democratic minimum must at least be open to claims of other communities and thus be willing to extend that minimum to all bearers of human rights. In this way, democracies would not merely act on behalf of humanity, but would *constitute* the human community. This does not require a world state, since the more institutionally differentiated such a community is at different levels, the better the dispersal of power condition is met. It is clear, however, that some of these obligations can be met only if some of those institutions are global in scope, particularly global juridical institutions such as the International Criminal Court. In terms of a republican conception of nondomination, human rights and the democratic minimum are two sides of the same coin: the political obligation to realize the civil condition necessary for the common liberty of humanity, a republic of humanity.

Conclusion

I have argued that universal human rights imply two different demands that we act for the sake of humanity. The first demand is the
obligation to respond to the fundamental injustice borne by those
whose membership in humanity as such has been so violated that they
have effectively become rightless. Even when their other rights have
been violated, they have not lost their status as members of the human
political community, precisely because other members respond to
their moral claims to justice. This obligation is also first-personal in
that it demands that we change our own normative statuses reflexively whenever we take up others' claims in order to do justice to their
humanity. Humanity in this sense functions as the open moral horizon
of all political communities. It is a moral status that grounds those
obligations not often fulfilled by international society as currently constituted. The second sense in which we are obliged to realize humanity is both legal and political: humanity ought to be realized in an
actual political community. The basic argument is that such a community is necessary to secure freedom from domination in two ways:
first, through institutional differentiation that enables citizens to
appeal to different overlapping statuses in various democratic institutions in order to achieve nondomination; and, second, through the
achievement of common liberty and a common civic status in a republic of humanity. Nondomination is secure only if all are free, if all share
the same liberty in virtue of their human political status. This common
liberty requires more than political inclusion in separate political communities and Kantian rights to hospitality. Rather, it must be realized
in the status of being a full member of the actual human political community constituted by such commitments.

This insistence on humanity as a political community may seem to
underestimate the significance of other forms of community that
might be attributed to humanity. For example, humanity is often said
to be realized as a moral community, the Kingdom of Ends. Such a
community is important, since it establishes obligations to individuals and concerns about their life chances that ought to constrain our
moral statuses and powers: they should not be inconsistent with
our moral obligations to humanity. Such moral demands may also be

thought to lead more directly to humanity as a legal rather than political community, in which human rights are taken to be juridical statuses and realized institutionally in the legal protection and recognition offered by the International Criminal Court and in the social goods provided by the UNHCR. While these institutions act on behalf of humanity as a legal entity (rather than for the sake of the humanity of individuals in the moral case), there are clear limitations on the extent to which legal enforcement and protections, however important, can realize the robust statuses and active powers necessary for nondomination and common liberty. The current human rights regime opens up a space for an emerging political community to the extent that the content of rights and the form of their implementation may be put up for democratic deliberation.[48] Such a global civil rights movement would serve not only to begin the process of forming a human political community, but it could also test the myriad possibilities for implementing and interpreting human rights both locally and globally. It would itself reflexively model essential features of publics and institutions that aim at this end. Although not advocating a cosmopolis, my argument is cosmopolitan in the sense that it suggests that human rights are best realized in a differentiated and democratically structured community, a community that ultimately aims at the common liberty of all human beings.

In her discussion of "the end of the rights of man," Hannah Arendt remained skeptical that human rights as such had been ever been fully realized. The same can be said about democracy in all current forms, whose commitments to incorporating a truly cosmopolitan perspective are contingent on the right circumstances. While it cannot be said that a well-ordered democracy with imperfect but fair procedures would always reflect the demands of global justice, we can say that by achieving the democratic minimum for citizens and noncitizens alike it would be able to realize the normative status of membership in the human political community. If everyone else has universal political rights, then democracy can become more just by making manifest the perspective of humanity as a requirement of democratic justification. And it can do this only if humanity becomes a novel political subject, a political community in which the full normative statuses of humanity and humanness are realized. This is the basic thesis of republican cosmopolitanism.

This political emphasis takes us well beyond the juridical focus of some theories of cosmopolitan democracy. Important as the rule of law is with respect to tyranny, it does not exhaust the linkages between human rights and democracy. As many have already noted, the formal rule of law cannot by itself eliminate those great iniquities that international human rights institutions aim to correct. I have emphasized the need for deliberation and a constitutional order because of their reflexivity and their capacity to make these very rights and institutional and normative frameworks open to the deliberation of those citizens acting within them. When considering the sort of political community that is necessary to realize basic human rights, it is important to distinguish the rule of law as a necessary condition for nontyranny from the democratic minimum as a necessary condition for nondomination. The rule of law requires democratic political activity in order to open the legal order, and even the constitutional essentials themselves, to challenge, revision, and amendment. Freedom as nondomination can best be realized in a highly differentiated, decentered polity with a commitment to common liberty. On normative grounds, many of the core commitments of constitutional democracy are inherently universalistic and thus cosmopolitan; on institutional grounds, humanity can best be realized in a complexly interconnected and overlapping deliberative and polyarchic structure. In the next chapter I discuss these structural features in an existing transnational polity: the European Union.

As my already quite frequent use of examples taken from its governance practices shows, I consider the European Union the best available instance of a transnational democracy. The European Union is a model for international democracy for this reason: it is unprecedented to the extent that the pooling of sovereignty has helped develop institutions whose *democratic* structure cannot resemble the unified structure of the nation-state that organizes a "people." In this sense, the EU is a highly differentiated, decentered political structure, both diverse and dispersed. It is diverse insofar as there are at any location many different peoples, and it is dispersed since political authority is exercised at many different sites and at many different levels. This is not to say, however, that it is in any sense ideal. In fact, it is in great need of democratic reform. It does nonetheless have a sufficiently complex and differentiated institutional structure, as well as a novel set of institutions and practices that are responsive to appeals made by those whose rights have been violated. Moreover, it is now likely to make explicit its already implicit constitutionalism and thus to acquire the sort of reflexivity necessary to solve its biggest democratic deficit from a republican point of view: its continued potential for legal domination as evidenced by its lack of deliberative and popular legitimacy.

In the next chapter, I offer a normative reconstruction of the EU's underlying transnational structure that brings out its features as a decentered democratic polity and an institutional regime. The central focus of the chapter is on a major failing of the European Union: its lack of the capability of its citizens to initiate legitimate processes of democratic reform. Overcoming this failure is central to the project of transnational democracy, because it is in initiating democratic reform that citizens not only become more secure in their nondomination, but also jointly exercise their common liberty.

4

Reforming the Transnational Polity: Deliberative Democracy and the European Union

Human rights are central to republican cosmopolitanism. Their justification is both republican and cosmopolitan to the extent that their implementation requires a political community of humanity. In this community, such rights are normative powers that are entailed by the minimal human status that is denied to slaves and to rightless persons. As legitimate claims against domination, rights are in the first instance addressed to a responsive political community. I have argued that such a responsive political community is a democratic one when the rights in question are not mere immunities or protections from arbitrary interference, but normative statuses and powers that are the fundamental basis of political rights, or of the right to have rights. Here democracy is not merely instrumental to the realization of human rights, but constitutive of justice, in that the achievement of democracy must also be the realization of a particular form of freedom: the freedom to initiate deliberation and to participate in processes that shape the duties and obligations that are necessary conditions for any fair scheme of social cooperation based on common liberty. In this chapter, I develop this conception further by examining the way in which the democratic minimum ought to figure in the European Union (EU), which I take to be an actual, if imperfect, transnational polity. I argue that the European Union does not suffer from a general democratic deficit, but rather from a deliberative deficit about the ends of the polity.[1] The specific context of deliberation here concerns the ends of democratic reform, and the lack of such deliberation indicates a failure to meet the democratic minimum.

In order to institute this normative power and link it to communicative freedom, the community and its decision-making processes must be organized in the proper institutional structure with sufficient reflexivity. Using the account of universal political rights developed in the last chapter as my guide, in this chapter I address the question of whether or not there is a distinctive form of constitutionalism for a polity whose institutions are both transnational and democratic. I put the arguments of the preceding chapters to work in order to develop a range of institutional possibilities for a transnational democracy in light of a case study of the European Union, currently the most developed project in transnational democracy. The EU is also a polity that has progressed to the constitutional phase, in which the democratic legitimacy of this form of polity is at issue.

Why discuss constitutionalism in the context of reform? Constitutionalism establishes one aspect of democratic legitimacy that is particularly important for the distribution of authority in an institutional structure as complex as the EU, which has grown by layers in the different treaties that have established and reestablished it. By attempting to build a diverse polity, the EU's arrangements have become transnational rather than intergovernmental in form, a fact seen most significantly in the emergence of distinctly European citizenship with its own rights and powers as established in the 1993 Maastricht Treaty.[2] In accordance with this treaty, normative powers of EU citizens are constitutionally independent of their powers as citizens of member states. The EU is for this reason a polity in the making, not merely a powerful organization of states, and as such needs constitutional legitimacy for its authority to be democratic. Without such legitimacy, the various *dêmoi* may find that some parts of their common institutional structures are impervious to democratic influence and popular control, no matter how much those structures resemble a parliamentary form. The impasse of the current constitutional convention shows the many difficulties that any polity inevitably confronts when creating legitimate institutions of democratic reform. Taken cumulatively, these difficulties lead to a potentially vicious circle: it is not democratic enough to propose the means and ends to achieve its own democratization. The unresolved problem of the so-called "democratic deficit" of transnational institutions is the legal and political domination that results from distinctly political methods of integration. The different possibilities for democratization beyond the nation-state remain open to the EU, each of which depends both on a different understanding of the type of political body the EU is supposed to be and on making European citizenship in some way comparable to the rich array of rights and opportunities associated with national citizenship that have emerged from long historical struggles for democratic reform within states.

Since the EU is not yet fully democratic, some kind of procedure is necessary to separate the normative husk from the contingent chaff of its many treaty layers. One might try to formulate general principles and deduce a general institutional form from them. This takes us only so far and leaves a great deal of indeterminacy between principles and their possible realization. This procedure also ignores the fact that a transnational democracy, as a democracy of democracies, already has established political norms. The alternative approach to both of these options is a rational reconstruction that begins with the best available example of an emerging transnational democratic polity. Given that the set of such polities currently has but one member, the EU is the logical choice. At the same time, any reconstruction of the EU as a transnational polity is a rational and thus a normative enterprise; that is, it is an account that seeks to select those features of its development that cohere best with the minimal criteria of democracy, human rights, and nondomination that I developed in the previous chapters. As such, the rational reconstruction I offer is contestable, precisely because it is an interpretation offered from the point of view of republican cosmopolitanism. From this republican point of view, the EU has already developed innovative practices of governance. International organizations such as the United Nations do not exhibit this same degree of coherence with republicanism, and features of its Charter, such as the commitment to noninterference in the internal affairs of other states, do not cohere with it at all.

If the EU is to be a transnational democracy, its citizens must be able to initiate democratic reform in both constitutional moments and everyday politics. This capacity further operationalizes the democratic minimum for transnational polities. In order to establish how such a minimum might be possible, I turn first to the necessary conditions for legitimate democratic reform: these include formal, deliberative, and popular conditions, all of which must be manifested within the reform process. Second, I argue that the fundamental reflexive aim of the constitution of a transnational democracy, as well as of the popular and deliberative processes of constitution-making, must be to create conditions for legitimate democratic reform. Central to the reform of the EU is the development of a more robustly deliberative citizenship, in which citizens have the minimum normative powers necessary for genuine democratization. Third, after reconstructing the EU as the ideal type of a transnational polity, I turn to the main issue of democratic reform as it emerges in everyday transnational politics: the problem of juridification, or the potential for formal legal rule making to be a source of transnational domination. Here, leaving deliberation to experts and officials will not be sufficient. The overall structure that would develop greater democratic legitimacy would be a form of decentered federalism, already manifested in the EU's novel deliberative practices. Above all, these practices must be linked to new popular and deliberative processes in order to establish legitimate democratic reform. If the EU could reform itself in such a way as to create conditions for deliberative and popular legitimacy, it would cease to be merely a potentially innovative structural model and become an actual democratic political community. I turn first to the conditions of democratic legitimacy necessary for reform.

Democratically Legitimate Reform

If the European Union is in some sense a democracy, then it must have mechanisms for its own reform, however inadequate they may be. In the existing structure of the EU, power of initiative is shared by the member states through the Council. More specifically, such a power resides in the executive branch, with a procedure for its being carried out by a mixed body. For this reason, the 2004 constitutional proposal was a product of the current treaty structure and inherited all of its problems of democratic legitimacy. I do not consider other possible sources of legitimacy, such as problem-solving capacity or effectiveness (emphasized by Fritz Scharpf as "outcome legitimacy").[3] In most constitutional democracies, there are three different aspects of democratic legitimacy, broadly understood, that play the role of legitimating democratic reforms. I will illustrate each of these aspects of such reform through processes that are part of constitution-making or constitutional change. The *formal legitimacy* of any process of reform is found in the institutional authority to initiate it, where this authority can be specifically delegated to some particular office or constitutionally specified in some explicit amendment procedure. *Popular legitimacy* is found to the extent that the people have genuine opportunities to shape or assent to such reform—minimally, the popular ratification of proposed changes or amendments—and that these opportunities are common knowledge among citizens. Popular legitimacy is not reducible to citizens' pro or con attitudes, which are always open to change. Finally, democratic reform has *deliberative legitimacy* to the extent that the deliberative process of citizens offering reasons to each other in mutual justification plays some role, such as exerting an influence over the process of drafting the constitution or parts of a constitution. Deliberative legitimacy is usually measured by the quality of deliberation: that is, either by qualities such as the freedom, openness, or publicity of the deliberative process, or by the quality of the reasons or outcomes as measured by some independent standard. While the latter, more epistemic standard is preferred in some forms of inquiry, it is unlikely that a constitutional proposal can be settled by appeal to some procedure-independent standard.

It is now clear that the proposed EU constitution has little more than formal legitimacy, especially since the process of its formation lacked any genuinely deliberative and popular features. Its deliberative resources were internal to the body formed by the Council and thus only served to increase popular illegitimacy. We might get the same result in Canada or the United States if proposed changes to the formal structure of NAFTA were put up for a vote, since NAFTA more clearly than the EU lacks the resources to reform itself democratically (given that its formal legitimacy could be met by the bylaws of the organization and its deliberative legitimacy refers to panels of experts as the subjects of deliberation). But such merely formal legitimacy is not yet democratic, precisely because it does not require that the opinions and interests of those outside the formally named bodies need to be heard and addressed. In fact, no one except these formally designated members has any legitimate say in the process of proposing such reforms, except in the ratification phase. Above all, the current proposed EU constitution codifies rather than improves the status quo and thus does not respond to the popular dissatisfaction with the current EU structure.

This difficulty has become even entrenched for the EU, since there is no "People" that it is supposed to organize into a subject. Instead, the more modest goal, as stated in its treaties, is that of "bringing the peoples of Europe together in an ever closer Union." The "peoples" that were to ratify the treaty were the national publics, not the citizens of Europe. When the citizens of EU member states were asked to put the proposal to a vote, the publics of France and the Netherlands rejected the democratic legitimacy of the constitution as a means to democratic reform. One main purpose of this democratic reform would be to address the issue of the potential loss of freedom from domination in a polity in which the political subject of democracy is plural, *dêmoi* rather than a *dêmos*. This attempt to create a democracy of *dêmoi* may seem paradoxical if citizens are to achieve the ideal of self-rule by becoming both authors and subjects of the laws of Europe.[4] Yet, as Bruce Ackerman has pointed out against such a "monistic" interpretation of constitutional structures, there is no one privileged place in which the popular will is located by some naïve synecdoche that takes the part for the whole. The EU has no legislative body since its Parliament does not have the authority to enact the law directly. And even if the European Parliament came to have this authority, its pluralistic structure as a democracy of *dêmoi* undermines any simple monism.

The only solution is then, as Henry Richardson has put it, to look for a way in which "the processes that form the popular will can be distributed across the various parts of the constitutional structure."[5] The difficulty here is that in the case of the European Union, it is the executive power of the Council, as empowered in the 2001 Laeken Declaration, that confers upon it the legitimate right to make such a proposal, independently of any exercise of the popular will. But if citizens are to be engaged as citizens both of Europe and of the member states, their will must be engaged at various stages and locations in the process. The challenge of democratic reform is that citizens have to appeal to normative powers that are not already constituted in some institutional structure. Thus they must first appeal to their intrinsic democratic authority to recreate those institutions that constitute their normative powers in the first place. This kind of reflexivity is the essential innovation of democracy that makes it the proper means to overcome institutional forms of domination.

For all the difficulties of formal legitimacy in the EU, the initiative of executive power need not exclude popular legitimacy. Here we might think of other institutions of legitimate democratic reform as providing superior models. For example, a Citizens' Assembly on Electoral Reform was empowered by the Premier of British Columbia to make a specific proposal for the reform of the province's electoral system. The proposal was the result of internal processes of deliberation among the randomly chosen ordinary citizens who made up the Assembly. Seen as a product of delegated executive power, something more than a transfer of normative powers is required for such an assembly to acquire fuller popular democratic legitimacy: namely, that the transparent process of its construction makes it a minipublic in the sense already discussed. As a minipublic, the Assembly used its delegated power by deliberating as citizen-representatives on behalf of the people, whose will could best be formed under the more ideal conditions that were fulfilled in the Citizen Assembly's deliberation (especially considering the complexities of various voting systems). The legitimating potential of such empowered participation in this case did not reside in the mere fact that the selection process somehow mirrored the opinions of the wider public, but rather in the way in which the Assembly's judgment helped to shape public judgment about reform processes in some normative sense—as the opinion that the public *ought* to hold. The force of such a claim must be tested when the powers of the Assembly are transferred back to the public as a whole. In order to secure popular as well as deliberative legitimacy, the Assembly's proposal had to be voted upon by all citizens. Nonetheless, the direct participation of citizens in the constitutional proposal stage permits many citizens to recognize its popular legitimacy even if the collective body of citizens was not actually present in deliberation. If this kind of procedure were repeated in various states or locations throughout the European Union, then it would not be at all paradoxical that the proposal voted upon would have some kind of popular credentials, and thus increased democratic legitimacy.

In order to understand popular legitimacy democratically, however, more needs to be said about how such delegated exercises of citizens' powers are consistent with popular rule understood distributively. Here we may appeal to some idea of minimum popular democratic legitimacy. The democratic minimum as I have developed it is sufficient for this purpose because it is constructed so as to make citizens sources of normative authority. Citizens would have to deliberate by employing just these shared normative powers ascribed to them in virtue of their being citizens, and not merely those specific powers delegated to them by the executive power of the EU Council. The Council itself, which delegated its powers to an intergovernmental body of representatives made up of heads of state and national parliaments and has no mechanisms for popular consultation, produced the current proposal. Thus the source of the legitimacy of the proposed EU Constitutional Treaty is merely intergovernmental, and its deliberations have not carried with them deliberative or popular legitimacy as accorded by the direct or indirect deliberation of citizens at large. Having no sense of the popular legitimacy of the constitution-making process, the French and Dutch *populus* asserted their normative powers and exercised their freedom by saying "no" in the absence of any other power.

The advantage of a constitution would be to give citizens fuller normative powers and political rights that include the power to change the assignment of rights and duties. However, it may be necessary to develop new institutions and forums for deliberation for this to be possible. More specifically, greater institutional differentiation and new normative powers may be necessary when the existing forms of will formation do not succeed in creating the proper distributive conditions for forming a popular will. Only in virtue of participating in forming such a popular will are citizens able to see the constitution as democratic rather than as arbitrarily imposed. Once initiated, the capacity of citizens to deliberate about the terms of democratic governance, including the rights, duties, and powers of citizenship, constitutes a source of democratic legitimacy: the popular legitimacy provided by the opportunity and the capacity of citizens to exercise their freedoms, and then to decide upon and authoritatively enact such reform, since this is what explains the value of ratification votes. The democratic minimum, rather than the veto exercised in voting, is the source of distributed popular legitimacy.

Even with this increased overall democratic legitimacy, citizens may still decide that the constitutional proposals for reform lack deliberative legitimacy for procedural reasons. Considered more fully, the claim to deliberative legitimacy is much stronger than popular legitimacy as such: if other citizens underwent a similar process, they too would arrive at a similar reasoned judgment, and this fact is manifest to other citizens in the deliberative role. Thus the judgment is not only for reasons that they could accept, but also for reasons that they could accept owing specifically to the recognition of the deliberative legitimacy of the minipublic that proposes the changes. The internal deliberative legitimacy achieved procedurally among participants does not automatically extend to those who have not participated in it. It is clear then that the procedures used to increase the deliberative legitimacy of democratic reform may fail to attain the proper threshold of popular legitimacy and are furthermore subject to the same sort of veto.

By putting all these aspects of legitimacy together we get a much more complex and demanding picture of democratic reform. Legitimacy does not arise from any one source in a democracy, but is distributed among legislatures, courts, and the administrative and executive bodies that implement its conditions. Distributive legitimacy requires well-established forms of institutional coordination and coherence. In the case of democratic and constitutional reform, the process is even more protracted and requires many different steps, but it can result in a popular will to change those very institutions that have not yet formed a popular will. In the end, formal, popular, and deliberative legitimacy should be manifested at various locations and stages of the process (even if in the case of democratically illegitimate institutions reform can be initiated without any formal legitimacy whatsoever). In this sense, Rousseau is right that popular sovereignty should not be alienated into any particular deliberative body or institutional location, but distributed across the whole constitutional structure and extended across long periods of will formation.

The power of initiative possessed by all citizens who participate in deliberation is crucial for judging the deliberative legitimacy of its results. While the attempt to make a minipublic or popular assembly duly and descriptively representative seems to be an appropriate goal in the case of constructing a minipublic for electoral reform, the distributed character of institutions of democratic change lessens the legitimating significance of representativeness. Once deliberation begins, issues such as procedural openness and the availability of a proper set of alternative proposals play a more direct role. One consequence of this complex process is that in cases of democratic reform, deliberation is historically extended, sometimes for decades, as the popular will is still being formed. At the very least, that is what the negative results of the current referenda indicate. In cases of conflict, citizens look to the quality and responsiveness of the process of deliberation to ensure that the addressees of the justification have been able to shape the discussion and its outcome in relevant ways.

This leads to the general conclusion that I want to draw from this section. The popular will that legitimates the reform itself could only be formed if the processes of constitution-making and ratification already had all the hallmarks of legitimate institutions of democratic reform. In the case of the European Union the process must not only be formally, popularly, and deliberatively legitimate, it must also have an added feature: it must to some degree instantiate the requirements of legitimacy of the kind of democracy it is meant to institute. It could well be constitutionally legitimate when judged ex post facto. For that reason, it must distribute the popular will in a way that is appropriate to the type of transnational polity that it is, rather than by a process that is based on an interpretation of its legitimacy as an intergovernmental body that is many degrees of delegation removed from democratic sources of political authority. This reflexivity is a further feature of legitimate institutions of democratic reform. Above all, for transnational polities such as the EU, the body of citizens or officials that proposes the new constitution must be a transnational rather than an intergovernmental one.

Democratic Legitimacy: Reconstructing the Ideal Type of a Transnational Polity

In the previous section I argued that the democratic core of constitutionalism is tied to its reflexive character—that is, to its capacity to make the basis of democracy *itself* the subject of the democratic deliberation of citizens. Such a self-transformative polity requires that a constitution enable its citizens to have just this normative power. If the institutional structure is large and multileveled (as the EU's surely is), then this power must be present not merely in its legislative and parliamentary core, but must also be distributed throughout its various levels and dispersed sites of deliberation. From the criterion of nondomination implied by the democratic minimum, it follows that some distinctly transnational form of federalism is the proper general type of institutional design, provided that it could be shown to be adequate to the democratic minimum with respect to the imposition of order and the possibilities of popular control. It also follows that the democratic deficit of the EU, is in the case of democratic reform, more properly a "deliberation deficit" that also leads to a "popular deficit."

One clear instance of this constitutionalism is implicit in the institutionalization of human rights in the 1950 European Convention for the Protection of Human Rights and the recent 2000 Charter of Fundamental Rights of the European Union. What is the purpose of this new layer of human rights enforcement beyond that already provided by the constitutions of member states? With the accompanying supranational European Court of Human Rights, which grants rights of individual petition, there are (at least in the juridical dimension) multiple new institutions and memberships that can be invoked in making claims about human rights. Such overlapping differentiated and polyarchical structures permit greater realization of these rights and their claims against domination, as the citizens of *dêmoi* exercise the various entitlements gained from their overlapping memberships. In such a structure, human rights are constitutive of membership in a plural democratic polity and become a secure basis on which to assess new governance institutions procedurally, including, for example, the transparency of committees and the broad inclusion of participants in deliberations related to committees and methods of policy coordination. Even without any police powers, such differentiated institutions best realize rights in multiple *dêmoi* with diverse entitlements rather than in a single form of citizenship that uniquely constitutes the *dêmos*. The Charter functions in just this transnational way, not as a binding document, but by reinforcing EU-level adjudicative institutions and case law already grounded in the constitutional traditions of the member states. This structure is based on a principle of institutional differentiation in which functions and powers become more accessible by being repeated at different levels.

Given the shape of the political institutions of the European polity, most cosmopolitans argue that the first step toward a supranational democratic order is to create a more effective and empowered European Parliament (EP), perhaps with a bicameral structure. The point here is not to see the EP as some privileged source of democratic legitimacy, but as one of the locations for distributing deliberative and popular powers. This would clearly shift the location of various normative powers in EU institutions—including the rights to initiate legislation, to set directives and objectives for administrative bodies, and to review implementation in conjunction with the Commission—from the Council to the people. As an elected body, the EP can potentially represent and empower more diverse interests. With the general weakening of legislative bodies now found in many large nation-states, however, it is unclear whether such a body would in fact overcome the gap between European institutions and the interests of the citizens they supposedly represent. The problem is not that the traditional separation of powers in federal constitutions would too radically alter the current shape of the EU, but that such a separation now needs to be understood in terms of a plurality of overlapping processes of distributed will formation.[6]

While the proposed constitution does indeed support greater parliamentary powers (through expanding the co-decision powers of national parliaments as a mechanism for democratization), it is unclear whether introducing a further source of legislative initiative is really so problematic in a structure that already has several, and needs them to promote a thickly institutionalized democratic minimum. So long as the EP is not the sole source of legislative legitimacy, a new constitutional right to be included among these institutional bodies with the ability to initiate policy debates could function as one among many mechanisms for public influence and accountability. It could do so in virtue of its tiered structure, which has the advantages of large and numerous legislatures that permit the emergence of a forum in which many diverse cultural and social perspectives are gathered. By reforming the EP with greater powers of initiative, the public spheres with which it interacts will thereby acquire greater access to the influence necessary for the constructive use of their communicative freedom to define the terms of debate and deliberation. This proposal thus helps the EU meet the democratic minimum, if only with increased indirect legitimacy.

Nonetheless, simply giving the EP greater powers is insufficient to meet the democratic minimum for processes of democratic reform. Rather, more direct forms of public deliberation must emerge within the polyarchy of various procedures for the responsive implementation of basic policies. This issue concerns the form of inquiry that institutions take to be necessary to inform their decision-making processes. As Charles Sabel and Joshua Cohen have argued, a "directly deliberative" design in many ways incorporates epistemic innovations and increased capabilities of economic organizations in the same way as, for instance, the New Deal institutions in the United States followed the innovations of industrial organization in the centralized mass production they attempted to administer and regulate.[7] Roughly, such a directly deliberative form of organization uses nested and collaborative forms of decision making based on highly collaborative processes of jointly defining problems and setting goals already typical in many large firms with dispersed sites of production. These forms of organization have been established in constitutional orders that do not require uniform policies, but permit a broad range of experimental initiatives, with public testing across levels and sites of mutual accountability and authority.

Given these necessary requirements for plural and dispersed polities, directly deliberative designs have a new salience, which is perhaps surprising only in light of previous turns toward centralization as the solution to problems of scale. Nondomination requires yet a different strategy, and I have already discussed the ways in which distributive publics or minipublics open up new directly deliberative possibilities for reform. Here we can see directly deliberative designs as a way of producing distributed rather than plebiscitary or mass popular legitimacy, such as the legitimacy to vote in a referendum on some democratic reform and to participate in a mass public that is persuaded by various appeals for its loyalty. Such mass publics are particularly important for saying "no" to inadequate or self-defeating democratic reforms that do not increase overall democratic legitimacy. We might think of these mass publics as mobilized when the issues of reform reach a broad enough audience to give them the popular salience they otherwise lacked.

However, such publics at best capture de facto public opinion and should best be seen as indicating that the popular will lacked sufficient opportunities to be more fully and deliberatively formed, even if initiative and policy coordination are still currently left entirely with the Commission. Distributing such powers to a single location, rather than across multiple levels and sites in the overall structure, violates the basic institutional principle of republican federalism that powers ought to be widely distributed and iterated at various levels. This principle ought then to be basic to any attempt to reform the EU in light of its potential for legal and bureaucratic domination. At present, practices such as the Open Method of Coordination lack the deliberative and popular legitimacy that would make them a means for democratic reform.[8] Nonetheless, in a democratically reformed EU they could become a source of deliberative legitimacy. I return to these issues below.

The biggest difference between the EU and such delegative institutions as the WTO is precisely that the EU is itself a polity and thus already has a constitutional framework for accountability through open and multiperspectival deliberative inquiry. The EU's explicit recognition of political rights as human rights invests all those affected by authoritative decisions with the normative powers and opportunities to exercise voice, including rights of participation. This makes it possible for citizens of the EU to make claims rather than simply challenge decisions; that is, they may appeal not only to basic principles of democracy and human rights, but also to political institutions that should be responsive to their claims.

Constitutionalism also has another wider and more important role, to the extent that it is internalized in deliberative institutions: not only does it create some broad institutional distinctions between good and bad reasons, it also creates the demand for reflective equilibrium in decision making. Such equilibrium is necessary because norms of deliberation are part of the normative framework of inquiry into possible institutional reforms, so that at the very least actors are constrained to show the coherence of specific decisions with basic norms. On the basis of this equilibrium effect of constitutionalization, Neyer argues that "noncompliance with the outcome of a deliberative procedure not only rejects the specific deal [that has been reached], but implicitly opposes the whole normative structure of which the specific norm is a part."[9] However, to be truly democratic and reflexive, participants must be empowered to change the normative framework as well. Otherwise, constitutions would not have the resources to institute the requisite change within the continuity necessary to retain their reflexive and polity-building roles. Calls for greater transparency or for participation by civil society are not really the answer, however, since the weaknesses here are more structural. The transnational principle of institutional differentiation (rather than the simple separation of powers) requires multiple and intersecting processes of public deliberation within a normative framework that is revisable when it no longer adequately institutionalizes the democratic minimum.

How do weaknesses in its deliberative institutions contribute to the EU's democratic deficit? Here the difficulty lies not with the breadth of its deliberative processes, but rather with their democratic depth. Even on the best interpretation offered by their defenders, committees currently function as forums for political processes and as coordinating bodies across various levels of governance; they are, however, deficient as argumentative forums to the extent that they are only semipublic and relate primarily to networks of administrative agencies and private policy experts. A committee-based procedure, however deliberative, retains the weaknesses of the hierarchical relations of experts, officials, and citizens within which it is embedded. In cases of democratic reform, a minipublic provides an institutionally constructed intermediary in popular will formation, although it could act in such as way as to become an agent for the creation of a larger public with normative powers.

If the constitutional order helps build the polity, this leaves open an important question: who are the citizens of the Europolity? Given the new immigration in Europe, the public sphere is undergoing a structural transformation with the potential for citizens to dominate noncitizen residents and immigrants, given the lack of the empowered participation and recognition of the latter as members of the public with communicative freedom. The transformation of inquiry in the EU on the effects of policies on human rights and normative powers depends on incorporating a cosmopolitan perspective of the generalized other into its public judgments and practices of assessment. The duties of EU citizens to the large numbers of noncitizens who reside in the EU currently include granting them some power to influence local deliberative processes, so that these remain democratically legitimate. With their commitments to human rights as contained in the Charter of Fundamental Rights explicitly constitutionalized, a more democratic EU would have greater constitutionally based obligations toward nonmembers: obligations that already exist in virtue of all residents of Europe having the normative powers that emerge from the commitments of a democracy of *dêmoi*.

This cosmopolitan perspective may also provide the impetus for ongoing collective learning at the constitutional level to go beyond some of the limits of the EU as a bounded community. For human political rights to be realized, the EU must be a community within a larger political community, a collection of *dêmoi* integrated as a larger democratic community. This transforms the problem of boundaries from an external to an internal one. With the recognition of the full range of human rights of all persons within a complex and differentiated institutional structure, the EU shifts from a regional to a cosmopolitan polity. Although the distributive publics and institutional deliberation can be iterated across regions as much as across states, this internalization of the perspective of the human political community provides the greatest potential for the democratization of the European polity. This requires a stronger and more demanding recognition of the right to nationality, with the danger that the failure to incorporate noncitizens "may lead to divided societies marked by severe inequalities and conflicts," including permanent minorities and excluded groups at the regional level.[10] Democracies with deep commitments to human rights have special obligations to humanity, and thus to the nondomination of noncitizens, in ways that nondemocratic polities do not. Such deep inequalities and conflicts also describe the source of the democratic deficit at the international level and the failure of international institutions and forms of authority to incorporate the perspective of humanity. It is in this respect, and not merely in its institutional structure and commitment to multilateral foreign policy, that the EU could provide a model for transnational democratization. Without this cosmopolitan dimension, the constitutional framework would lack the universality needed to locate developing claims to rights of citizenship within a highly differentiated institutional order.

This discussion of the democratizing role of European juridical and legal institutions also raises the possibility of an opposing tendency. With their predominately legal rather than political form, a distinctive form of domination arises in emergent transnational polities. Legal domination is distinct from tyranny also in the sense that its effects are not global; it may be specific to some particular area of authority that is immunized from democratic influence. While not unique to the particular political form of the EU, such domination cannot be overcome by simply creating representative legislative institutions, but requires other, more deliberative means. The lack of a transnational-level democratic minimum that enables citizens to secure their freedom and their power against the characteristic legal form of transnational domination is behind overly general talk of a democratic deficit. In order to overcome legal domination, an analysis is needed of the potential location and character of the freedom to initiate deliberation within a transnational institutional structure. The potential for juridification raises in more general form the issue of the lack of popular and deliberative legitimacy in the EU, even as the EU has developed novel deliberative institutions and practices. These practices should now become the basis for access to this sort of influence, on the basis of common liberty. Everyday politics in a transnational polity must be based on the republican principle of common liberty. As such, deliberative legitimacy must be manifested not just in constitutional moments, but also in the hierarchies of everyday administrative and legislative rule making in which the rules themselves can become a source of domination. The next section undertakes a sociological analysis of such pitfalls of transnational politics already manifested in the EU's problems of legitimacy.

Juridification, Domination, and Formal Legitimacy

Juridification denotes the tendency toward the increasing expansion of law and law-like methods of formal rules and adjudication to new domains of social life. As Habermas argues, this tendency has the consequence that many social relations and informally regulated domains of social life become "formally organized," and are thus increasingly opened up to the state and the market.[11] As a long-term trend in modern societies, juridification has until recently taken place by means of the territorial state. Yet more and more areas of economic life and transactions are being juridified in ways over which there is little popular or public deliberative influence, especially in international society. With the emergence of institutions that regulate global trade and capital, such as the WTO, NAFTA, and certain aspects of the EU, it has now become a global phenomenon. Indeed, the EU is quite advanced in the replacement of state forms of juridification, given that an increasingly larger proportion of legal policy in the EU derives from Community directives and intergovernmental proceedings.[12] This supranational form of juridification is based on the doctrines of direct effect and the legal supremacy of EU law over national law; other such regulatory institutions (such as the WTO) have the same effect of creating a system of obligations for individuals, states, and corporations, all the while imposing a scheme of global economic cooperation that bypasses the democratic mechanisms of the representative constitutional state.[13]

Given these main differences with such international organizations, the EU constitutional debate is paradigmatic for transnational democracy because it is part of a larger trend of global juridification: the more directly it interacts with democratic state organizations, the more explicit become the debates about redemocratization as a response to such hierarchical and administrative juridification. In order to solve the problem of legal domination, this process requires more than mere reparliamentarization alone. Whatever the laudatory consequences of giving the European Parliament (EP) more powers, this constitutional act will not suddenly constitute a *dêmos* or unitary public sphere. A more differentiated structure of institutions and procedures is needed if the EU is to solve the problem of juridification democratically. In this respect, the EP could play a much greater role than it currently does, but only with respect to specific powers related to reflexively implementing a new and nonhierarchical normative framework.

Juridification takes place even in political contexts where formal legitimacy is already present and legislative authority is tied to representative institutions. Such authority is delegated by legislative principals to various agents in the many situations of epistemic dependence and asymmetrical information that are already pervasive in modern societies.[14] The potential for domination lies in the specific character of the agent/principal relationship that has replaced formal political authority. Unlike many forms of the agent/principal relationship in economic life, the new transnational agents are acting in a more general regulatory capacity, primarily regulating the very political authorities for which they are agents. As I have argued, the challenge to democracies is precisely that such authority is incompletely defined, since it is precisely the incompleteness of the definition of authority that marks shifts in the structure of accountability away from a legally defined framework of political authority within the constitutional state. In response to this problem, some organizations could create their own internal constitution, establishing a new hierarchy by assigning a principal to supervise each agent. While in the global economic sphere this shift has been marked mainly by deregulation, even in the reduction of market barriers the EU requires a positive shift in the location of authority and the source of legislation. In this respect, the problem is one of reconstitionalization, of constituting democratic authority at a different level in order to place such hierarchical and incompletely defined authority under democratic control.

Put in this context of shifts in political authority, the debate about EU constitutionalism is not a response to any specific historical event or crisis, but to a long-term learning process concerning state authority and power. This problem of legal domination in modern democracies has been heightened by the emergence of principal/agent hierarchies and by the new forms of coordination that larger political structures demand. Constitutionalization has produced a learning process aimed at solving the pressing problems of internal legitimacy that result from the use of law without institutionalizing the principle of democratic nondomination. The issue of democratic nondomination emerges in this context of multiple *dêmoi*, in which there is no determinate exercise of a singular popular sovereignty. So long as there are multiple or pooled forms of sovereignty, domination by transnational authority is still possible, even with the features of the formal rule of law present and institutionally protected. Thus, the main criterion for successful constitutionalization of the EU is whether or not it can democratize the transnational polity just as representative institutions previously democratized the constitutional state, by making its political agents more accountable and diverse. The solution is at a different level of democratic arrangement than that of the simple delegation of elected legislative authority and executive decision-making power.

Instead of polity building that would place such authority in a distributed constitutional structure, we might think that such delegated power would best operate through its diffusion into various expert and policy networks. As Anne-Marie Slaughter argues, such networks are certainly part of the "new world order" that operates effectively without centralized coercive authority. Because they disperse power, they are one of the central transnational features of the intergovernmental order of both international organizations and the EU. Tied to the committee system, government networks have become "the signature form of governance of the European Union, which is itself pioneering a new form of regional collective governance that is likely to prove far more relevant than the experience of federal states" precisely because it has instituted governance by networks.[15] I have already argued against Dryzek's similar view of transnationalism. While such networks are certainly decentered, they nonetheless entirely lack popular legitimacy, even if they might open up informal channels of influence, primarily for civic and corporate nongovernmental organizations. As opposed to minipublics of representative citizens, the deliberation within such networks lacks any democratic basis upon which to transfer the internal legitimacy of their deliberation to the broader external popular and deliberative legitimacy. While networks have the proper decentered and transnational form, they should be connected to distributive publics rather than to civil society if they are to solve the problem of the transfer of their deliberative legitimacy to the larger publics and constituencies they inevitably affect. To this extent, they are consistent with juridification rather than its solution. Epistemic communities could be better democratized by interaction with broader publics than with the self-defining constituencies of NGOs, as the case of AIDS activism in the United States shows. Deliberation in such communities is democratized only when they act as intermediaries for broader publics, so that they facilitate interaction among various constituencies, collect information, make policy alternatives and comparisons available, and fund innovative practices. As a part of transnational governance, however, networks are no replacement for polity building.[16] Network governance without democracy puts extraordinary faith in the quality of expert reasoning. Contrary to self-consciously created minipublics of representative citizens, the deliberative legitimacy internal to policy networks is not transferable outside the official networks. Its claims to outcome legitimacy through effectiveness are often temporary and self-validating without public scrutiny and popular legitimacy.

The reflexivity of democratic constitutions makes them the historically appropriate response to shifts in authority brought about through juridification. Constitutions are neither simply institutional designs nor merely first-order legislative practices, but also make issues of social order and democracy themselves open to deliberative decision making as they are reflexively institutionalized. Juridification in constitutions has had several stages, including regularizing expectations in the formal rule of law and creating a private sphere protected from legal intervention. But such constraints on the legal power of the state are not yet democratic. The crucial step in that direction is the institution of reflexivity in the legal order; it entails the juridification of the legitimation process itself, as was achieved by the legal protections of universal suffrage and of the political dimensions of freedoms of expression and association. The legal specifications of democratic legitimacy constitute political freedom in such a way that the constitution itself can be challenged and remade; they create rights as conditions of freedom and entitlement, even while opening the interpretation and implementation of these very rights to the democratic deliberation of citizens. It is precisely these special reflexive features that are inadequately institutionalized in the EU, and thus require a constitutional moment.

If this analysis is correct, then the purpose of a transnational constitutionalism is to create just such a reflexive, deliberative, and dispersed order. It can do so only if the contours of this order are continually subject to the deliberative assessment of its citizens, even while that same order makes juridical these conditions for reflexive legitimation. While it is indeed correct that the current design of constitutional states with representative democracies provides no real guide, constitutionalism as such is still required to solve the problems of juridification. It should also be clear that this constitutionalism must normatively empower citizens to deliberate and to act distributively as *dêmoi*. The crucial points at which democratic legitimacy is at stake in the EU have to do with the institutional distribution of normative powers of initiative and the institutional capacity of these regularized powers of initiative and reform to respond to the claims made by communicatively free participants in various public spheres. Before turning to this particular criterion of minimal democratic legitimacy, however, the larger and more differentiated structure in which this power can be instituted and regularized must be developed. For this reason, the principle of subsidiarity, with its emphasis on devolving power to the lowest possible level, should be complemented by a principle of federalism that transfers power to higher-level institutions to the extent that such a transfer enhances the normative powers of citizens (here, the citizens of Europe). I argue in the next section that a multilevel polity is necessary for non-domination and for the democratic minimum.

Deliberative Legitimacy and Transnational Politics

In the previous section I argued that the democratic core of constitutionalism is tied to its reflexive character, that is, to its capacity to make the basis of democracy *itself* the subject of the democratic deliberation of citizens. Such a self-transforming polity requires that a constitution enable citizens to have just this normative power, a power that can be exercised in the capability to initiate deliberation that may change the terms of democratic cooperation. If the institutional structure is large and multileveled (as the EU surely is), then this power must be present not merely in its legislative and parliamentary core, but also distributed throughout the various levels and dispersed sites of deliberation. From this same criterion of democratic nondomination it also follows that federalism is the proper form of institutional design, provided it can be shown to be adequate to the democratic minimum of nondomination with respect to the imposition of order and the possibilities of popular control.

It is important to keep in mind why republicanism has traditionally been suspicious of the imperium of the state, one source of which may be expertise turned directly into political authority. But the reverse is true according to the standard of nondomination that I have been employing: namely, that larger political units are conducive to democracy under certain circumstances, especially if the population is diverse enough to make the domination of minorities less likely in contexts of collective self-determination. Properly organized with dispersed power, there are also deliberative advantages to large and numerous units. It can be shown that existing practices of the EU employ particular institutional structures of cooperation to take advantage of the dispersal of power and deliberation in multileveled and polycentric polities.

These structures are democratic insofar as they are constitutional orders that provide for deliberation about the proper location for any political deliberation and authorization. Without access to political influence over just such questions, the larger democracies in transnational polities have the potential to dominate the smaller ones. Republican arguments for the separation of powers within the state can then be used against classical modern sovereignty, so that republican cosmopolitan institutions ought to further separate powers by disaggregating state monopolies and functions into a variety of institutional levels and locations, as well as by disaggregating centralized transnational powers. In classical federal arrangements, however, all participate in a polity qua members of a *dêmos* of a common regime, which is then split into various levels of increasing scale. More than simply adding a layer of authority, however, the difficulty to be overcome requires redefining this hierarchical pattern of relationships among the local, the national, and the supranational levels of scale. Nor is subsidiarity the proper principle for the EU as a transnational polity, since it gives priority to lower units when the issue is the distribution of authority at all levels. Exercising authority at the lowest levels is a desirable feature of transnational institutions, but it is achievable only when deliberative legitimacy is distributed across the interconnected levels and sites of the polity.

Some have argued that deliberative legitimacy is local, rising to no higher level that that of a nation-state.[17] A structure with a variety of different unit types has considerable deliberative advantages, especially with regard to mutual correction. This problem can be addressed by creating institutional spaces for joint deliberation in a variety of interacting units at different levels, a process that makes for the exercise of common liberty as European citizens.

What sort of deliberation might go on in such an institution? One common application of dispersed deliberative procedures is in the construction and testing of National Action Plans (NAPS) in various policy areas, such as employment, regional development, and education. Such highly focused deliberation on specific policies permits publics to identify problems and gaps in accountability. More importantly, such deliberation is typically structured around collective and recursive reasoning about ends and means. In the case of NAPS, the Commission empowers a committee to set broad ends or targets that the various national plans must minimally achieve, say in literacy or numeracy in education. Once these ends are set, they are not fixed but serve as the basis for further reasoning about means in parallel processes at various locations, which in turn may lead to the revision and specification of ends given the variety of circumstances among locales within the EU. These newly set ends and means are then passed on to a higher level, and so on, where these become premises for further deliberation. At the EU level, the committee then collects the various plans and begins a deliberative process of comparative evaluation, suggesting improvements when there are clearly best practices.

Such a process is "learning by monitoring," where deliberation serves as the means by which such inquiry takes place. Such a process depends "not on harmony and spontaneous coordination, but on the permanent disequilibrium of incentives and interests imperfectly aligned, and on the disciplined, collaborative exploration of the resulting differences."[18] This sort of process thus institutionalizes a process of ongoing reform by shared deliberative inquiry within everyday political decision making. Even with such potentially innovative practices, their actual application does not yet produce the requisite deliberative legitimacy necessary to overcome juridification. The Open Method of Coordination (OMC) could be useful as a deliberative procedure in such cases, in that citizens submit means and ends to parallel public deliberation that begins at the local level and continues up to the national and regional levels, then back down again after higher-level institutions put together the results for the purpose of comparing and sharing information. Publics then are informed with and interact with other publics, so that all publics can say that they have jointly and reflexively shaped the means and ends that are the outcome of rule-making decisions.

As they are currently constituted, however, many such distributed deliberative processes in the EU, including the OMC, are not yet fully public. They are semipublic, to the extent that contributions to deliberation are aimed primarily at other experts rather than the public at large. As in the case of democratic reform, such processes are likely to be considered popularly illegitimate to the degree that citizens lack the common knowledge that they can shape the course of actual decision making. While such processes may already have the appropriate transnational structure, they rely only on indirect popular legitimacy and thus still lack the means to overcome juridification. Legitimate decision making must not only distribute authority as such across borders, but also use these institutions to distribute and constitute the popular will democratically through public shaping and testing decisions.

Organized in this way, institutionalized deliberation becomes more responsive by virtue of strengthening and shortening the feedback loops necessary for implementation and learning in decentered yet public decision making. Democracy could be deepened by such empowerment, and it could also be broadened by facilitating interaction between institutions and publics, especially if they institute something closer to what Frank Michelman calls the "full blast condition" for deliberation.[19] In other respects, the current constitutional moment is also an institutional learning process that is rather like the case of the New Deal–type reforms of the American nation-state, motivated by both democratic and functional failures of its existing, not fully constitutionalized use of administrative and political power. It might also permit the emergence of wider and deeper forms of deliberative interaction across institutions and *dêmoi* than have been realized thus far. Since deliberation in transnational polities does not aim at the same solutions to all problems, it requires only that EU-level institutions serve to establish legitimate diversity, which would be constitutionalized in provisions related to the normative status of membership, with these in turn based on human rights. In order to institutionalize experimental practices, the constitution must reflect such a multilevel division of normative powers. Deliberative legitimacy is then tied directly to the presumption of plurality, which could be built into the constitution of a transnational democracy. But this plurality is at the same time manifestly a common liberty, exercised together in deliberatively legitimate institutions that are distributed across the structure of the EU.

Many critics have expressed doubts about the democratic credentials of some of the deliberative practices developed in the European Union. To the extent that they have not closed the deliberative deficit, such criticisms have a large measure of truth. However, these criticisms often go further and claim that these practices do not capture the proper relation between democracy and human rights. Gould argues that directly deliberative polyarchy is merely "quasi-democratic" and circular. "The rights required to ensure that these processes are democratic are said to be determined at least in part by the course of deliberation and thus such rights are left open for redefinition."[20] Of course, it cannot be asserted that in any actually existing democracy, liberal or otherwise, rights are not also open to redefinition in various institutional contexts. Given that there is no history of jurisprudence and no workable cross-cultural agreement on the substantive force of human rights as standards, the policies for implementing human rights as ends should be deliberated upon publicly and in ways permitting comparisons across democratic units. The OMC as defended by Cohen and Sabel is simply one of many different ways to provide an institutional basis for such recurrent deliberation about standards, including the legal and political interpretation of various rights.

More importantly, Gould's criticism of opening rights to public deliberation can be answered normatively in two ways. First, the redefinition of rights in the course of deliberation has been part of any historical process of democratization and indeed is the means by which democracy has historically been used as a means to justice. More often than not, democratic transformations bring with them new rights and innovative reinterpretations of old ones. Second, such a process of redefinition is legitimate only if the process meets the democratic minimum (rather than the fully maximal requirements of some putative democratic ideal); that is, if the process permits more than just consultation or contestation, but rather allows the development of robust normative powers of initiation and deliberation by participants, including deliberation about the terms of democracy itself. It is precisely when the interpretation of the substance of rights is open to debate that the dialectic between rights and democracy takes place. The dialectic is fully reciprocal—if rights are to bring about greater democratization, it is only by incorporating them as norms within various democratic processes. This kind of reflexivity is an essential feature of constitutional democracy, which institutionalizes exactly the sort of deliberative process to which Gould objects.

Gould's criticisms of directly deliberative polyarchy bring us back to perhaps the most fundamental question of the EU's democratic legitimacy: who are the citizens of Europe? This question can only be answered by considering all the dimensions of democratic and constitutional legitimacy, including the implementation of human rights. It is clear that the European Court of Justice as well as EU judicial bodies already recognize strong obligations toward noncitizens of any member states who reside in the EU, including their rights of political participation in local elections and other forms of empowerment and inclusion. The democratic basis for such human rights policies expresses the transnational republican principle of common liberty: that freedom from domination within a transnational polity is possible only if it is extended to *all* persons who reside within it. Otherwise, the EU simply repeats the very problem it is supposed to solve. EU citizens would come to dominate resident noncitizens, and the public space for full blast, legitimate deliberation among *dêmoi* is once again closed in a bounded community. These obligations can ultimately be fulfilled if the European Union is embedded in at least some global institutions. In order for these institutions to avoid the problems of global juridification, their formal structure of executive, legislative, and judicial institutions will also need to be reformed. A decentered federalism aims to secure nondomination by instituting a distributed popular will in everyday politics and rule-making, and does so only if this will is distributed beyond the EU's borders.

Decentering Federalism: Parliamentary Institutions as Intermediaries

The sort of deliberative processes described in the last section are so extended and distributed that they require some large-scale institutions to organize them. Cosmopolitan republicans often appeal to federations as the proper institutional form of transnational politics. To be sure, federalism has been used to provide legitimacy in polities in which various peoples are constitutionally recognized. It does so not by decentralizing power through delegation from the central apex, but by dispersing it widely in many different sites and centers. Guided by the account of iterated and differentiated democratic structures and the normative powers required for nondomination, other avenues for access to influence are desirable. Indeed, it can be argued that European practices of governance are already "heterarchical," in that authority is neither centralized nor decentralized, but shared.[21] The Community Method provides ways to share power and to pool sovereignty through the institutions of the Commission, the Council, and the European Parliament, each of which have different orientations representing the interests of the member states, the common good of the Community, and the indirect influence of the people. If this sharing of powers already suggests heterarchy, then the reconstruction of this development could play a role in the EU's democratic regime along with its emerging innovative, decentered institutions and experimental, flexible, and dynamic practices in various policy domains. New actors and powers have evolved so that processes of deliberation and the implementation of various legislative directives and regulations have also become more inclusive. Such inclusive and public participation in practices offers new sources for legitimacy that do not so severely tax the system of representation and the types of interests that were balanced in the EU's original constitutionalism. With these new practices has also come an increased emphasis on human rights, including the drafting of a Charter of Fundamental Rights that now shapes and informs the practices of governance and deliberation. Let me turn first to more standard democratic institutions related to the separation of powers before discussing the importance of specific deliberative practices of inquiry in the EU that permit publics to interact with and influence their ongoing and iterated processes.

As I noted earlier, given the rather traditional shape of some of the European polity's political institutions, most cosmopolitans argue that the first step toward a supranational democratic order is to create a more effective and empowered European Parliament, perhaps with a bicameral structure. Such a claim overestimates the capacity of elected legislatures in large polities to represent the diverse interests of their constituencies so as to close the gap between citizens and public officials. Indeed, an EP based on traditions of territorial representation from member states is likely to repeat this same deficit, no matter what its structure. Bicameralism would make sense only if at least one body of the EP were organized on a nonterritorial and inclusive basis. Such a conception of constituency would transform the EP from its traditional role of democratic self-legislation to an institution that initiates and organizes public deliberation and thus provides a forum in which diverse social and cultural perspectives are gathered. If distributed deliberative processes are to be subject to Michelman's full blast condition, then the aim of such a forum is to provide citizens with access to two sorts of influence directly relevant to everyday politics: first, the influence that comes from the exercise of communicative freedom and the creation of new associations, constituencies and publics; and, second, discursive influence that is based on the capacity to define and change the terms of public debate. As EU institutions become the focus of a European-wide political public sphere, their forums provide a common focus of attention for various national and linguistic public spheres that discuss and deliberate upon the nature and scope of the EU polity.

One specific federal role this interaction with the Europe-wide public sphere could facilitate is that of monitoring the human rights records of member states and thus testing the legitimacy of their

exercise of normative powers. Through the progress reports conducted by the EP since 2002, the status of membership in the EU is
itself open to the test of nondomination. Such a process could be
reconstructed as a test for legitimate diversity based on an ongoing
and explicit overlapping consensus of the diverse constitutional traditions reflected in the Parliament. This overlapping consensus is
quite minimal in Article 6 of the Treaty of the European Union, and
includes principles of liberty, respect for human rights and fundamental freedoms, the rule of law, and the diversity of national identities as "principles common to member states." Member states are
obligated to respect and implement these rights and principles and
are held accountable to this obligation by each other (in Article 7),
and if these obligations were monitored through a directly deliberative application of the OMC process, the EP could facilitate the deliberative legitimacy and openness of such a process.

Similarly, more standard federal institutions can be granted more
deliberative roles. Just as in American case law, one role of the courts
is to interpret the doctrine of federalism itself. The European Court
of Justice and various national supreme courts have already taken on
the judicial task of interpreting the various treaties and their principles, and they will continue to do so even if the structure becomes
more elaborate, or principles of jurisdiction and transparency more
explicitly adapted to a multilevel and differentiated framework.
Besides increasing the individual's normative powers to appeal to
these bodies about human rights violations as discussed earlier, this
role also protects the democratic process through the establishment
of procedures and processes for reviewing the extent of public
accountability. Furthermore, such courts continue to have a direct
relation to individuals (rather than to publics) across various levels
of governance.

Normative powers granted to individuals may also have important
deliberative effects. When individuals directly petition the independent European Court of Human Rights, there is an important analogy
to features of constitutional adjudication involved in federal civil rights
prosecutions and suits that Owen Fiss has described as "structural
reform."[22] Confronting these organizations with the basic norms of
human rights is one kind of adjudication. Such adjudication is part of

the process by which the European political community undertakes
to promote the restructuring of large-scale organizations and institutional arrangements that have failed to treat individuals as citizens
with equal rights and normative powers. I have already discussed one
instance of structural reform in the way in which EU courts have protected the rights of resident aliens, immigrants, and third party
nationals (including various political rights, such as normative powers of voice or entry and exit from the EU). Doing so does not merely
make such bearers of human rights secure in their political nondomination, but it also strengthens the democratic minimum for all
residents of the EU. The multilevel system of courts in the EU makes
it possible for the perspectives of individuals or groups to be brought
directly to bear on the legality of standards and norms that make up
the normative framework in which authority operates. These courts
provide a test for the most dominating forms of the exercise of
normative powers by institutions. Thus, at least judicially, the EU
exhibits the sort of differentiated and overlapping democratic structure that not only makes peoples' basic rights less vulnerable to legal
domination, but also provides a means for structural reform in the
case of local structures of domination and juridification.

Finally, what role do executive powers play in such a federal structure? New forms of public deliberation have emerged in which distributive publics open up new, directly deliberative possibilities for
administrative reform. By placing all authority in a democratic framework, delegated authority is embedded in a polity and a reflexive legal
order that constrains its exercise by empowering citizens to make legitimate claims independently of the particular epistemic community
typically given such authority in functional organizations. From the
point of view of a decentered federalism, what is needed is precisely to
embed the relation between committees and the Commission in a
larger and more public process; the process would have to be institutionalized so that normative powers are widely distributed across levels
in order to encourage greater and more diverse discursive interaction
with publics in deliberation. The transnational principle of institutional differentiation once again calls for multiple and iterated
processes within a revisable normative framework, and the possibilities
of reform through deliberative processes should not be confined to

the constitutional debate alone. These directly deliberative processes could also distribute and decenter popular legitimacy.

In this way, institutions such as the European Parliament, the European Court of Justice, and even various administrative bodies could, if suitably reformed, have a democratic role; but their new role is transnational rather than supranational in that they enable and coordinate deliberation across various sites and levels of the polity. These familiar institutions become more concerned with second-order issues and are reflexively concerned with the normative framework for democratic deliberation, maintaining it by testing for legitimacy. By contrast, the democratic legitimacy of the decision-making process involving minipublics empowered to make policy decisions is dependent on the quality of the deliberation, which can be tested through the perspectives of other publics. Federal institutions are, nonetheless, necessary not only to organize such a dispersed and diverse process, but also to create the multiple channels of influence and communication that enable the deliberation across multiple perspectives needed for a large and diverse polity to be peaceful and democratic. The democratic legitimacy of these enabling and intermediary institutions is thus more indirect, and depends upon the standards, objectives, and membership conditions that make the EU a polity with a normative legal framework. In both dispersed and federal institutions, testing and decision-making powers are separated more clearly than in typical federal states. Since deliberation in transnational polities does not aim at the same solutions to all problems, it requires only that EU-level institutions serve to establish the domain of legitimate diversity, which would be constitutionalized in provisions related to the normative status of membership, with these in turn based on human rights. In order to institutionalize experimental practices, the constitution must reflect such a multilevel and distributive division of normative powers.

If extending and deepening democracy are among the aims of the constitutional reform of the EU, it is easy to see why such a project is the continuation of what is best in the EU. In order to be democratic, the EU must not only achieve a democratic form of regional integration, it must also meet the repeated challenge of creating the conditions for democratic nondomination given the polity building of European integration. Given that meeting this challenge demands a transnational democratic minimum, the constitutional debates in the EU could well be a precursor to a process that is iterated in many different polities and institutions. From a constitutional perspective, the signal innovations of the EU could be given greater coherence by putting them in the service of realizing a democracy of *dêmoi* rather than a single *dêmos*. Once the EU achieves a more fully reflexive order and a more differentiated institutional structure, the question shifts away from whether the EU is a democracy to how it can be more deliberatively and popularly legitimate. Such deliberation might be made more feasible if it were to attain greater popular legitimacy and more vibrant publics. The task of its reform is to create just these conditions.

In terms of the overall argument of this chapter, the last two sections have made two important points about institutions that might support deliberative and popular legitimacy in everyday transnational politics. First, they have shown why the differentiated institutional structure is the best way to realize human rights against nondomination in a transnational polity. At the same time, this diverse and dispersed structure is also able to make use of the distributive character of transnational public spheres in its institutional deliberation. This is a feasible transformation because a differentiated institutional structure works best if it convenes and empowers citizens as publics in diverse settings, thereby increasing the opportunities for participation as well as the effectiveness of institutional inquiry and problem solving. Second, decentered federal institutions can take advantage of the fact that in a federal system no single body of citizens can exercise final control over the agenda. The formal institutions in which powers are dispersed derive their legitimacy by securing the conditions for deliberative access to influence, whether for individual citizens in adjudicative institutions or in legislative facilitation of directly deliberative procedures.

Seen in the light of the requirements of nondomination, distributed normative powers might become more fully realized transnationally than in most national federal systems. Distributed power is thus a democratic virtue of nondominating institutions, not a reason to doubt whether decentered multiunit systems "can in principle ever be fully democratic."[23] In fact, the opposite is true. Such sharing of authority and other normative powers is necessary to take advantage of differentiated structures, so that citizens deliberate together rather than merely alongside each other. This feature explains why transnational democracy adopts a distinctively dynamic and interactive form of federalism. It also explains why it is cosmopolitan, given that such a perspective must be institutionalized in any process of multiperspectival deliberation and inquiry that manifests the common liberty of all citizens.

Conclusion: Legal Nondomination as a Transnational Constitutional Ideal

While many see public deliberation in constitutional moments as tied to crises or founding events, I have argued that in the case of the EU it is better to see such deliberation in terms of long-term learning processes that issue in the normative framework that is the solution to problems of governance. The difficulties of democratic legitimacy are not the result of failure, but of the EU's prodigious, if one-sided, success at integration through law. With its increasing juridification, organizing a self-legislating European *dêmos* is hardly the solution to this potential for domination. A democratic constitution for Europe will not create a *dêmos* but it will create a basis for legitimate democratic reform that is currently lacking in the EU. I have emphasized the democratic and deliberative features of constitutionalism: its reflexivity and its capacity to make rights and political order open to deliberation by those citizens who act within them to initiate processes of democratic reform. This reflexivity, linked with the basic human freedom to initiate deliberation about claims to justice, provides the minimal requirement for political nondomination and for the exercise of communicative freedom and normative powers in a constitutional regime. Transnational polities will become democratic when they have solved the problem of democratic reform by establishing the normative power of citizens in their constitutional states, which is not yet part of the common liberty shared by the citizens of Europe.

Once democratically legitimate enough to be able to reform themselves democratically, it is plausible that such transnational deliberative institutions might extend the limits of political possibility toward an ever-wider scope of democracy. If this is one of the motivations of constitutional reform, it is easy to see why such a project is the continuation of what is best in the EU. From the perspective of a decentered form of federalism, based on the dispersal of power condition rather than the simple and ambiguous principle of subsidiarity, the core innovations of the EU can be interpreted as showing the greater coherence of realizing democracy and human rights in multiple *dêmoi* rather than in a *dêmos*. Subsidiarity needs to be decentered. Once the EU achieves a more fully reflexive order and a more differentiated institutional structure, then the question shifts to considering lower and higher levels as equally important democratically: it is not whether the EU is democratic, but rather what aspects of it still need to become the subject of ongoing public deliberation.

The analysis I have proposed changes how we view the relationship between constitutionalism, reform, and governance, to the extent that deliberative and popular legitimacy demand that citizens have the power to initiate deliberation and place items of reform on the agenda. How are we to understand other types of polities? What is the transformed role for states? How can they become decentered and multiperspectival? Similar questions can be asked concerning the current international system, including the United Nations, various Courts and adjudicative bodies, and functional organizations such as the World Bank or the World Trade Organization. Two issues emerge in both cases. The first is the transformation of the current system of delegated political authority into a distributive and democratic form that is open to direct deliberative influence through transnational publics; the second is whether or not borders can be shown, contrary to the democratic theory implicit in the nation-state, to be settled by democratic criteria. These issues show the theoretical advantages of republican cosmopolitanism for diagnosing problems and proposing solutions under the current circumstances of justice.

In the concluding chapter, I use this account of transnational democratic institutions to solve two important problems: the problems of democratically arbitrary borders and the declining potential for an expanding democratic peace. First, I argue that a fully decentered and reflexive transnational democracy no longer takes the units of democracy, whether territorial or jurisdictional, as fixed. Current democratic structures cannot solve the *dêmoi* problem. As conceived in traditional democratic form, the delimitation of the *dêmos* that is empowered to make any particular decision is, from a democratic point of view, fundamentally and irredeemably arbitrary and thus a potential dominator of other *dêmoi*. Second, I turn to traditional issues of international order, peace, and security. I argue for a version of democratic peace that reestablishes a positive feedback relationship between democracy and the international order. The current structure of the international system of security is democratically self-defeating for good republican reasons: it attempts to achieve security without the common liberty of a shared political order, and thus undermines democracy even within states.

Conclusion: Democracy, Peace, and Justice across Borders

My defense of the ideal of transnational democracy has followed two lines of argument that go hand in hand. First, the central task of the first three chapters has been to offer ways to rethink some of the historically contingent democratic conceptions that we have inherited. Second, in light of these revisions, I have suggested various institutional reforms that are necessary to maintain certain important features of the democratic ideal related to nondomination. In arguing for transnational democracy in these two ways, I have sought to fulfill the two normative tasks that Dewey saw as the essential intellectual contribution to any successful transformation of democracy: clarifying and deepening our conceptual resources related to the core ideals of democracy, and then using these resources normatively to criticize and remake existing political and institutional forms.

The ideal of a transnational democracy as I have developed it accomplishes the first task by taking up the republican conception of freedom from domination that had already found expression in republican philosophers such as Kant and Diderot, who, along with other republicans, saw transnational federalism in part as a response to colonialism. By analyzing the conditions of international civil society and the new distributive public spheres, I have argued that freedom from domination outside the state is not merely a utopian ideal, but is rather a feasible extension of current political possibilities. Far from a condition of anarchy, the international sphere is already quite dense with networks of communication and associations that are often connected to informal political processes and domain-specific international regimes. Furthermore, international institutions already both hold actors accountable to widely endorsed norms of human rights (including political rights) and justify thinking of humanity as a political subject and community. Emerging regulatory and legal institutions such as the World Trade Organization and the International Criminal Court are already able, for better or worse, to override national self-interests and impose certain obligations on states. These organizations have various sorts of normative powers to impose obligations and duties, even on nonmembers. Nonetheless, they currently lack regularized and vigorous interaction with publics exercising communicative freedom that would not only make them accountable but also permit affected publics to change their frameworks of accountability. Finally, the European Union provides an instance of an ongoing experiment in political integration (whatever its current misfortunes) that has resulted in innovative deliberative practices and an emergent transnational institutional design with democratic ambitions. I have provided a reconstruction of these practices not only to show the feasibility of their further development according to relevant democratic standards, but also to establish the possibility of the emergence of genuinely novel institutions. These arguments fulfill Dewey's second desideratum by showing the feasibility of the transnational ideal when it is cast in broadly republican terms.

Prior to the debates about global governance in the 1990s, which resulted in a new awareness of the destructive consequences of globalization without political integration, most philosophical discussions of cosmopolitanism focused on issues of global distributive justice, especially on the moral obligations of developed countries to aid distant strangers who suffer from destitution and hunger. Such obligations derive most often from basic rights, which include rights to food and other primary goods. In political cosmopolitanism, these problems are the result of highly uneven social processes and the institutions and forms of authority that entrench them. In republican terms, these forms of authority may also be discussed in terms of freedom from domination, where destitution is often the product of social relations and political institutions that deny the most basic entitlements to the exercise of normative powers. Problems of distribution can then be cast in terms of capabilities and substantive freedoms rather than simply in terms of resources, as has been shown, for example, by the empirical fact that the capability to avoid famine and destitution may be tied to the existence of other freedoms (such as freedom of the press and public expression and association), as well as to the presence of democratic institutions and dense relationships of mutually recognized entitlements and obligations. Defensible commitments to a local democracy of this sort are fully consistent with the differentiated form of transnational democracy that I have defended, but are also more secure under current political circumstances.

The final task to be completed in this chapter is to show that transnational democracy can be justified with respect to general considerations of justice. Justifications of democracy have been intrinsic, instrumental, or both.[1] The most common arguments in favor of cosmopolitan or transnational democracy are made in terms of its intrinsic value. One way or another, these arguments hinge on the idea that intrinsic features of democracy systematically promote the requirements of justice. One version of this type of justification is the idea that a global democracy would be more just than democracy confined to the nation-state to the extent that it realizes the values of freedom and equality for all individual persons as demanded by universal human rights. Such justifications are common among moral cosmopolitans and comprehensive liberals who take enormous global inequalities to be the result of global institutions that do not respect the moral worth of each individual human person, or do not fairly distribute the opportunities for leading a good human life.[2] A more common strategy for social or political cosmopolitans is to see a cosmopolitan order as intrinsically valuable to the extent that it realizes the values that are constitutive of the democratic ideal, such as self-rule, or that all those affected ought to be able to participate in decisions that affect them. I have argued here that the best intrinsic justification of a transnational democracy is based on the republican ideal of freedom as nondomination as constitutive of the powers of citizenship.[3]

In applying this justification, I want to show that the argument I have given supplies a solution to the problem of borders. The democratic minimum could fail to obtain, not only because individuals or groups are dominated by nondemocratic means, but also because they are dominated democratically to the extent that the *dêmos* of one unit is subordinated to others. I have called this the *dêmoi* problem. This problem of democratic domination is overcome so long as the capacity to initiate deliberation about the terms of democracy itself is distributed among the *dêmoi* of the various units and levels. This requirement leads to the need to justify borders democratically by the criterion of nondomination, without which they remain democratically arbitrary and a source of conflict. This argument does not suggest a borderless world, but that the issue of borders should not be treated as exogenous to democracy, as simply given. Transnational democracy rejects Dahl's overly simple assertion that the borders of democracy cannot be decided democratically, at the risk of an infinite regress.

But these arguments do not exhaust the possible justifications for transnational democracy. It could also be thought to be instrumentally valuable to the extent that global democracy is a necessary means to achieve particular valuable ends or to avoid terrible evils. Such instrumental value can be tested empirically and supported by robust social scientific generalizations. Strong evidence suggests that democracy is instrumentally valuable in preventing great evils such as war, famine, and human deprivation generally. One such generalization that is used to lend support to the benefits of a democratic order is the so-called "democratic peace hypothesis," which has often been used by moral cosmopolitans and liberal nationalists to justify the policy of fostering democracy within states as the best means of creating a peaceful international order of politically organized peoples.[4] It is sometimes thought that this argument could justify military intervention by democratic states into nondemocratic ones for the sake of establishing more democracies as a means for peace and security.

In "Perpetual Peace" and other writings, Kant rejects the idea that democracies or constitutional republics alone are sufficient for the attainment of peace, which Kant considered the highest political good that demanded the reorganization of political power under the constraints of cosmopolitan law. In one form or another, this realistic utopia of peace has informed the creation of the international system, culminating in the emergence of international law and a zone of peaceful relations among democracies since 1945. The success of this practical vision of peace has been based on the idea of an ever-expanding democratic peace, and thus the claim that the zone of peace among democratic states plays a role in the emergence of a pacific federation.

Compelling as this historical vision still is, I want to argue that the current forms of political violence challenge this and similar Kantian state-based mechanisms, even if the latter affirm the fact that peace is to be understood politically. At this juncture in global dynamics, the democratic peace is no longer expanding. Indeed, it has become potentially self-defeating for democracies: much as the rivalries among states did in the past, new forms of international conflict have begun to undermine the democratic quality of liberal states and with it the prospects for democracy as the key to a new pacific international order. The current situation shows that the democratic peace is not genuine, but a peace whose dynamic requires the discovery of the means by which both democratic states and the international system may become more democratic in a mutually reinforcing way. Broadly speaking, the new potential for warlike tendencies among democracies marks a social fact in Dewey's sense, a problematic situation that opens up a new field of possibilities for peace.[5] As such, the democratic peace hypothesis needs to be reformulated in ways that take into account the possibility of nonarbitary endogenous democratic borders.

The first issue is, then: Given the democratic minimum, what are the conditions for nondomination among *dêmoi*? The democratic theory of the constitutional state regards the achievement of a democratic minimum as the result of an already existing constitution containing a fixed set of rights exercised within a given set of boundaries. This is true only in a form of democracy that constitutes a single *dêmos*. In a sufficiently reflexive democracy where citizens can deliberate up on and change the terms of their association as well as exercise their normative powers and communicative freedoms so as to achieve justice, fixed boundaries cannot even be a necessary condition for democracy. In order to be secure, the democratic minimum must be multiply realized in a democracy of *dêmoi*.

The Democratic Circle Revisited: The Regress of *Dêmoi*

As I have developed the concept, the democratic minimum describes the necessary but not sufficient conditions for democratic arrangements to be a means of realizing justice. As such, even if these conditions were realized, a single democratic polity would not necessarily be just in all its dealings. It may not be just in all domains in which citizens are obligated, and it may not be just in relation to noncitizens affected by its decisions. The minimum can be represented in terms of political rights related to the normative powers of citizens to assign and modify rights themselves and other terms of democracy. In some cases these powers are used for democratic reform in order to overcome democratic domination. Democracy and justice are in this case mutually dependent normative concepts: a democracy becomes just only by becoming more democratic so that democracy and justice can in these cases only be realized together. But what about situations in which those who suffer injustice are noncitizens?

The scope of citizenship and the boundaries between citizens and noncitizens must also be open to creative reinterpretation under new circumstances of politics, and publics must be the primary creative agents of democratic renewal as well as the intermediaries of claims to democratic justice. Since democracy flourishes through the constant interaction between the creative powers of communicative freedom and the normative powers of citizens, the best argument for transnational democracy across borders is simply that it secures nondomination by promoting such interaction. But this is clearly not yet sufficient. There are other problems of institutional design in established democracies whose institutions have entrenched conditions of ever-increasing pluralism, complexity, and interdependence. Under these circumstances, it may also be the case that citizens in one or more units have lost their constituent power to initiate deliberation. The *dêmoi* problem, as I have defined it, emerges wherever there are multiple units necessary for good governance, yet there exists a unitary institutional design that is still guided by the principle that democracy requires control by a singular *dêmos*. When thought to constitute a *dêmos*, the conditions of the democratic minimum are realized only in a particular set of institutions and no other. As Dahl puts it, "the criteria of the democratic process presuppose the right-fulness of the unit itself."[6] Dahl is suggesting that the question of the boundaries of democracy is not a democratic one, but must be regarded as fixed from the point of view of democratic procedure in order to stop a vicious regress. Similarly, Richardson thinks that for this reason radical populists are wrong to think that constitutions can be established by an act of the popular will, since the procedures by which this would be possible would also have to be established by an act of the popular will, and so on. This regress can be avoided, they contend, only through a constitution that clarifies "who the people are by defining a jurisdiction and indicating who is to be counted as a citizen."[7] But this solution leaves the problem of the domination of noncitizens without a solution and breaks the linkage between democracy and justice. Moreover, it would condemn those who have the misfortune to live within the jurisdiction of a failed state to have no way to achieve those human rights that are constitutive of justice and nondomination.

One obvious solution to this problem is to develop an account of those institutional arrangements in which citizenship is decen-tered into a variety of different units and jurisdictions. But even this arrangement, once regarded as constitutionally fixed, could simply repeat the same difficulty, as when particular social groups or politi-cal units acquire salience for the exercise of normative powers that are not anticipated in the formal constitutional arrangements. In American federalism, the legal and political system proved inade-quate with respect to large cities, as the polity became more urban-ized throughout the last century. As a unit in this system, cities have limited power of legislative initiative and their citizens lack the capa-bility to initiate and carry out decisions. They also lack the demo-cratic minimum necessary to make their democratic governance a means to greater justice for their members. This condition is made worse by interdependence with autonomous units in their region, such as towns and suburbs, which need not take into account the externalities of their decisions. As a consequence, citizens in their subunits are vulnerable to domination, just as people in less well-off parts of the world may lack political rights against powerful actors such as multinational corporations or powerful neighboring states.

In these cases, citizens do not have the normative powers to set the terms of their own association but rather can only hope that they are members of a *dêmos* that is able to set such terms. A potential regress of *dêmoi* ensues with no nonarbitrary, democratic stopping point. Instead of this search for an optimal and thus sovereign *dêmos*, the better solution is to organize the relations among the *dêmoi* democratically. Otherwise, once we grant multiple *dêmoi*, each one of them would inevitably fall short of democratic criteria to the extent that the citizens of such a federation, in Dahl's words, "do not exercise final control over their agenda."[8] This normative power is one of the concrete indications of the freedom to initiate deliberation that is part of the democratic minimum. Each way out of the regress seems to lead to yet another dilemma. What is required is the decentering of this sort of control in a democracy of *dêmoi*.

As Dahl's remark about popular control over the agenda as fundamental to democracy suggests, part of the problem lies in linking democracy to a particular kind of sovereignty: democracy as understood to require a single subject, the people, who exercise a particular sort of freedom, freedom as control over a territory. If to possess sovereignty is to have the ultimate control or the highest power to decide, then democratic sovereignty is not a matter of degree, especially if its agenda is assumed to have a universal domain, and is able to make decisions that affect indefinite numbers of people. In a transnational polity this assumption of a universal domain is abandoned for a distributive approach that takes the powers of citizenship as distributed across many domains and institutions. We should expect the regress of *dêmoi* to remain vicious in the international arena, and democratically self-defeating, for the same reasons that a unitary polity cannot rule without oppression and domination in large, pluralist, and interdependent polities. Even if outsiders have the right to speak and communicate as part of Kant's "right to hospitality" to strangers and nonmembers (a right that explicitly transcends and thus relativizes claims to sovereignty), this normative power falls well short of the necessary minimum for nondomination.

Most of all, requiring a democratic justification of borders breaks the constitutive connection between sovereignty and self-determination on the one hand and bounded political communities on the other. Doing so also stops the regress of *dêmoi* that ends only in contests for de facto control over territory. Instead, the democratic minimum can be achieved for a *dêmos* among *dêmoi* only if political rights to introduce items on the political agenda and to initiate deliberation can be exercised across borders. If it fulfills the basic conditions of the democratic minimum, any democracy, transnational or otherwise, must be decentered and permit the inclusion of those perspectives that lead to changing the distribution of normative powers. In a decentered deliberative democracy, one subject of inquiry will be the organization of inquiry itself, the nature and scope of which is "something to be critically and experimentally determined."[9]

As Polanyi pointed out in his *Great Transformation*, opening borders to unregulated world trade in the late nineteenth century led to new demands for political closure as the socially destructive consequences of the first wave of economic globalization become apparent in the early twentieth century. Yet, renewed political closure in this instance neither produced greater democratic consequences, nor was it successful in providing polities with the means to achieve justice or freedom from nondomination. Instead, as Polanyi points out, political closure led to the undermining of the democratic aspects of the state form and to support for the rise of fascism, as well as to exclusivist political identities and to thousands of stateless persons displaced by struggles for sovereignty.[10] New, more functional borders and properly protective constraints on arbitrary authority are more likely to be effective in a differentiated institutional structure of *dêmoi* that multiply realizes human rights. It follows then that the challenge of the democratic domination of noncitizens can be overcome once we regard borders as a proper subject for democratic deliberation and an issue of establishing a common liberty from domination. The challenge is to realize that form of democracy which can make democracies more just precisely by making them more democratic. This is possible only if the terms of democracy itself, including issues of borders and jurisdictions, are themselves democratic questions for deliberation across *dêmoi* that aims at common liberty that is nonarbitrary from a democratic point of view.

I turn now to the instrumental benefits of such a transnational democratic order, most especially its promotion of those democratic capabilities that permit citizens to avoid the great evils of domination: famine and war.[11] In this regard, democracy has two different effects that ought to be distinguished: its capacity to protect the rights of those who are juridical subjects under its laws, and its political capacity to empower its citizens to actively change their circumstances. This latter effect, I shall argue, is crucial to having the capability to avoid a variety of these great evils and represents both the core of human political rights and an indication of freedom from domination. Once again, this capacity of democracy to realize justice can best be realized transnationally.

Democracy, War, and Famine: Transnational Democracy as a Means for Avoiding Evils

There are two main social scientific generalizations about the beneficial effects of democracy, both of which concern what might be thought of as negative facts: the first is that there has (almost) never been a famine in a democracy, and the second is that democracies have (almost) never gone to war with each other. The relative absence of these two great causes of human suffering can be tied to the operation of distinctive features of democracy. Without some fine-grained explanation of the mechanisms behind them, there is no reason to believe that these generalizations have always held or will always hold in the future, especially if the causes of famine and war are always changing and are sometimes brought about by democratic institutions themselves. Both generalizations have been hotly disputed, leading their defenders to introduce more and more ceteris paribus clauses to limit their scope. For example, Bruce Russett has argued that the generalizations have only held since the first half of the twentieth century, given the relative paucity of democratic states before then.[12] Yet, even with such ceteris paribus clauses, different mechanisms may do the explanatory work in the cases of famine and war.

Sen's analysis of the relation between famines and democracy begins with two striking facts. The first is that they "can occur even without any decline in food production or availability."[13] Even when this is the case, Sen argues that more equitably sharing the available domestic supply is nearly always an effective way to get beyond the crisis. Indeed, famines usually affect only a minority of the population of any political entity, and Sen's hypothesis is that their vulnerability to starvation is explained by the loss of certain powers and entitlements that they had before the crisis. The second striking fact goes some way in this direction by showing that when food shortages do occur, they do not have the same disastrous consequences. These facts yield the robust generalization that "there has never been a famine in a functioning multiparty democracy," so that we may conclude that "famines are but one example of the protective reach of democracy."[14] It would be tempting to associate this sort of security with the achievement of various instrumental freedoms or with one's status as a subject or client of a state or similar institution with an effective and well-funded administration. But even in the case of the protective function of the state, much more is required of democracy to create (or sustain in a crisis) the conditions of entitlement and accountability, as well as the reflexive capacity to change the normative framework. Once the explanation is put in the normative domain, so is the practical understanding of remedies and solutions.

The practical effects of democracy are not directly tied to more effective administrative institutions or even to the consistent application of the rule of law, both of which democracy may achieve. As Sen notes, there are limits to legality: "other relevant factors, for example market forces, can be seen as operating *through* a system of legal relations (ownership rights, contractual obligations, legal exchanges, etc.). In many cases, the law stands between food availability and food entitlement. Starvation deaths can reflect legality with a vengeance."[15] In this sense, the presence of famine must also be explained via the operation of social norms conjoined with citizens' lack of the effective social freedom to deliberate about their content. The deplorable treatment of native populations in famines caused by colonial administrators is often due to domination, manifested in the natives' lack of substantive freedoms such as free expression or political participation. Thus, famine prevention can be gained through fairly simple democratic mechanisms of accountability such as competitive elections and a free press that distribute effective agency more widely than in their absence.

Sen clearly goes further and sees democracy as more than a protective mechanism that can empower certain agents to act and thus enable them to defend the entitlements of citizens. It is also more active and dynamic, offering genuine opportunities to exercise substantial freedoms, including the ability to not live in severe deprivation or to avoid the consequences of gender norms for overall freedom. It is clear that such substantive freedoms depend on normative powers and the emergence of deliberative practices among citizens. For example, India's general success in eradicating famines is not matched in other areas that require facing problems such as gender inequality, in which the normative powers necessary for effective agency are differentially distributed. There is certainly no robust empirical correlation between democracy and the absence of these problems; they exist in affluent market-oriented democracies such as the United States. The solution for these ills of democracy is not to discover new and more effective protective mechanisms or robust entitlements, since it is hard for some democracies to produce them. Rather, the solution is, as Sen puts it, "better democratic practice" in which citizens are participants in a common deliberative process and sufficiently protected and empowered to change the distribution of normative powers and take advantage of improved practices.

To put it somewhat differently, the issue is not merely to construct a more protective democracy, but to create conditions under which an active citizenry is capable of initiating *democratization*, that is, using their power to extend the scope of democratic entitlements and to establish new possibilities for creative and empowered participation. Democracy is on this view the project in which citizens (and not just the agents for whom they are principals) exercise those normative and communicative powers that would make for better and more just democratic practice. This kind of enabling condition is essential to the explanation of the role of democratically produced phenomena that serve as Sen's explanans: citizens' powers and entitlements.

The democratic peace hypothesis is similar to Sen's generalization about famines in that fairly minimal democratic conditions figure in the explanation of the absence of certain types of wars. The generalization is, however, more restricted in the case of war than famine. Democracies do go to war against nondemocracies, although almost never against other democracies. Many explanations have been offered for why this is the case, and many of these do not depend on any transformative effects of democratic institutions other than that they provide channels for influence and the expression of citizens' rational interests and presume amity among democracies across borders as the basis for trust. Seen in light of the explanation of the absence of famines, democracy might reasonably be given a similar, more dynamic and transformative role than is usually offered: by being embedded in democratic institutions, agents acquire the normative role of citizens and thus the freedoms and powers that provide means by which to avoid the ills of war.

If this is the explanation of peace, it is important to make clear why war and the preparation for war often have the opposite effects. The institutional capability to wage war increases with the executive and administrative powers of the state, which often bypass democratic mechanisms of deliberation and accountability and thus work against democratization. At the same time, participation in national self-defense has often been accompanied by the emergence of new rights or their broader attribution to more of the population. Charles Tilly has argued that warfare may have historically been an important mechanism for the introduction of social rights, as the state became more and more dependent on the willingness of citizens to accept the obligations of military service.[16] As modern warfare became increasingly lethal and professionalized, however, the institutional powers of the state have outstripped this and other democratic mechanisms. The institutionally embedded normative powers of citizens are no longer sufficient to check the institutional powers of states to initiate wars, and these arrangements have left citizens vulnerable to the expanding militarization that has weakened these same entitlements. A new dialectic between the capacities of citizens and the instrumental powers of states has not yet reached any equilibrium, so that there has now emerged a strong negative influence on democratic practices and human rights generally because of the use of state force for the sake of security. Further, liberal democracies have not only restricted some civil rights, but have violated human rights, with the use of extralegal detention centers and torture in order to achieve security. As such, they might be said to have become less democratic, at least in the active sense of creating enabling conditions for the exercise of normative powers.

These remarks indicate that the democratic peace generalization depends on a set of historically specific institutional and normative presuppositions having to do with states as the primary sources of organized political violence. When war is no longer the sole form of political violence, then the significance of the internal democracy of states as a means toward peace is greatly diminished. This is particularly true of the Kantian normative inference that democracies would somehow assure that the political federation of peaceful states is ever-expanding. But once the institutional mechanisms of war-making shift from representative bodies toward much less accountable administrative and executive functions, and thus undermine the balance of institutional powers within a democracy, the expansive effect created by democratically organized institutions of domestic politics is less likely. This occurs when security requires the limitation of the freedoms and entitlements of one's own citizens.

Beyond these internal effects, the overvaluation of security brings to a halt the expansion of the zone of peace among liberal democracies. This means that the borders of the zone of peace become a source of political conflict with those outside it. Various transnational publics are now increasingly aware of the problematic fact of this zone of liberal peace and prosperity and regard it as having inherent and systematic asymmetries. The increased potential for violence from those outside the zone of peace requires that democratic states adapt to these new threats to their security, often by restricting both the liberties of their citizens and their own commitments to human rights, and thus leads to a tendency for democracies to restrict their own democracy and political inclusion within their own states.

With these institutional responses to the international order, the conditions and institutions that once promoted a democratic peace among states now act as part of a negative feedback mechanism, affecting particularly the liberties and rights that have permitted an active citizenry to possess enormous influence over the use of violence. Instead of democracies making international relations among states more peaceable, the new constellation of political violence is potentially making democratic states less democratic and less open to applying their standards of human rights and legal due process to those they deem to be threats to security.

Recent events show, then, that sustaining the democratic peace depends on a positive feedback relation between the internal structure of states and the international political system, where democracy is internally promoted by external peace and external peace is promoted by wider powers of citizenship, including transnational citizenship. When citizenship is transnational, citizens can appeal directly to other institutions and associations in order to make states accountable, as is already the case with human rights violations. This mechanism has not been able to counteract the new negative feedback on democracy in the international system, and the negative and interactive effects of the emergence of the actual zone of peace indicate that its continued existence no longer depends solely upon the increased democratization of states. The fact that democracies do not wage wars against other democracies now means that the borders of conflict are externalized by means that exact a cost from their internal democratic character. The republican linkage between an empowered citizenry and international peace is in fact systematically severed.

If the practical import of these negative feedback relationships undermines the prospect of expanding peace through a political union of existing democracies, then peace and security are no longer reducible to the absence of war. Here we need to modify some deep assumptions about the proper location for democracy and the exercise of the powers of citizenship in order to determine what would help democratic states avoid the weakening of internal democracy as a means to maintain security. One possibility is that some supranational institutions could exist that would make democratic states more rather than less democratic. Peace requires not democracies, but democratization at positively interacting levels.

In his analysis of the reasons why famines almost never occur in democracies, it is readily apparent that Sen emphasizes not merely the protective functions of democratic state institutions, but also the various powers of individuals: to challenge officials by demanding an account of these policies and actions, to engage in public debate and deliberation, and so on. These powers and entitlements are distinctly normative in the sense that they are powers to interpret and create norms, rights, and duties. This takes the account of normative powers one step further than Sen's account, by showing how democracy entails a particular understanding of the public exercise of such normative powers (for example, in deliberation). Such a process is free, not because it issues in consensus or voluntary agreement, but because it produces obligations as the result of the joint exercise of normative powers in deliberation. Security is not increased by the voluntary surrender of such active powers, since this undermines democratic practice itself.

This support for the active aspects of democracy is inherently cosmopolitan, since it emphasizes the entitlement of all who possess such powers to be able to exercise them. This broadens considerably the cosmopolitan conception beyond the Kantian emphasis on law as the fundamental mechanism for the protection of individuals as bearers of human rights. In order for democracy to promote justice and human rights, it must recognize the claims made in deliberations initiated by those who have the same rights and obligations. In its active dimension of rights as normative powers, democracy thus promotes peace through nondomination. The guiding principle here is not just that democracy promotes such active powers of citizens, but also that such rights and powers are best protected and promoted when there are differentiated and overlapping institutional locations for their exercise. Security-minded states do not function well democratically, precisely because they are missing the checks on executive power that the dispersal of the powers of citizenship across various institutions and levels would provide.

If democracy is conceived actively in terms of the joint exercise of normative powers and rights, a different analysis of the presuppositions of a reconstructed democratic peace must be provided. According to this view, democracies would be more likely to promote human rights if they had a high degree of internal institutional differentiation *and* external interconnectedness with other democratic polities, such as would be provided by a high level of participation in multilateral and international institutions. While this would be a good start, it is still not sufficient for democratization. In order to increase the capability of citizens to exercise such normative powers in these contexts, new and better transnational democratic practices are required, with many more institutionally differentiated and distributed processes of deliberation than are currently available in democratic states or in current multilateral institutions. From the standpoint of those who lie outside the zone of democratic peace, those institutions are not sufficient to solve the problem of domination inherent in most international institutions, including many multilateral ones. What is needed is a kind of distributed and differentiated deliberation that is already apparent in emerging global public spheres. For those who lack democratic citizenship, participation in these transnational public spheres establishes social ties that may become the basis of democratization through communicative interchange and mutual claim making through which mutual respect can be established and deepened.

The European Union provides a more appropriate model than liberal multilateralism for such a conception of a transnational democracy. As I have noted, EU-level institutions can in some instances require member states (and now even applicant states) to better realize human rights and to enhance participation by diverse actors, with the overall effect of making member states more democratic. In this way, the EU presents a different positive feedback relationship of pooled sovereignty that enables democratization to occur, in which it is precisely the transnational-level institutions that enhance democracy at the lower levels. Certainly, even in the EU the interaction can go the other way: democracy exercised at the lower levels (in cities, regions, and states) can enhance the democracy of higher levels, especially as these suffer from the potentially dominating effects of juridification that often make transnational institutions so distant and alien. With such mutual interaction across levels and locations, a highly differentiated polity works not merely in policy areas, but also in creating a regime of human rights that can multiply realize the powers of citizenship and make them more rather than less robust.

If we are to continue the democratic project, at least in part because of its connection to the ideals of peace and the obligation to end pointless human suffering, it is best to recognize that democracy's capacity to do so is a contingent historical fact and a fragile achievement. The European Union examples show that robust interconnections between democracies at local, national, and transnational levels can create and entrench the conditions for democratization that would begin to address the conflict between the privileged citizens of the zone of democratic peace and those who lack normative powers and are potentially dominated by the protective apparatus of the liberal state. Democracy not only allows citizens to avoid the evils of war, it is also the case that the democracy that can achieve this end must now be transnational, giving a new normative significance to the idea of a democratic peace.

In the previous two sections, I have argued that transnational democratic institutions have both an intrinsic justification in terms of the democratic ideal and an instrumental one based on more robust realizations of rights and powers in a transnational polity. Transnational polities can be justified in terms of ideals and conditions intrinsic to the democratic ideal. They can also be justified instrumentally in terms of reconnecting the hope that democracy can produce the capacity to avoid war and other forms of suffering. Both arguments show the transnational democracy overcoming the democratically self-defeating character of current democratic arrangements.

Conclusion: Realizing Transnational Democracy

I began this book by arguing that the only way to extend democracy beyond the nation state is to think of it in terms of a democracy of *dêmoi*, a democracy across rather than beyond borders. I have now given both constitutive and instrumental justifications of this claim. The improvement of democratic practice that Sen sees as crucial to maintaining its capacity to enable citizens to avoid evils such as war and famine is now a matter of its extension to the transnational level. Given the difficulty of overcoming domination without democracy, citizens should demand an international system of institutions that would afford such protections and limit the imperial ambitions of their own states. If this is the case, then citizens and publics must begin to transform their democracy transnationally, not only if it is to remain a means to promoting justice, but also if it is to continue to be a democracy at all.

Many states are still effective democracies, but with problems of immigration and economic volatility, they can become more democratic only if they begin to practice democracy across borders. In this way they may also become more just, less likely to become a thousand tiny fortresses in which the oldest form of domination is practiced at many different levels: the domination of noncitizens by citizens, of nonmembers by members, using their ability to command noninterference much like those who live within gated communities. They do so at a price, the price of the benefits of common liberty. Transnational democracy in this context is then instrumental not only to justice, but also to peaceful relations and mutually beneficial economic interaction. Its institutional principles based on interlocking and shared powers may also provide models of federalism that could create social peace within states without mutually destructive contests for singular sovereignty.

I have discussed two sets of conditions that suggest that transnational democracy is already a realistic extension of current political possibilities. The first is the existence of transnational public spheres and civil society. Such public spheres are particularly important for creating conditions of communication that enable the exercise of public influence across diverse and dispersed institutional structures. The second is the emergence of new institutions with great but as yet unrealized democratic potential, primarily in the European Union and in international regimes. Taken together, such conditions would permit the emergence of transnational democratic institutions that could be constitutionally, democratically, and deliberatively legitimate in novel ways.

These developments suggest that there are two primary agents for a possible transnational democratization. The first are democratic states, which pool their sovereignty and pursue broadly federalist and regional projects of political integration. The European Union exhibits how this possibility may develop beyond initial intentions and become a project of polity building. The second sort of transformative agent is less institutional: namely, the participants in transnational public spheres and associations, the citizens who inhabit networks of communication and interaction. These citizens become agents when they create the means by which they gain voice across borders. They do so not merely by employing new technologies and networks of communication, but also by using them self-consciously to create public spheres to pursue justice, create innovative practices, establish common liberty, and further democratic ends.

Following Dewey's dictum, I have sought to criticize and remake our understanding of democracy in two ways. First, I criticized the deeper assumptions about self-legislation and bounded territoriality underlying the limitations of democracy's historically contingent insistence on a unitary rather than a plural political subject and its search for the optimally sized polity as a bounded community committed to freedom and equality. Second, I proposed an alternative account that significantly transforms the current political markers of democratic institutions. This alternative is not simply cosmopolitan in the hierarchical or juridical sense. It does not merely demand bigger and better institutions, but that we reshape familiar state institutions and understand them on the same transnational model, as a democratic polity of democratic polities within a distributed system of democratic authority. The goal of my argument has been the same as that of the first transnational republicans, who saw the deep connection between transnationalism and nondomination in a political order that does justice to our deepest commitments to freedom and justice.

Notes

Introduction

1. Franck, *Fairness in International Law*, 83–145.

2. Dewey, "The Public and Its Problems," 325. On the significance of this work for the application of the international public spheres, Cochran, *Normative Theory in International Relations*.

3. Dewey, "The Public and Its Problems," 327.

4. Weber, "Politics as a Vocation," 77–126.

5. See, for example, Miller's arguments for the distinction between duties of concern and of respect, based on spatial proximity, intensity of interaction, and other criteria in Miller, "Cosmopolitan Respect and Patriotic Concern," 202–224.

6. For a good summary of the current state of the globalization debate, see Hirst and Thompson, "Global Myths and National Policies" and the reply by Perraton in *Global Democracy: Key Debates*, 47–72.

7. Rawls, "The Idea of an Overlapping Consensus," 424.

8. Richardson, *Democratic Autonomy*, 34.

9. Dewey, "The Public and Its Problems," 327.

10. MacCormick, "Democracy, Subsidiarity and Citizenship in the 'European Commonwealth,'" 345.

11. For this formulation see Held and McGrew, *Globalization/Antiglobalization*, 1. For the best comprehensive treatment of globalization in its many dimensions, see Held, et al., *Global Transformations*.

12. Dewey, "The Public and Its Problems," 255.

13. Ruggie, *Constructing the World Polity*, 195.

14. Weiler, "A Constitution for Europe?," 569.

Chapter 1

1. For an excellent treatment of this history, see Linklater, *The Transformation of Political Community*.

2. Ackerman has argued against the idea that the legislature (or any one institution) is the legitimate "People Assembled." See Ackerman, *We the People*, vol. 1, 181. Popular control over decisions and the formation of the popular will are thus institutionally distributed.

3. Dahl, *Democracy and Its Critics*, 224.

4. On the various positions on and controversies over globalization, see Held et al., *Global Transformations*.

5. See Held, *Democracy and the Global Order*, 98–101, for an argument of this sort that emphasizes the scope of interconnections and their consequences for the realization of autonomy as the key problem for democratic governments.

6. Kant, "On the Common Saying" in *Kant's Political Writings*, 90. Kant argues that it is both a practical and a moral necessity to enter into a civil society subject to coercive public law; the analogy to the state of nature here is the "universal violence and distress" of the state of nature that applies in the context of forming a state or a "lawful federation according to a cosmopolitan constitution." While he later weakens this form to "a confederation without the sovereign power of a civil constitution," the achievement of peace is still a moral ideal of pure practical reason, an expression of the highest good, and thus a moral duty. See also *Kant's Political Writings*, 165ff.

7. Kant, "Perpetual Peace" in *Political Writings*, 106.

8. Brown, "International Political Theory," 93. Beitz at one time suggested such a direct inference from empirical interdependence through trade, but he later retracted such a view. See Beitz, *Political Theory and International Relations*, 5ff. For a criticism of this inference, see Barry, "Humanity and Justice in Global Perspective," 232ff.

9. Kant, *Political Writings*, 133, 135.

10. Young, *Inclusion and Democracy*, 223–224. For a similar argument that the scope of obligations derives from sharing a "world," see Lichtenberg, "National Boundaries and Moral Boundaries," 79–100.

11. Held et al., *Global Transformations*, 27.

12. For a republican criticism of Held's account of globalization for failing to begin with such asymmetries rather than with mere scope or intensity, see Dobson, *Citizenship and the Environment*, 12–22.

13. Ibid., 213. For various dimensions of this issue, see Hurrell and Woods, *Inequality, Globalization, and World Politics.*

14. O'Neill, *Towards Justice and Virtue,* 119.

15. Ibid., 120–121.

16. See Buchanan, "Rawls's Law of Peoples," 705.

17. On the "circumstances of politics" see Weale, *Democracy,* 8–13; also Waldron, *Law and Disagreement,* 114–117.

18. On the conception of freedom from domination as "robust noninterference," see Pettit, *Republicanism.* For the problem of freedom and social dependence, see Neuhouser, *The Foundations of Hegel's Social Theory,* chapter 3.

19. Held, *Democracy and the Global Order,* 145.

20. Held and Habermas offer such a legal interpretation of cosmopolitan democracy.

21. Pettit says that nondomination is "not an instrumental good, but enjoys the status of a primary good." See *Republicanism,* 91. See also Shue, *Basic Rights.* For Shue, economic rights such as the right to subsistence are included among the basic rights; my argument sees them as derivative of basic membership rights in the human political community. This civic republican argument can be put to cosmopolitan purposes when linked to nondomination as constitutive of the status of membership.

22. Pettit bases this claim on nondomination as a condition for planning. "For most all the things a person is likely to want, the pursuit of those things is going to be facilitated by their ability to make plans." See Pettit, *Republicanism,* 91. For a more direction connection between primary goods and rights, for which there are human rights to all such goods, see Nussbaum, *Women and Development,* 138–143.

23. See Walzer, *Spheres of Justice,* 50.

24. Pettit, *Republicanism,* 69.

25. Rousseau, *On the Social Contract,* Book 1, chapter 7; Book 3, chapter 16.

26. Young, *Inclusion and Democracy,* 35.

27. On the first, see Sen, *Poverty and Famine;* on the second, see, among others, Doyle, "Kant, Liberal Legacies and Foreign Affairs, Parts I and II." These two fairly robust generalizations concerning the absence of famines and war offer evidence for democracy as a means to justice or at least as a means of avoiding great ills.

28. Habermas, *The Postnational Constellation,* 63. See also Benhabib, *The Rights of Others,* 219. Benhabib says that there is "no way to cut the Gordian knot linking territoriality, representation, and democratic voice" and thus to go beyond the current understanding of democratic community and membership.

29. See Habermas, *Between Facts and Norms,* 296. Also on decentering, see Frug, *City Making,* Part II.

30. Young, *Inclusion and Democracy*, 46.

31. Sunstein, *Republic.com.*

32. See Dahl, "Federalism and the Democratic Process," 96.

33. Weiler, *The Constitution of Europe*, 268ff.

34. Since writing this chapter and other articles using this term, I have discovered that the term "demoicracy" has some currency. See Nicolaidis, "We the Peoples of Europe," 22–33. However, Nicolaidis uses to term to denote a "democracy of states and of peoples," and thus not in the manner I am using *dêmoi* here.

35. Dahl, *Democracy and Its Critics*, 337.

36. As Pagden puts it in *Lords of All of the World*: "the Enlightenment was, perhaps more than has been recognized, the product of a world which was ridding itself of its first, but by no means, alas, its last imperial legacy" (200).

37. Shapiro makes a similar claim that the purpose of deliberation among citizens is "to minimize domination in their collective endeavors." See Shapiro, *The State of Democratic Theory*, 5.

38. Buchanan, *Justice, Legitimacy and Self-Determination*, 176.

39. Ibid., 189.

40. Ibid., 326.

41. Schumpeter, *Capitalism, Socialism and Democracy*, 271–272.

42. Held, *Democracy and the Global Order*, 145.

43. See Habermas, *Der gespaltene Westen*, 113–193.

44. For an alternative account that sees such phenomena in terms of political networks, see Slaughter, *A New World Order*.

45. Habermas, *Postnational Constellation*, 107, 117.

46. Ibid., 109.

47. Habermas, *Der gesplatene Westen*, 130–131.

48. Held and McGrew, *Globalization/Antiglobalization*, 95.

49. Held, *Democracy and the Global Order*, 234.

50. Ibid., 154, 236.

51. Dryzek, *Deliberative Democracy and Beyond*, 93.

52. This is precisely the theme of Dryzek's most recent book, in which he claims that "deliberative and democratic global politics can most fruitfully be sought in the

more informal realm of international public spheres." See Dryzek, *Deliberative Global Politics*, vii.

53. Dryzek, *Deliberative Democracy and Beyond*, 133.

54. Universal Declaration of Human Rights, Article 28.

55. Rawls, *The Law of Peoples*, 32; and "The Idea of Public Reason Revisited," also reprinted in this work, 172.

56. Arendt, "What Is Freedom?," 143–172.

57. Besides Sen's work on capability failure, see the dismal statistics of extreme destitution and suffering cited in Pogge, *World Poverty and Human Rights*.

58. See Pettit, *Republicanism*, 88ff.

59. Ibid., 185.

60. Ibid.

Chapter 2

1. See, among other works, Richardson, *Democratic Autonomy*, Sunstein, *Designing Democracy*, and Michelman, "Law's Republic," 1493–1537.

2. See Onuf, *The Republican Legacy*.

3. Habermas, *The Structural Transformation of the Public Sphere*.

4. Dewey, "The Public and Its Problems," 327.

5. Kymlicka, *Politics in the Vernacular*, 94; for criticisms of the idea of a European-wide public sphere along these lines, see Schlessinger and Kevin, "Can the European Union Become a Sphere of Publics?," 206–229.

6. Dryzek, *Democracy in Capitalist Times*, 79ff.

7. According to the common definition, regimes are "sets of implicit and explicit principles, norms, rules, and decision-making procedures around which actors' expectations converge in a given area of international relations." See Krasner, "Structural Causes and Regime Consequences," 2. Agreements reached that form a regime constitute rules and norms regulating specific activities or domains of activities: commercial whaling, the rights of children, trade, nuclear accidents, and so on.

8. For a critique of such an idea of participation of civil society through NGOs interacting with experts, see Chatterjee, *The Politics of the Governed*, 68–69.

9. On the idea that the people speak only in "constitutional moments," see Ackerman, *We the People*, vol. I, chapter 1. Pettit generalizes this idea by making the useful distinction between the authorial and the editorial dimensions of the people with regard to the content of laws. See Pettit, "Democracy, Electoral and Contestatory," 105–146.

10. Arrow, "The Economics of Agency," 37.

11. Shapiro, "The Social Control of Impersonal Trust," 627.

12. On this issue, see Bohman, "Democracy as Inquiry, Inquiry as Democratic," 590–607.

13. Llewellyn, "Agency," 483.

14. Miller, *Managerial Dilemmas*, 16.

15. See Pogge, *World Poverty and Human Rights*, chapter 1, especially 20ff.

16. Sassen, *Losing Control?*, 10.

17. Ibid., chapter 1.

18. Llewellyn, "Agency," 484; also White, "Agency as Control," 205.

19. See Ewig, "Strengths and Limits of the NGO Women's Movement Model," 97.

20. See Dewey, "The Public and Its Problems," 255 and 314.

21. See Soysal, *Limits of Citizenship*.

22. Aristotle, *Politics*, 1261b.

23. For a further development of these conceptual issues, see Bohman, "Expanding Dialogue," 131–155.

24. Lessig, *Code*, 141.

25. Habermas, *Between Facts and Norms*, 360.

26. Habermas, *The Structural Transformation*, 38.

27. Ibid., 60.

28. Garnham, "The Mass Media," 243–271.

29. Hurley, "Rationality, Democracy, and Leaky Boundaries," 274. Here, and earlier in her *Natural Reasons*, Hurley argues that borders can be more or less democratic in terms of promoting epistemic values of inquiry and the moral value of autonomy as constitutive of democracy. For examples of this form of cognition in social settings, see Hutchings, *Cognition in the Wild*.

30. Lessig, *Code*, 217.

31. Smith and Smythe, "Globalization, Citizenship, and Technology," 183.

32. Ruggie, *Constructing the World Polity*, 195.

33. Kymlicka, "Citizenship in an Era of Globalization," 120.

34. Dahl, "Can International Organizations Be Democratic?," 19ff.

35. On the distinction between strong and weak publics, see Fraser, "Rethinking the Public Sphere," 109–142. Habermas appropriates this distinction in his "two-track model of democracy" in *Between Facts and Norms*, chapter 7. The requirements of a strong public sphere for both are closely tied to access to influence over legislation that produces coercive law.

36. Dorf and Sabel, "The Constitution of Democratic Experimentalism," 292.

37. Cohen and Sabel, "Directly-Deliberative Polyarchy," 3–30. For a more direct application to the EU, see Cohen and Sabel, "Sovereignty and Solidarity." My description of the OMC as a deliberative procedure owes much to their account.

38. Dorf and Sabel, "Democratic Experimentalism," 288–289.

39. On accountability in "delegative democracy," see Guillermo O'Donnell, *Counterpoints*, 162–173, especially 171.

40. See, for example, Joerges and Neyer, "Intergovernmental Bargaining," 273–299.

41. See Fung, "Recipes for Public Spheres," 338–367.

42. For this sort of criticism, see Peters, "Public Discourse, Identity and Legitimacy." Peters and others who make this criticism are too demanding and would in the end eliminate the applicability of the public sphere in most contemporary settings: the European public sphere could no more be realized as shared and common than could the public sphere of a large pluralist and complex nation-state. Peters is correct, however, in arguing against Habermas's conception of a public sphere that is somehow united in virtue of shared attention to the same problems and debates. Even a nonunitary distributed public sphere is always interactive; shared attention is episodic and usually related to crises—the Iraq war, global warming, and so on.

43. Cohen and Sabel, "Sovereignty and Solidarity," 368.

44. Moraviscik, "Explaining International Human Rights Regimes, 158.

45. Dewey, "Liberalism and Social Action," 50–51.

46. Dewey, "The Public and Its Problems," 281.

47. O'Neill, *Towards Justice and Virtue*, 119.

48. Rawls, *The Law of Peoples*, 121–122.

49. Held, *Democracy and the Global Order*, 145.

50. Pettit, *Republicanism*, 52.

51. Richardson, *Democratic Autonomy*, 34.

52. Ibid.

53. Pettit, *Republicanism*, 35.

54. Pettit, "Freedom as Antipower," 589.

55. Habermas, *Between Facts and Norms*, 147.

56. Hollis, *Models of Man*, 181.

57. Rawls, *A Theory of Justice*, 113. In my terms, natural duties are those normative powers that a person has to make claims upon humanity.

58. Mead, *Mind, Self, and Society*, 270–271.

Chapter 3

1. Universal Declaration of Human Rights, Article 28.

2. UNCHR Resolution 1999/57, paragraphs 1 and 2.

3. See *Universal Declaration of Human Rights*, article 21; also the *International Covenant on Civil and Political Rights*, article 25. The status of these claims is highly ambiguous: the right to participate in public affairs is often used interchangeably with weaker rights of a people to "consultation in the selection of governments." One of my aims here is to provide a plausible justification for the participatory interpretation. For a general discussion of these various documents, see the essays in Fox and Roth, *Democratic Governance and International Law*.

4. See Williams, "Making Sense of Humanity," 88. Historically the distinction is much richer. It involved "a quality of the subject, one of his or her faculties; a franchise, freedom or a power; and a possibility of acting." See Villey, "La gènese du droit subjectif," 97–126. Rather than returning to natural law or accepting a kind of moral minimalism about rights, I reintroduce this more complex structure of subjective rights as related to normative powers in the human political community. Such a complex analysis of rights as normative powers and relational duties is broadly Hohfeldian. See Hohfeld, *Fundamental Legal Conceptions*, 36ff. For the broader context of humanity and rights in European history, see Pagden, "Human Rights, Natural Rights," 171–199.

5. See Arendt and Jaspers, *The Hannah Arendt and Karl Jaspers Correspondence*, 413. In republican fashion, Arendt argues that Nuremberg marks the beginning of political claims made for humanity as *Menschheit*. See also Arendt, *Eichmann in Jerusalem*.

6. Kant, *Metaphysics of Morals*, 553.

7. See Darwall, "Fichte and the Second-Personal Standpoint," 91–113. For Darwall dignity is both a specific set of moral requirements for the treatment of persons and also the attributed authority *to require* that we comply with them and hold others accountable if they do not.

8. See Korsgaard, *Creating the Kingdom of Ends*, 106ff.

9. Buchanan argues that democracy is a reliable form of "governance for the protection of basic human rights" and includes rights of political association among them. Such an instrumental justification cannot justify the full democratic entitlement. If democracy were a basic human right, then this would be contradictory to the

extent that democracy also instantiates and does not merely protect political rights to participation. See Buchanan, *Justice, Legitimacy, and Self-Determination*, 328.

10. See Berlin, "Two Concepts of Liberty," 129. The text continues: "The despot who leaves his subjects a wide area of liberty may be unjust, or encourage the wildest inequalities, care little for order, or virtue, or knowledge; but provided he does not curb their liberty, or at least curbs it less than many other regimes, he meets with Mill's specification" of the greatest possible liberty. Similarly, Pettit argues that a benevolent slave master who does not actually interfere is still a dominator.

11. Arendt, *The Origins of Totalitarianism*, 297.

12. Nussbuam, *Women and Human Development*, 96ff.

13. See Bohman, "Punishment as a Political Obligation," 101–139; see also my "Is Democracy a Means to Global Justice," 101–116. For a similar view of human rights as explicable through the idea of membership, see Cohen, "Minimalism about Human Rights," 190–213. Cohen argues that the encounter with human rights demands the re-elaboration of various traditions; however, these encounters also re-elaborate human rights doctrines as well. See also Benhabib, *Rights of Others*, 134–143.

14. See, for example, Arendt, *Eichmann in Jerusalem*, 268, or Glendon, *The World Made New*, 9.

15. For this formulation, see Luban, "A Theory of Crimes against Humanity," 88.

16. For a justification of punishment for international crimes along these lines, see Bohman, "Punishment as a Political Obligation," 121ff.

17. See Luban, "A Theory of Crimes Against Humanity," 137.

18. Ibid., 126.

19. Arendt, *Origins of Totalitarianism*, 357.

20. See Chan, "The Right to a Nationality," 1–14.

21. Habermas, *The Inclusion of the Other*, 190–191.

22. For such a republican skepticism directed at rights as juridical statuses, see Bellamy, "Constitutive Citizenship versus Consitutitonal Rights, 16–39.

23. See Fletcher, *The Political Works*, 129–175.

24. See Pagden, *Lords of all the World*, 188.

25. Kant, "The Idea of a Universal History," in *Kant's Political Writings*, 47.

26. Benhabib, *The Claims of Culture*, 140–141.

27. See Schauer, "Amending the Presuppositions of a Constitution," 145–162. Thus, constitutional revision does not take place exclusively through the explicit amendment process or by popular sovereignty, but along with the historical development of the community and its practices.

28. Kant, *Metaphysics of Morals*, 92. Gregor translates the passage as "mere underlings of the commonwealth." These "auxiliaries" lack the independence necessary to acquire full status as citizens, and include women, children, and propertyless servants, as well as foreigners, strangers, and visitors. As such, they are not just unequal, but also dependent and dominated.

29. On the "fusion of horizons" as the result of the practical testing of presuppositions, see Gadamer, *Truth and Method*, 306–307.

30. On this point, as well as on the limits of the UN declaration on the rights of colonized peoples, see Tully, "The Struggles of Indigenous Peoples," 53–54.

31. Ibid., 47.

32. Reflective equilibrium in Rawls's sense moves back and forth between theories and intuitions, adjusting the weights given to various principles in cases of conflict. This process need not be monological (as some critics have argued), but could well be both dynamic and interpersonal. By moving back and forth among various perspectives, novel interpretations may transform intuitions and principles. As developed by Rawls, reflective equilibrium remains a first-person plural method for developing a theory of "our intuitions" in all their rich possibilities.

33. See Kant, *Critique of Judgment*, section 40. For an interpretation of Kant along these lines, see Arendt, *Lectures on Kant's Political Philosophy*. For an impartialist interpretation, see Benhabib, *The Claims of Culture*, 170–171.

34. George Herbert Mead, *Mind, Self and Society*, 280.

35. Weiler, "A Constitution for Europe?," 569.

36. Mead, *Mind, Self, and Society*, 282.

37. Ibid., 157.

38. Ibid., 270.

39. Tully, "The Freedom of the Ancients," 217.

40. Sabel, "Constitutional Orders," 159.

41. Kymlicka, "The Evolving Basis."

42. Joseph Weiler points to the case of *Gayusuz v. Austria* that went to the European Court of Human Rights and led to the extension of social security benefits to third country nationals. See Weiler, "An 'Ever Closer Union,'" 719.

43. On the democratizing role of the EU with respect to human rights, see Bowman, "The European Union Democratic Deficit," 191–212. On the rights of immigrants to political participation in the EU on republican grounds, see Honohan, *Civic Republicanism*, 238–239.

44. Habermas, *Between Facts and Norms*, chapter 8. Also see Frug, *City Making*, especially chapter 4.

45. Schmitter, "Is it Possible to Democratize the Europolity?," 32.

46. Pettit, *Republicanism*, 177–180.

47. For such criticisms, see Dahl, "Can International Organizations Be Democratic?," 19–37.

48. See Bunch, "Women's Rights as Human Rights," 489–490.

Chapter 4

1. On deliberating about "ends in view," see Dewey, "Theory of Valuation," 189–251.

2. One of the purposes of the Maastricht Treaty was to democratize the EU. However, some provisions with this aim may have had unintended undemocratic consequences, such as making decision making less transparent. See Curtin, "The Constitutional Structure of the Union," 17–69.

3. See Scharpf, *Governing in Europe*, chapter 1.

4. Ackerman, *We the People*, vol. 1, 6.

5. Richardson, *Democratic Autonomy*, 70.

6. Shaw, "The Interpretation of European Citizenship," 293–317.

7. Cohen and Sabel, "Sovereignty and Solidarity," 345–375. More generally on the constitutional significance of directly deliberative polyarchy, see Dorf and Sabel, "The Constitution of Democratic Experimentalism," 267–473.

8. Jacobsson and Vifell, "Integration by Deliberation?," 411–451.

9. Neyer, "Discourse and Order in the EU," 293.

10. Castles and Miller, *The Age of Immigration*, 2nd edition, 39.

11. Habermas, *The Theory of Communicative Action*, Vol. II, 356ff.

12. Habermas, "Why Europe Needs a Constitution," 5–6.

13. See Tully, "Introduction," 5ff; also Bohman, *Public Deliberation*, chapter 4.

14. See Bohman, "Cosmopolitan Republicanism," 3–22.

15. Slaughter, *A New World Order*, 11.

16. See Bohman, "Democracy as Inquiry," 590–607.

17. Kymlicka, "Citizenship in an Era of Globalization," 112–126; for similar arguments, see Dahl, "Can International Organizations Be Democratic?," 19–37.

18. Cohen and Sabel, "EU and US Sovereignty and Solidarity," 366.

19. Michelman, *Brennan and the Supreme Court*, 59.

20. Gould, *Globalizing Democracy and Human Rights*, 205.

21. See Neyer, "Discourse and Order in the EU," 689.

22. See Fiss, "The Supreme Court 1978 Term," 2.

23. See Dahl, "Federalism and the Democratic Process," 96.

Conclusion

1. On the distinction between instrumental and intrinsic justifications of deliberative democracy, see Christiano, "The Significance of Public Deliberation," 243–279. Christiano argues that public deliberation is best regarded as having instrumental value, to the extent that it promotes correct reasoning and good outcomes.

2. On the distinction between moral and social cosmopolitanism as the difference between the focus on the moral worth of individuals and on institutional order, see Beitz, "Social and Cosmopolitan Liberalism," 515. Political cosmopolitanism is a subspecies of social cosmopolitanism.

3. See Bohman, "Republican Cosmopolitanism," 336–352.

4. For his version of the idea of a democratic peace see Rawls, *The Law of Peoples*, 44ff.

5. According to Dewey, understood practically "facts are such in a logical sense only as they serve to delimit a problem in a way that affords indication and test of proposed solutions." See John Dewey, "Logic: The Theory of Inquiry," 499.

6. Dahl, "Federalism and the Democratic Process," 95.

7. Richardson, *Democratic Autonomy*, 67.

8. Dahl, "Federalism and the Democratic Process," 103.

9. Dewey, "The Public and Its Problems," 281.

10. See Polanyi, *The Great Transformation*, especially the discussion of the regulation of free trade in the last chapter. A similar argument about the socially destructive aspects of contemporary globalization is developed in Rodrik, *Has Globalization Gone Too Far?* On the development and consolidation of power in the nation-state, see Mann, *The Sources of Social Power*, vol. I, 15ff. On the complex relation between gains in national citizenship and military obligations, see the work of Charles Tilly. My argument suggests that new gains in rights and powers must be transnational.

11. For a further discussion of these issues, see my "Beyond the Democratic Peace," 127–138.

12. As Russett puts it: "Depending on precise criteria, only twelve to fifteen states qualified as democracies at the end of the nineteenth century. The empirical significance of the rarity of war between democracies emerges only in the first half of the

twentieth century, with at least twice the number of democracies as earlier, and especially with the existence of perhaps sixty democracies by the mid-1980s." See Russett, *Grasping the Democratic Peace*, 20.

13. Sen, *Development as Freedom*, chapter 5.

14. Ibid., 184.

15. Sen, *Poverty and Famine*, 165–166.

16. Tilly, *Coercion, Capital, and European States*.

Bibliography

Ackerman, Bruce A. *We the People,* vol. 1. Cambridge: Harvard University Press, 1991.

Arendt, Hannah. *Between Past and Future.* New York: Viking, 1961.

Arendt, Hannah. *Eichmann in Jerusalem: A Report on the Banality of Evil.* New York: Viking, 1965.

Arendt, Hannah. *Lectures on Kant's Political Philosophy.* Chicago: University of Chicago Press, 1982.

Arendt, Hannah. *The Origins of Totalitarianism.* New York: Harcourt Brace, 1951.

Arendt, Hannah, and Karl Jaspers. *The Hannah Arendt and Karl Jaspers Correspondence.* New York: Harcourt Brace, 1993.

Aristotle. *Politics.* Trans. C. D. C. Reeve. Indianapolis: Hackett, 1998.

Arrow, Kenneth. "The Economics of Agency." In *Principals and Agents,* ed. J. Pratt and R. Zeckhauser, 37–51. Cambridge, Mass.: Harvard Business School Press, 1985.

Barry, Brian. "Humanity and Justice in Global Perspective." In *Ethics, Economics and the Law,* ed. J. R. Pennock and J. W. Chapman, 219–252. New York: New York University Press, 1982.

Beitz, Charles. *Political Theory and International Relations.* Princeton: Princeton University Press, 1979.

Beitz, Charles. "Social and Cosmopolitan Liberalism." *International Affairs* 75 (1999): 525–530.

Bellamy, Richard. "Constitutive Citizenship versus Constitutional Rights: Republican Reflections on the EU Charter and the Human Rights Act." In *Sceptical Essays on Human Rights,* ed. T. Campbell, K. D. Ewing, and A. Tomkins, 15–40. Oxford: Oxford University Press, 2001.

Benhabib, Seyla. *The Claims of Culture*. Princeton: Princeton University Press, 2002.

Benhabib, Seyla. *The Rights of Others*. Cambridge: Cambridge University Press, 2004.

Berlin, Isaiah. "Two Concepts of Liberty." In *Four Essays on Liberty*. Oxford: Oxford University Press, 1969.

Bohman, James. "Beyond the Democratic Peace: An Instrumental Argument for Transnational Democracy." *Journal of Social Philosophy* 37 (2006): 127–138.

Bohman, James. "Constituting Humanity: Universal Political Rights and the Human Community." *Canadian Journal of Philosophy* (forthcoming).

Bohman, James. "Constitution Making and Institutional Innovation: The European Union and Transnational Governance." *European Journal of Political Theory* 3:3 (2004): 315–337.

Bohman, James. "Cosmopolitan Republicanism." *Monist* 84 (2001): 3–22.

Bohman, James. "Democracy as Inquiry, Inquiry as Democratic: Pragmatism, Social Science, and the Cognitive Division of Labor." *American Journal of Political Science* 43 (1999): 590–607.

Bohman, James. "Expanding Dialogue: The Public Sphere, the Internet, and Transnational Democracy." In *After Habermas: Perspectives on the Public Sphere*, ed. J. Roberts and N. Crossley, 131–155. London: Blackwell, 2004.

Bohman, James. "From *Dêmos* to *Dêmoi*." *Ratio Juris* 18 (2005): 293–314.

Bohman, James. "Is Democracy a Means to Global Justice? Human Rights and the Democratic Minimum." *Ethics and International Affairs* 16 (2005): 101–116.

Bohman, James. *Public Deliberation*. Cambridge, Mass.: MIT Press, 1996.

Bohman, James. "Punishment as a Political Obligation: Crimes against Humanity and the International Political Community." *University of Buffalo Criminal Law Review* 5 (2002): 101–139.

Bohman, James. "Republican Cosmopolitanism." *Journal of Political Philosophy* 12 (2004): 336–352.

Bowman, Jon. "The European Union Democratic Deficit: Federalists, Skeptics, and Revisionists." *European Journal of Political Theory* 5 (2006): 191–212.

Brown, Chris. "International Political Theory and the Idea of World Community." In *International Relations Theory Today*, ed. K. Booth and S. Smith, 90–110. University Park: Penn State University Press, 1995.

Buchanan, Allen. *Justice, Legitimacy, and Self-Determination*. Oxford: Oxford University Press, 2004.

Buchanan, Allen. "Rawls's Law of Peoples." *Ethics* 110 (2000): 697–721.

Bibliography

Bunch, Charlotte. "Women's Rights as Human Rights: Towards a Revision of Human Rights." *Human Rights Quarterly* 12 (1990): 486–498.

Castles, Stephen, and M. J. Miller. *The Age of Immigration.* London: St. Martin's, 1999.

Chan, Johannes. "The Right to a Nationality as a Human Right." *Human Rights Law Journal* 12 (1991): 1–14.

Chatterjee, Partha. *The Politics of the Governed.* New York: Columbia University Press, 2004.

Christiano, Thomas. "The Significance of Public Deliberation." In *Deliberative Democracy,* ed. J. Bohman and W. Rehg, 243–279. Cambridge, Mass.: MIT Press, 1997.

Cochran, Molly. *Normative Theory in International Relations.* Cambridge: Cambridge University Press, 1999.

Cohen, Joshua. "Minimalism about Human Rights: The Most We Can Hope For?" *Journal of Political Philosophy* 12 (2004): 190–213.

Cohen, Joshua, and Charles Sabel. "Directly-Deliberative Polyarchy." In *Private Governance, Democratic Constitutionalism, and Supranationalism,* ed. C. Joerges and O. Gerstenberg, 3–30. Florence: European Commission, 1998.

Cohen, Joshua, and Charles Sabel. "Sovereignty and Solidarity: EU and US." In *Governing Work and Welfare in a New Economy: European and American Experiments,* ed. J. Zeitlin and D. Trubek, 345–375. Oxford: Oxford University Press, 2004.

Curtin, Deirdre. "The Constitutional Structure of the Union: A Europe of Bits and Pieces." *Common Market Law Review* 30 (1993): 17–69.

Dahl, Robert. "Can International Organizations Be Democratic? A Skeptic's View." In *Democracy's Edges,* ed. C. Hacker-Cordon and I. Shapiro, 19–37. Cambridge: Cambridge University Press, 1999.

Dahl, Robert. *Democracy and Its Critics.* New Haven: Yale University Press, 1989.

Dahl, Robert. "Federalism and the Democratic Process." In *Liberal Democracy,* ed. J. R. Pennock and J. W. Chapman, 95–108. New York: New York University Press, 1983.

Darwall, Stephen. "Fichte and the Second-Personal Standpoint." *International Yearbook for German Idealism* 3 (2005): 91–113.

Dewey, John. "Liberalism and Social Action." In *The Later Works, 1925–1937,* vol. 11. Carbondale, Ill.: Southern Illinois University Press, 1991.

Dewey, John. *Logic: The Theory of Inquiry.* In *The Later Works, 1925–1937,* vol. 12. Carbondale, Ill.: Southern Illinois University Press, 1986.

Dewey, John. "Theory of Valuation." In *The Later Works, 1925–1937,* vol. 13. Carbondale, Ill.: Southern Illinois University Press, 1988.

Dewey, John. "The Public and Its Problems." In *The Later Works, 1925–1937,* vol. 2. Carbondale, Ill.: Southern Illinois University Press, 1988.

Dobson, Andrew. *Citizenship and the Environment.* Oxford: Oxford University Press, 2003.

Dorf, Michael, and Charles Sabel. "The Constitution of Democratic Experimentalism." *Columbia Law Review* 98 (1998): 267–473.

Doyle, Michael. "Kant, Liberal Legacies, and Foreign Affairs, Parts I and II." *Philosophy and Public Affairs* 12 (1983): 205–235.

Dryzek, John. *Deliberative Democracy and Beyond.* Oxford: Oxford University Press, 2002.

Dryzek, John. *Deliberative Global Politics.* Cambridge: Polity Press, 2006.

Dryzek, John. *Democracy in Capitalist Times.* Oxford: Oxford University Press, 1996.

Ewig, Christina. "Strengths and Limits of the NGO Women's Movement Model." *Latin American Research Review* 34 (1999): 75–98.

Fiss, Owen. "The Supreme Court of 1978 Term; Foreword: The Forms of Justice." *Harvard Law Review* 93 (1979): 1–58.

Fletcher, Andrew. *The Political Works.* Ed. J. Robertson. Cambridge: Cambridge University Press, 2006.

Fox, Gregory H., and Brad R. Roth, eds. *Democratic Governance and International Law.* Cambridge: Cambridge University Press, 2000.

Franck, Thomas. *Fairness in International Law and Institutions.* Cambridge: Cambridge University Press, 1995.

Fraser, Nancy. "Rethinking the Public Sphere." In *Habermas and the Public Sphere,* ed. C. Calhoun, 109–142. Cambridge, Mass.: MIT Press, 1992.

Frug, Gerald. *City Making: Building Communities without Building Walls.* Princeton: Princeton University Press, 1999.

 Fung, Archon. "Recipes for Public Spheres." *Journal of Political Philosophy* 3 (2003): 338–367.

Gadamer, Hans-Georg. *Truth and Method.* New York: Seabury, 1992.

Garnham, Nicholas. "The Mass Media, Cultural Identity, and the Public Sphere in the Modern World." *Public Culture* 5 (1993): 243–271.

Glendon, Mary Ann. *The World Made New: Eleanor Roosevelt and the Universal Declaration of Human Rights.* New York: Random House, 2001.

Gould, Carol. *Globalizing Democracy and Human Rights.* Cambridge: Cambridge University Press, 2004.

Habermas, Jürgen. *Between Facts and Norms.* Cambridge, Mass.: MIT Press, 1996.

Habermas, Jürgen. *Der Gespaltene Westen.* Frankfurt: Surhkamp Verlag, 2004.

Habermas, Jürgen. *The Inclusion of the Other.* Cambridge, Mass.: MIT Press, 1998.

Habermas, Jürgen. *The Postnational Constellation.* Cambridge, Mass.: MIT Press, 2001.

Habermas, Jürgen. *The Structural Transformation of the Public Sphere.* Cambridge, Mass.: MIT Press, 1989.

Habermas, Jürgen. *The Theory of Communicative Action,* vol. 2. Boston: Beacon Press, 1988.

Habermas, Jürgen. "Why Europe Needs a Constitution." *New Left Review* 11 (2001): 5–26.

Hanohan, Iseult. *Civic Republicanism.* London: Routledge, 2002.

Held, David. *Democracy and the Global Order.* Stanford: Stanford University Press, 1995.

Held, David, Anthony McGrew, David Goldblatt, and Jonathan Perraton. *Global Transformations: Politics, Economics, and Culture.* Stanford: Stanford University Press, 1999.

Held, David, and McGrew, Anthony. *Globalization/Antiglobalization.* Cambridge: Polity Press, 2002.

Hirst, Paul, and Grahame Thompson. "Global Myths and National Policies." In *Global Democracy: Key Debates,* ed. B. Holden, 47–72. London: Routledge, 2000.

Hohfeld, Wesley Newcomb. *Fundamental Legal Conceptions.* Westport: Greenfield Press, 1978.

Hollis, Martin. *Models of Man.* Cambridge: Cambridge University Press, 1977.

Hurley, Susan. *Natural Reasons.* Oxford: Oxford University Press, 1989.

Hurley, Susan. "Rationality, Democracy, and Leaky Boundaries." In *Democracy's Edges,* ed. C. Hacker-Cordon and I. Shapiro, 273–295. Cambridge: Cambridge University Press, 1999.

Hurrell, Andrew, and Ngaire Woods. *Inequality, Globalization, and World Politics.* Oxford: Oxford University Press, 1999.

Hutchings, Edwin. *Cognition in the Wild.* Cambridge, Mass.: MIT Press, 1995.

International Covenant on Civil and Political Rights. United Nations General Assembly res. 2200A (XXI), U.N. Doc. A/6316 (1966).

Jacobsson, Kersten, and Asa Vifell. "Integration by Deliberation? On the Role of Committees in the Open Method of Coordination." In *European Governance, Deliberation, and the Quest for Democratization,* ed. E. Eriksen, C. Joerges, and J. Neyer, 411–451. Oslo: ARENA, 2003.

Joerges, Christian, and Jürgen Neyer. "From Intergovernmental Bargaining to Deliberative Political Processes: The Constitutionalization of Comitology." *European Law Journal* 3 (1997): 273–299.

Bibliography

Kant, Immanuel. *Critique of Judgment*. Indianapolis: Hackett, 1987.

Kant, Immanuel. *Metaphysics of Morals*. In *Practical Philosophy*, trans. and ed. M. Gregor. Cambridge: Cambridge University Press, 1996.

Kant, Immanuel. *Political Writings*. Ed. H. Reiss. Cambridge: Cambridge University Press, 1970.

Korsgaard, Christine. *Creating the Kingdom of Ends*. Cambridge: Cambridge University Press, 1996.

Krasner, Stephen. "Structural Causes and Regime Consequences: Regimes as Intervening Variables." In *International Regimes*, ed. S. Krasner, 1–21. Ithaca: Cornell University Press, 1983.

Kymlicka, Will. "Citizenship in an Era of Globalization." In *Democracy's Edges*, ed. C. Hacker-Cordon and I. Shapiro, 112–127. Cambridge: Cambridge University Press, 1999.

Kymlicka, Will. *Politics in the Vernacular*. Oxford: Oxford University Press, 2001.

Kymlicka, Will. "The Evolving Basis of European Norms of Minority Rights: Rights to Culture, Participation, and Autonomy." In *European Integration and the Nationalities Question*, ed. J. McGarry and M. Keating. Routledge, forthcoming.

Lessig, Lawrence. *Code and Other Laws of Cyberspace*. New York: Basic Books, 1999.

Lichtenburg, Judith. "National Boundaries and Moral Boundaries." In *Boundaries*, ed. P. Brown and H. Shue, 79–100. Lanham: Rowman and Littlefield, 1981.

Linklater, Andrew. *The Transformation of Political Community: Ethical Foundations of the Post-Westphalian Era*. Cambridge: Polity Press, 1998.

Llewellyn, Karl. "Agency." In *Encyclopedia of Social Sciences*, vol. 1. New York: Macmillan, 1930.

Luban, David. "A Theory of Crimes against Humanity." *Yale Journal of International Law* 29 (2004): 86–167.

MacCormick, Neil. "Democracy, Subsidiarity, and Citizenship in the 'European Commonwealth.'" *Law and Philosophy* 16 (1997): 331–356.

Mann, Michael. *The Sources of Social Power*, vol. 1. Cambridge: Cambridge University Press, 1986.

Mead, George Herbert. *Mind, Self, and Society*. Chicago: University of Chicago Press, 1934.

Michelman, Frank. *Brennan and the Supreme Court*. Princeton: Princeton University Press, 2002.

Michelman, Frank. "Law's Republic." *Yale Law Journal* 97 (1988): 1493–1537.

Miller, Gary. *Managerial Dilemmas: The Political Economy of Hierarchy*. Princeton: Princeton University Press, 1992.

Miller, Richard. "Cosmopolitan Respect and Patriotic Concern." *Philosophy and Public Affairs* 27 (1998): 202–224.

Moraviscik, Andrew. "Explaining International Human Rights Regimes: Liberal Theory and Western Europe." *European Journal of International Relations* 1 (1995): 157–189.

Neuhouser, Frederick. *The Foundations of Hegel's Social Theory*. Cambridge: Cambridge University Press, 2000.

Neyer, Jürgen. "Discourse and Order in the EU." *Journal of Common Market Studies* 41 (2003): 687–706.

Nicolaidis, Kalypso. "We the Peoples of Europe." *Foreign Affairs* 82 (2004): 22–33.

Nussbaum, Martha. *Women and Human Development*. Oxford: Oxford University Press, 1999.

O'Donnell, Guillermo. *Counterpoints*. South Bend: University of Notre Dame Press, 1999.

O'Neill, Onora. *Towards Justice and Virtue*. Cambridge: Cambridge University Press, 1996.

Onuf, Nicholas Greenwood. *The Republican Legacy in International Thought*. Cambridge: Cambridge University Press, 1998.

Pagden, Anthony. "Human Rights, Natural Rights, and Europe's Imperial Legacy." *Political Theory* 31 (2003): 171–199.

Pagden, Anthony. *Lords of All the World*. New Haven: Yale University Press, 1995.

Peters, Bernard. "Public Discourse, Identity, and Legitimacy." In *The Making of the European Polity*, ed. E. Eriksen and E. Fossum, 84–123. London: Routledge, 2005.

Pettit, Phillip. "Democracy, Electoral and Contestatory." In *Designing Democratic Institutions*, ed. I. Shapiro and S. Macedo, 105–146. New York: New York University Press, 2000.

Pettit, Phillip. "Freedom as Antipower." *Ethics* 106 (1996): 576–604.

Pettit, Phillip. *Republicanism*. Oxford: Oxford University Press, 1998.

Pogge, Thomas. *World Poverty and Human Rights*. Cambridge: Polity Press, 2002.

Polanyi, Karl. *The Great Transformation*. Boston: Beacon Press, 1957.

Rawls, John. *A Theory of Justice*. Cambridge, Mass.: Harvard University Press, 1971.

Rawls, John. "The Idea of Overlapping Consensus." In *Collected Papers of John Rawls*, ed. S. Freeman, 421–229. Cambridge, Mass.: Harvard University Press, 1999.

Rawls, John. *The Law of Peoples*. Cambridge, Mass.: Harvard University Press, 1999.

Richardson, Henry. *Democratic Autonomy: Public Reasoning and the Ends of Policy.* Oxford: Oxford University Press, 2002.

Rodrik, Dani. *Has Globalization Gone Too Far?* Washington, D.C.: Foreign Affairs Press, 1997.

Rousseau, Jean-Jacques. *On the Social Contract.* Indianapolis: Hackett, 1987.

Ruggie, Gerald. *Constructing the World Polity.* London: Routledge, 1996.

Russett, Bruce. *Grasping the Democratic Peace.* Princeton: Princeton University Press, 1993.

Sabel, Charles. "Constitutional Orders: Trust Building and Response to Change." In *Contemporary Capitalism*, ed. J. R. Hollingsworth and R. Boyer, 154–197. Cambridge: Cambridge University Press, 1997.

Sassen, Saskia. *Losing Control? Sovereignty in the Age of Globalization.* New York: Columbia University Press, 1996.

Scharpf, Fritz. *Governing in Europe: Effective or Legitimate?* Oxford: Oxford University Press, 1999.

Schauer, Frederick. "Amending the Presuppositions of a Constitution." In *Responding to Imperfection*, ed. S. Levinson, 145–162. Princeton: Princeton University Press, 1995.

Schlessinger, Phillip and Deirdre Kevin. "Can the European Union Become a Sphere of Publics?" In *Democracy in the European Union: Integration through Deliberation?*, ed. E. Eriksen and J. Fossum, 206–230. London: Routledge, 2000.

Schmitter, Philippe. "Is It Possible to Democratize the Europolity?" In *Democracy and the European Union*, ed. A. Follesdal and P. Koslowski, 13–36. Berlin: Springer Verlag, 1998.

Schumpeter, Joseph. *Capitalism, Socialism, and Democracy.* New York: Harper Collins, 1947.

Sen, Amartya. *Development as Freedom.* New York: Knopf, 1999.

Sen, Amartya. *Poverty and Famine.* Oxford: Oxford University Press, 1986.

Shapiro, Ian. *The State of Democratic Theory.* Princeton: Princeton University Press, 2003.

Shapiro, Susan. "The Social Control of Impersonal Trust." *American Journal of Sociology* 93 (1987): 623–658.

Shaw, Jo. "The Interpretation of European Citizenship." *Modern Law Review* 40 (1999): 293–318.

Shue, Henry. *Basic Rights.* Princeton: Princeton University Press, 1996.

Slaughter, Anne-Marie. *A New World Order.* Princeton: Princeton University Press, 2004.

Smith, Peter, and Elizabeth Smythe. "Globalization, Citizenship, and Technology: The Multilateral Agreement on Investment Meets the Internet." In *Culture and Politics in the Information Age: A New Politics?*, ed. F. Webster, 183–207. London: Routledge, 2001.

Soysal, Yasemin. *Limits of Citizenship: Migrants and Postnational Membership in Europe.* Chicago: University of Chicago Press, 1994.

Sunstein, Cass. *Designing Democracy: What Constitutions Do.* Oxford: Oxford University Press, 2001.

Sunstein, Cass. *Republic.com.* Princeton: Princeton University Press, 2001.

Tilly, Charles. *Coercion, Capital, and the European State.* Oxford: Blackwell, 1990.

Tully, James. "Introduction." In *Multinational Democracies*, ed. J. Tully and A. Gagnon, 1–35. Cambridge: Cambridge University Press, 2001.

Tully, James. "The Freedom of the Ancients and the Unfreedom of the Moderns in Comparison to Their Ideals of Constitutional Democracy." *Modern Law Review* 65 (2002): 204–228.

Tully, James. "The Struggles of Indigenous Peoples for and of Freedom." In *Political Theory and the Rights of Indigenous Peoples*, ed. D. Ivison, P. Patton, and W. Sanders, 36–60. Cambridge: Cambridge University Press, 2000.

Villey, Michel. "La genèse du droit subjectif chez Guillaume d'Ockham." *Archives de la Philosophie du Droit* 9 (1969): 97–126.

Waldron, Jeremy. *Law and Disagreement.* Oxford: Oxford University Press, 1999.

Walzer, Michael. *Spheres of Justice.* New York: Basic Books, 1983.

Weale, Albert. *Democracy.* London: St. Martin's, 1999.

Weber, Max. *From Max Weber: Essays in Sociology.* Ed. H. H. Gerth and C. Wright Mills. Oxford: Oxford University Press, 1946.

Weiler, J. H. H. "An 'Ever-Closer Union' in Need of a Human Rights Policy." *European Journal of International Law* 9 (1998): 658–723.

Weiler, J. H. H. *The Constitution of Europe.* Cambridge: Cambridge University Press, 1999.

White, Harrison. "Agency as Control." In *Principals and Agents*, ed. J. Pratt and R. Zeckhauser, 187–212. Cambridge, Mass.: Harvard Business School Press, 1985.

Williams, Bernard. "Making Sense of Humanity." In *Making Sense of Humanity and Other Philosophical Papers*, 79–90. Cambridge: Cambridge University Press, 1995.

Young, Iris. *Inclusion and Democracy.* Oxford: Oxford University Press, 2002.

Index